MULTICULTURAL EDUCATION SERIES
James A. Banks, Series Editor

The Making – and Remaking – of a Multiculturalist
CARLOS E. CORTÉS

Transforming the Multicultural Education of Teachers:
Theory, Research, and Practice
MICHAEL VAVRUS

Learning to Teach for Social Justice
LINDA DARLING-HAMMOND, JENNIFER FRENCH, AND
SILVIA PALOMA GARCIA-LOPEZ, EDITORS

Culture, Difference, and Power
CHRISTINE E. SLEETER

Learning and Not Learning English:
Latino Students in American Schools
GUADALUPE VALDÉS

Culturally Responsive Teaching:
Theory, Research, and Practice
GENEVA GAY

The Children Are Watching:
How the Media Teach About Diversity
CARLOS E. CORTÉS

Race and Culture in the Classroom:
Teaching and Learning Through Multicultural Education
MARY DILG

The Light in Their Eyes:
Creating Multicultural Learning Communities
SONIA NIETO

Reducing Prejudice and Stereotyping in Schools
WALTER STEPHAN

We Can't Teach What We Don't Know:
White Teachers, Multiracial Schools
GARY R. HOWARD

Educating Citizens in a Multicultural Society
JAMES A. BANKS

Multicultural Education, Transformative Knowledge, and Action:
Historical and Contemporary Perspectives
JAMES A. BANKS, EDITOR

THE MAKING
—*AND REMAKING*—
OF A
MULTICULTURALIST

CARLOS E. CORTÉS

TEACHERS COLLEGE, COLUMBIA UNIVERSITY
NEW YORK AND LONDON

Published by Teachers College Press, 1234 Amsterdam Avenue, New York, NY 10027

Library of Congress Cataloging-in-Publication Data

Cortés, Carlos E.
    The making, and remaking, of a multiculturalist / Carlos E. Cortés
        p. cm—(Multicultural education series)
    Includes bibliographical references and index.
    ISBN 0-8077-4252-X—ISBN 0-8077-4251-1 (pbk.)
      1. Cortés, Carlos E. 2. Educators—United States—Bibliography. 3. Multicultural
education—United States—History. I. Title. II. Multicultural education series (New York,
(N.Y.)
    LA2317.C637 A3 2002
    370'.92–dc21
    [B]   2002021140

ISBN 0-8077-4251-1 (paper)
ISBN 0-8077-4252-X (cloth)

Printed on acid-free paper
Manufactured in the United States of America
09 08 07 06 05 04 03 02   8 7 6 5 4 3 2 1

To Alana—
No father has ever been prouder

CONTENTS

PART TWO
SELECTED ANTHOLOGY

THEME I. EXPERIENCING TRANSFORMATIONS

THEME II. BUILDING BRIDGES

THEME III. EXPANDING VISIONS

THEME IV. GRAPPLING WITH NEW CHALLENGES

SERIES FOREWORD

THE NATION'S DEEPENING ETHNIC TEXTURE, INTERRACIAL TENSION AND CONFLICT, AND increasing percentage of students who speak a first language other than English make multicultural education imperative in the 21st century. The United States Census Bureau (1998) estimated that people of color would make up 28% of the nation's population in the year 2000, 38% in 2025, and 47% in 2050.

American classrooms are experiencing the largest influx of immigrant students since the beginning of the 20th century. About a million immigrants are making the United States their home each year (Martin & Midgley, 1999). More than seven and one-half million legal immigrants settled in the United States between 1991 and 1998, most of whom came from nations in Latin America and Asia (Riche, 2000). A large but undetermined number of undocumented immigrants also enter the United States each year. The influence of an increasingly ethnically diverse population on the nation's schools, colleges, and universities is and will continue to be enormous.

In 1998, 34.9% of the students enrolled in U.S. public schools were students of color. This percentage is increasing each year, primarily because of the growth in the percentage of Latino students (Martinez & Curry, 1999). In some of the nation's largest cities and metropolitan areas, such as Chicago, Los Angeles, New York, San Francisco, Seattle, and Washington, D.C., half or more of the public school students are students of color. During the 1998–1999 school year, students of color made up 63.1% of the student population in the public schools of California, the nation's largest state (California State Department of Education, 2000).

Language and religious diversity is also increasing among the nation's student population. In 1990, 16% of school-age youth lived in homes in which English was not the first language (United States Census Bureau, 1998). Harvard professor Diana L. Eck (2001) calls the United States the "most religiously diverse nation on earth" (p. 4). Most teachers now in the classroom and in teacher education programs are likely to have students from diverse ethnic, racial, language, and religious groups in their classrooms during their careers. This is true for both inner-city and suburban teachers.

An important goal of multicultural education is to improve race relations and help all students acquire the knowledge, attitudes, and skills needed to participate in cross cultural interactions and in personal, social, and civic actions that will help make our nation more democratic and just. Multicultural education is consequently as important for middle-class White suburban students as it is for students of color who live in the inner city. Multicultural education fosters the public good and the overarching goals of the commonwealth.

The major purpose of the *Multicultural Education Series* is to provide preservice educators, practicing educators, graduate students, scholars, and policy makers with a comprehensive set of books that summarizes and analyzes important research, theory, and practice about diversity that is related to the education of ethnic, racial, cultural, and language groups as well as mainstream students in the United States. The books in the series present research, theoretical, and practical knowledge about the behaviors and learning characteristics of students of color, language minority students, and low-income students. They also provide knowledge about ways to improve academic achievement and race relations in educational settings.

The definition of multicultural education in the *Handbook of Research on Multicultural Education* (Banks & Banks, 2001) is used in the series: "Multicultural education is a field of study designed to increase educational equity for all students that incorporates, for this purpose, content, concepts, principles, theories, and paradigms from history, the social and behavioral sciences, and particularly from ethnic studies and women's studies" (p. xii). In the series, as in the Handbook, multicultural education is considered a "metadiscipline."

The dimensions of multicultural education, developed by Banks (2001) and described in the *Handbook of Research on Multicultural Education,* provide the conceptual framework for the the books in the series. They are: *content integration, the knowledge construction process, prejudice reduction, an equity pedagogy,* and *an empowering school culture and social structure.* To implement multicultural education effectively, teachers and administrators must attend to each of these five dimensions of multicultural education. They should use content from diverse groups when teaching concepts and skills; help students understand how knowledge in the various disciplines is constructed; help students develop positive intergroup attitudes and behaviors; and modify their teaching strategies so that students from different racial, cultural, language, and social-class groups will experience equal educational opportunities. The total environment and culture of the school must also be transformed so that students from diverse groups will experience equal status in the culture and life of the school.

Although the five dimensions of multicultural education are highly interrelated, each requires deliberate attention and focus. Each book in the series focuses on one or more of the dimensions, although each book deals with all of them to some extent because of the highly interrelated characteristics of the dimensions.

This engaging book is a landmark publication in the life of a discipline and a scholar. As one of the constructors of the field of multicultural education, Cortés' life during the last three decades mirrors the historical development of the field. Like most of the scholars who played key roles in constructing multicultural education, Cortés became involved in multicultural education for both personal and professional reasons. The richly textured autobiographical essays in this book, which contextualize and foreground its thirteen essays, tell the story of Cortés' professional life as well as the emergence, growth, problems, and promises of the field of multicultural education. Cortés shares not only his successes and triumphs but his concerns, frustrations, and dilemmas. This generous sharing enriches and enlivens his odyssey.

Cortés' book is an important contribution to the history of multicultural education and is an extension of the work described in the first book in the series (Banks, 1996). That book is a part of *Studies in the Historical Foundations of Multicultural Education,* a series of studies begun at the Center for Multicultural Education at the University of Washington in 1992 (Banks, 2002). The purpose of this research project is to uncover the roots of multicultural education, to identify the ways in which it is connected to its historical antecedents, and to gain insights from the past that can inform school reform efforts today related to race and ethnic diversity (Banks, 1996).

This book will enable scholars and practitioners to compare Cortés' life and work with those of ethnic studies scholars such as Carter G. Woodson, John Hope Franklin, and George I. Sánchez. Cortés' saga reveals important ways in which scholars doing work on race and ethnicity today are connected to those in the past. The construction of the history of multicultural education is essential for its academic legitimacy and institutionalization. The history of a field helps its scholars and practitioners to better understand its present and to envision and construct its future.

I am personally pleased to welcome this book to the *Multicultural Education Series* because of the significant ways that my life and career have intersected with Cortés' academic and personal journeys. We met in 1971 when Wilson Riles, the state superintendent of public instruction in California, created a task force to evaluate the social science textbooks in that state during an acid controversy over the treatment of minority groups in these books.

Subsequently, I invited Cortés to contribute a chapter to *Teaching Ethnic Studies: Concepts and Strategies* (Banks, 1973), the National Council for the Social Studies 43rd Yearbook which became a landmark and widely used publication. In 1976, Cortés served on the National Council for the Social Studies Task Force on Ethnic Studies Curriculum Guidelines that I chaired (Banks, Cortés, Gay, Garcia, & Ochoa, 1976/1991). We served as co-instructors of an inservice course in the Portland Public Schools during a year in the mid-1970s. Our personal and professional interactions have been continuous since we met on the California textbook task force in 1971.

During our thirty-year journey I have been greatly enriched by Cortés' keen insights, vast knowledge, candor, wit, and unwavering commitment to human liberation and social justice. The fortunate readers of this book will be able to share this enrichment.

James A. Banks
Series Editor

REFERENCES

Banks, J. A. (Ed.). (1973). *Teaching ethnic studies: Concepts and strategies* (43rd yearbook). Washington, D.C.: National Council for the Social Studies.

Banks, J. A. (Ed.). (1996). *Multicultural education, transformative knowledge and action: Historical and contemporary perspectives.* New York: Teachers College Press.

Banks, J. A. (2001). Multicultural education: Historical development, dimensions, and practice. In J. A. Banks & C. A. M. Banks (Eds.), *Handbook of research on multicultural education* (pp. 3–24). San Francisco: Jossey-Bass.

Banks, J. A. (2002). Race, knowledge construction, and education in the United States: Lessons from history. *Race, Ethnicity and Education, 5*(1), 7–27.

Banks, J. A., & Banks, C. A. M. (Eds.) (2001). *Handbook of research on multicultural education.* San Francisco: Jossey-Bass.

Banks, J. A., Cortés, C. E., Gay, G., Garcia, R. L., & Ochoa, A. S. (1976/1991). *Curriculum guidelines for multiethnic education.* Washington, D.C.: National Council for the Social Studies. (Revised edition published in 1991 as *Curriculum guidelines for multicultural education*).

California State Department of Education. (2000). Available: http://data1.cde.ca.gov/dataquest.

Eck, D. L. (2001). *A new religious America: How a "Christian country" has become the world's most religiously diverse nation.* New York: HarperSanFrancisco.

Martin, P., & Midgley, E. (1999). Immigration to the United States. *Population Bulletin, 54*(2), 1–44. Washington, D.C.: Population Reference Bureau.

Martinez, G. M., & Curry A. E. (1999, September). *Current population reports: School enrollment—social and economic characteristics of students* (update). Washington, D.C.: U.S. Census Bureau.

Riche, M. F. (2000). America's diversity and growth: Signposts for the 21st century. *Population Bulletin, 55*(2), 1–43. Washington, D.C.: Population Reference Bureau.

United States Census Bureau (1998). *Statistical Abstract of the United States* (118th edition). Washington, D.C.: U.S. Government Printing Office.

INTRODUCTION

WHEN JIM BANKS ASKED ME IF I WOULD BE INTERESTED IN PUBLISHING A COLLECTION of my articles in his *Multicultural Education Series* with Teachers College Press, my immediate, nearly predictable, ego-driven response was an enthusiastic "Yes," if for no other reason than vanity. Imagine that! An entire book of *my* articles. Then reality set in.

As I glanced through my older writings—sometimes containing dated references, out-dated insights, infelicitous prose, and occasionally passé thinking—vanity surrendered to embarrassment. This was hypertrophied by uncomfortable recollections of others' books and articles that had drawn upon, even quoted, some of my ancient writings, citing predictions that had proven to be erroneous and attributing to me beliefs that I no longer held. After all, as John Maynard Keynes reportedly responded when faced with criticism for having abandoned some of his previous beliefs, "When I get new information I change my opinions. What, sir, do you do with new information?"

Then came the third reaction . . . mysterious excitement. Somewhere at the intersection of vanity and embarrassment emerged a new idea. Maybe republishing some of those articles—even dated ones—might not be a bad idea if I could approach that enterprise as a historian.

After all, by education and vocation I am a historian. However, I also participated in the birth of the contemporary multicultural education movement, have remained active in it for more than three decades, and, as a historian, bring perspectives from *outside* of the field of education. In those years I have been involved in multicultural education's development, rejoiced in its accomplishments, done public battle with its critics, become dismayed at times by its directions, and critiqued what I felt were its errors of omission and commission. Maybe, I thought, I could use this collection as the basis for an autobiographical history of that movement—a sort of "testimonial literature"—with my past articles serving as personal, idiosyncratic historical artifacts.

This concept raised a series of "if's": *If* I could revisit my articles, reconsider them, and reframe them to highlight their historical significance by placing them in the autobiographical context of the development of both multicultural education and my own thinking about diversity. . . . *If* I could approach them not merely for what they said but also for what they revealed as temporal records—albeit very personal records—of that young and still evolving field. . . . *If* I could use them as launching pads for re-examining the transformation of my own ideas about diversity, society, and education. . . .

Fortunately, both Jim Banks, the series editor, and Brian Ellerbeck, executive acquisitions editor at Teachers College Press, were receptive to the idea. They encouraged me to proceed with the project, although my ideas were still inchoate. The result of this exploration is *The Making—and Remaking—of a Multiculturalist.*

THANKS

As I proceeded through this retrospection I was helped by observations and comments from those who have read some or all of my autobiographical pieces: my University of California, Riverside, colleagues Eugene Cota-Robles, Kenneth Barkin, Roger Ransom, and Irwin Wall; Clifford Baden, one of my mentors at the Harvard Graduate School of Education; Carol Geary Schneider, president of the Association of American Colleges and Universities; Dan Holt of the California Department of Education; Karen Bartz, vice president of Hallmark Corporate Foundation; Andrew Smith, president of the American Forum for Global Education; Steven Petkas and Rhondie Voorhees, two of my coinstructors during my postretirement residency at the University of Maryland, College Park.

Over the years I have had many fine graduate research assistants, but I want to thank two of them for their special contributions to this book: Tom Thompson, for his superb insights during the formative stages of my research into media and diversity; and Lore Kuehnert, for her critical suggestions and dependability in the preparation of the manuscript. I lack the words to sufficiently thank my three editors—Jim Banks of the University of Washington and Brian Ellerbeck and Amy Kline of Teachers College Press—for their careful reading and perceptive comments on my manuscript, as well as their patience as I struggled with the challenges created by the special nature of this book. Finally, there are the two most important people in my life . . . my wife, Laurel, and my daughter, Alana, who, over the years, have provided me with love, companionship, and inspiration.

BOOK STRUCTURE

Because of its heterogeneous contents, this book required a series of structural decisions, both minor and major. In making these decisions, I benefited from the insights and recommendations of my three fine editors: Jim

Banks, Brian Ellerbeck, and Amy Kline. Each of them raised structural issues and made suggestions, most of which were incorporated into the book.

The book is composed primarily of thirteen new autobiographical pieces and thirteen related, reprinted selections. I chose these selections not because they were the best of my writings, certainly not the most scholarly. Rather I selected them because of their value as historical documents, illustrating transitions in my involvement with multicultural education and the development of my thinking about diversity.

Both the autobiographical pieces and the reprinted selections are roughly organized in chronological order. I say "roughly" because my professional world has not evolved in a neat, linear pattern. Like most of life, my career has been messy, tortuous, sometimes chaotic. It has been dotted with detours, dead ends, and unexpected doorways to unforeseen ventures, yet from it has emerged a comprehensible, meaningful, overall sweep. As has the field of multicultural education, my career has been buffeted by a series of temporally overlapping, conceptually linked, sometimes conflicting, and continuously transformative forces, resulting in numerous changes of thought, action, and direction. These I explore in my autobiographical pieces and document with my reprinted selections.

Beyond chronology, the most challenging structural issue was the placement of the book's various components. I originally planned to divide the book into thirteen topical sections, each consisting of a new autobiographical piece examining a personal or professional transition followed immediately by a list of selected books and articles of mine related to that transition, and then by one representative republished selection from that list. The obvious advantage of such an organization was that it would keep together all of the elements related to the thirteen individual topics.

However, the closer I came to completing the autobiographical essays, the more I began to view this organization as choppy, with the reprinted selections and selected bibliographies interrupting the narrative flow of the new pieces. I concluded that the narrative would be more coherent if the new autobiographical pieces were kept together rather than broken up. Therefore, I proposed beginning the book with the thirteen autobiographical essays, followed by the republished selections grouped together as a historical document set illustrating the development of my thinking about multicultural education and diversity.

This proposal provoked lengthy interchanges with my editors over the pros and cons of different structural alternatives. My suggested structure created certain risks, such as the possibility—unlikely, I hope—that some readers might go directly to a reprinted piece without first reading the related context-setting autobiographical essay. However, after weighing the editors' differing perspectives, I finally decided to go with my proposed structure because it facilitates what I believe is the most valuable way to read and use this book. First, the reading of the thirteen autobiographical essays gives an overall grasp of the historical development of both multicultural education and the societal dialogue about diversity. Second, the joint reading of each individual context-setting autobiographical piece along with its related reprinted selection provides a more intensive examination of the different issues raised in the book.

As a result, the book is divided into two sections. The first section contains the thirteen autobiographical essays organized under four themes: Experiencing Transformations; Building Bridges; Expanding Visions; and Grappling with New Challenges. These are followed by a selected bibliography of my writings, grouped according to the same thirteen topics. The second section contains reprints of thirteen selections (eleven of my previously published articles, one book chapter, and an interview), each historically documenting one autobiographical essay, which in turn establishes the context for reading the reprinted selection.

I believe that the final structure most effectively highlights, explores, and documents the trajectory of my ideas both about multicultural education per se and about broader issues of unity and diversity. It also captures my diversity-related personal and professional transitions and dilemmas, successes and frustrations, accomplishments and concerns. Through its historical and personal examination of diversity, this book should contribute to a better understanding of the multicultural education movement as well as the changing societal context in which it has operated.

HOPES

This book is a study of change and continuity—of my ideas, of my participation in multicultural education, and of my involvement in many issues relating to unity and diversity in the United States. Moreover, the changes I explore have been more than *professional.* My involvement first in ethnic studies, then in multicultural education, and finally in a variety of related endeavors has also brought numerous *personal* transformations. These changes, in turn, have caused me to reflect and re-reflect on the course of both my life and my career. They have certainly changed me as a grandson, son, husband, father, and, most recently, grandfather.

Nehru of India once said, "Life is like a game of cards. The hand that is dealt you is determinism; the way you play it is free will." Yet even with the hindsight of time, the line between the dealt hand and the way I have played it remains fuzzy, sometimes puzzling. The process of looking back on my career—a career still in progress—has made me more introspective. It has pinpointed personal crossroads, magnified dilemmas I have encountered, clarified my choices, etched my frustrations, illuminated my accomplishments, and boldfaced the costs and benefits of my professional journey.

My hope is that this book will offer insight into and thereby provide greater clarity concerning the ongoing story of multicultural education and diversity in the United States. But beyond this I hope it will also provoke readers into reflecting on their own lives, careers, professional goals, and involvement in our increasingly multicultural society and shrinking globe. Finally, I hope that the book will help those concerned about education and our nation's future to interrogate their own purposes, practices, beliefs, and behaviors, especially their personal reasons for participating in the struggle for the hearts and minds of Americans, particularly young people.

Maybe this sounds too audacious, and it may be. But it is my hope . . . not just a professional one but also a personal one. After all, I am a grandfather. And as one of my chapters suggests, I have not been working simply to improve education. I have also been trying to help build a better multicultural future for my grandchildren. To them I say thanks for making me care more deeply and understand more clearly.

Carlos E. Cortés
Riverside, California

THE MAKING
—AND REMAKING—
OF A
MULTICULTURALIST

PART ONE

AUTOBIOGRAPHICAL ESSAYS

CHAPTER 1

FROM LATIN AMERICANIST TO CHICANO STUDIES ADVOCATE

IN LATE NOVEMBER OF 1967 I RETURNED FROM TWENTY MONTHS in Brazil, where I had been conducting research for my doctoral dissertation on historically important Rio Grande do Sul, Brazil's southernmost state. When, less than two months later, I took up a professorial position in the History Department at the University of California, Riverside (UCR), I had every intention of pursuing an academic career dedicated to Latin American history. But, as would happen many times throughout the next three decades, fate intervened. It came first in the person of another UCR professor, Eugene Cota-Robles, an internationally eminent microbiologist.

Toward the end of my initial spring quarter, in May of 1968, I received a call from Gene, whom I had never met. His voice betrayed a certain hesitancy, but he finally got around to raising the issue. He had noticed my name on the list of new UCR faculty and wondered if I might be a Mexican American. I answered tentatively in the affirmative.

LUNCHEON REVELATIONS

Over a subsequent lunch I explained the tentativeness of my answer. My grandfather came from Guadalajara, Mexico. While studying engineering in California, he met and married an American. This led to my father being born in San Francisco although, shortly thereafter, the family returned to Guadalajara, where my father grew up.

Several years later, like so many others, Dad's family fled to the United States because of the 1910–1920 Mexican Revolution. My grandfather had been *jefe político* (political chief) of Guadalajara under the revolutionary government of

3

President Francisco Madero. When Madero was overthrown and assassinated by General Victoriano Huerta, my grandfather's name appeared on Huerta's "hit list." It was leave now or else. Forced to flee immediately, my grandparents left without my dad, who remained in Mexico and was reared by an aunt until he could rejoin his parents in the San Francisco Bay area at age eleven.

Then I added my caveats. While my father was Mexican, my mother was not. Rather she was born in Kansas City, Missouri, the Jewish offspring of a Russian immigrant father and Austrian immigrant mother. My parents met in California, where I was born, but I grew up in Kansas City. We did not live in the local Mexican American *barrio,* although Dad participated to a modest degree in Latino affairs. Moreover, even though Dad emphasized my Mexican identity, fostered my love for our Mexican heritage, and took us to spend time with relatives in Guadalajara and Mexico City, we spoke limited Spanish at home. I studied it, along with Portuguese, in school. Finally, due to the unpredictability of genetics, I turned out to be a *güero,* a light-skinned Latino.

Therefore, as I told Gene, I was not sure if my background "qualified" me as Mexican American. He assured me that my background was just fine, that lots of Mexican Americans came from mixed heritages, and that physical "brownness" was not a requirement for being Chicano.

Gene was desperate for ethnic reinforcements on campus. UCR, circa 1968, was hardly a hotbed of minority students or faculty. Affirmative action had not yet seen the light of day. At that point UCR had only two Black faculty members and Gene had been the lone Chicano. My arrival had doubled the corpus of UCR's Mexican American faculty, to go along with fewer than 150 Chicano students.

He then launched into the specific purpose of our meeting. He was directing the Educational Opportunity Program (EOP), an outreach effort to recruit and assist minority and poor students. Would I be willing to become involved? And he was helping form a new organization, United Mexican American Students (UMAS). Would I be willing to assist him?

These requests could not have come at a more inopportune time. I was just preparing to write my doctoral dissertation, working under tremendous time pressure. Upon arriving on campus in January of 1968 as an acting assistant professor, I had received a letter from the vice chancellor informing me that I had until June of 1969 to complete my dissertation or I would forfeit my position. At that point I had not yet written word one. And since I had never previously taught, other than TAing one semester in graduate school, I needed to prepare all new courses.

The wise answer to Gene's requests would have been "I'd love to help, but I can't until I complete my dissertation." However, for reasons I cannot clearly recall, I found myself answering "yes." That answer would change the course of my life, not just my career.

TAKING CARE OF BUSINESS

During my first seventeen months at UCR I taught all new classes and finished my dissertation, thus removing the stigmatic "acting" from my title and averting the threatened termination. Simultaneously, however, I became deeply involved in Mexican American activities. In addition to working with EOP and UMAS I attended Chicano conferences throughout the state and, to begin to compensate for my knowledge deficit (there had been no courses on Mexican Americans when I was in graduate school), I audited the Sociology of Mexican Americans, taught by Joan Moore, one of the pioneers in that field.

Then, in spring of 1969, enveloped by the euphoria of the civil rights movement, UCR decided to establish Mexican American Studies and Black Studies B.A. programs. The administration asked me to become the first chair of Mexican American Studies . . . the law of supply and demand in all of its glory. The demand was there—I was the supply.

But this was too much, too soon. I had just completed my dissertation and first had to take care of business, namely earning tenure. In particular, this meant transforming my dissertation into a book. Moreover, a couple of senior professors in my department had already informed me—gently but firmly—that they took a dim view of my growing Chicano involvement, advising me to steer clear of this Chicano stuff and stick to being a Latin Americanist. So I turned down the chairmanship, with Gene accepting it for a year while we could search nationally for a chair. Yet I agreed to establish a course on Chicano history, which I had never studied in college.

My decision not to accept the chairmanship turned out to be a wise one. My revised dissertation, accepted for publication as *Gaúcho Politics in Brazil: The Politics of Rio Grande do Sul, 1930–1964,* won a prize from the Pacific Coast Council on Latin American Studies. And in spring of 1972 came promotion to associate professor with tenure aided, I should add, by tempting offers from two other universities to help build their ethnic studies programs. Instead, greatly in response to the touching appeal from a delegation of Chicano students, I decided to remain at UCR and become chair of Mexican American Studies (soon renamed Chicano Studies), serving for seven-and-one-half years until the end of 1979.

While over the subsequent years I stayed involved with Latin American history through teaching, supervising dissertations, lecturing on Latin America, and to some extent research, as well as chairing UCR's Latin American Studies Program for two years, I had found a new calling, Chicano Studies. Yet, in all honesty, my research on Chicano history per se yielded relatively modest results: one article in a never-completed book project on the Chicano experience in the communities surrounding UCR; various historiographical reviews, conceptual pieces, and historical overviews, culminating in the publication of a lengthy essay on Mexicans for the *Harvard Encyclopedia of American Ethnic Groups* (1980); three edited reprint series—*The Mexican American, The Chicano Heritage*, and *Hispanics in the United States*—totalling 106 volumes; and a movie.

MOVIEMAKER

Through a process too complex to relate in detail here, Mario Barrera, a UCR political scientist, R. Alex Campbell, a San Francisco Bay area filmmaker, and I hatched the idea of making a documentary film about the expedition of Mexican pioneer Juan Bautista de Anza, which resulted in the founding of San Francisco. We drew up a grant proposal to present the Anza expedition as a south-to-north alternative to the standard east-to-west portrayal of the colonization of the American West, an idea we felt might appeal to the National Endowment for the Humanities. It did. Receiving a small grant and operating on less than a shoestring budget, we made *Northwest from Tumacácori* (1972), a 33-minute documentary film of which I was coauthor and coexecutive producer. This media dabbling would also prove to be prophetic of the directions that my career would take.

A few years later, when asked to write an article for a U.S. bicentennial publication, *The Revolutionary Era: A Variety of Perspectives* (1976), I revisited the film in "'Northwest from Tumacácori': A Chicano Perspective on the American Revolution Bicentennial" (Selection 1). As illustrated by the film, I argued that the story of the American West, traditionally presented from an east-to-west perspective, was incomplete without a thorough consideration of south-to-north Hispano-Mexican expansion into the area that ultimately would become part of the United States. This was hardly a novel idea, as borderlands historians had been championing this view for decades, although their appeals seldom reverberated beyond recondite academic circles and even then were generally dismissed other than for a few token pages at the beginning of some U.S. history textbooks. That south-to-north argument became one of my basic lecture/workshop themes throughout the 1970s.

PERSONAL TRANSFORMATION BEGINS

But the movement from dedicated Latin Americanist to committed Chicano Studies advocate proved to be as much a personal as a professional transformation. Particularly through the inspiration of Gene Cota-Robles, the mentoring of Joan Moore, and my involvement with Mexican American students, who drew me into what had become known as the Chicano movement, I had discovered a new, more meaningful focus for my life.

For the first time I had become deeply involved in the genesis of a social movement. It was as if the Mexican seeds sown by my father during my youth had finally sprouted. Yet many of the professional aspects of that blossoming would occur not in the field of history, my graduate specialty, but in the field of education, which I had never studied. My second transformation on the road to becoming a multiculturalist was about to begin.

The corresponding Selection for this Chapter can be found on pg. 71.

CHAPTER 2

FROM HISTORIAN TO EDUCATION ACTIVIST

M Y SECOND TRANSFORMATION, FROM BEING STRICTLY A COLLEGE history and ethnic studies professor to also becoming a K–12 diversity activist, may have been virtually inevitable. Having introduced a Chicano history course in winter of 1970, I found myself being invited to speak on that topic for local school districts, teacher education courses, and even community events.

Talk about learning on the run! Published sources were limited, featuring more gaps than content. It would be two years before the publication of the first movement-spawned, college-level Chicano history textbooks—most notably Rodolfo Acuña's *Occupied America* and Matt Meier and Feliciano Rivera's *The Chicanos: A History of Mexican-Americans.* But demand does not wait for supply. My Chicano history course became an annual event, ready or not. The same "ready-or-not" applied to my entrance into the K–12 educational arena.

STATEWIDE DEBUT

In the fall of 1970 psychologist Alfredo Castañeda became the new chair of UCR's Mexican American Studies Program. He and I, along with a few other interested professors, organized a two-day conference, Mexican Americans and Educational Change, to be held at UCR in May of 1971. Of course I would be one of the speakers.

That conference became my statewide coming-out party as an analyst, spokesperson, and champion of integrating the Chicano experience into the mainstream curriculum. My talk, later published in the conference proceedings, which I coedited, was called "Revising the 'All-American Soul Course':

A Bicultural Avenue to Educational Reform." That title provided an ironic twist to the then-widespread criticism that ethnic studies programs mainly offered "soul courses," intended primarily to improve ethnic self-identities. At that point ethnic studies courses seldom received credit for dealing seriously with a societally and academically important topic or for helping to build scholarly bridges of intergroup understanding. In my talk I challenged those criticisms by arguing that U.S. education itself was an extended "soul course" for fostering American identity, except that in doing so it generally excluded those groups that did not fit neatly into calcified ways of recalling and teaching about U.S. history, literature, and other subject areas.

The talk and article were part history (for example, I discussed the development of the Black legend of Spanish depravity, particularly Spanish subjugation of Indian peoples), part contemporary analysis (a cursory examination of the treatment and exclusion of Mexican Americans in U.S. history textbooks), part recommendations (ideas on greater Chicano curricular inclusion), and part posturing (exhorting the choir of three hundred present at the conference). For some listeners and readers, a few of my claims, criticisms, and suggestions, as well as my tone, might have seemed radical for their time. Yet my basic argument—that K–12 and college textbooks and curricula had essentially excluded Chicanos and that Chicanos should be regularly included in the study of U.S. history and culture—seems remarkably unremarkable from today's perspective.

Regardless, the talk drew a standing ovation. Yet I did not fully realize the extent of that enthusiasm until the following fall. Even more unexpected was that this response to my talk—my statewide educational debut—would also draw me deeper into the K–12 arena.

TEXTBOOK TASK FORCE

At that time California was going through the statewide adoption cycle for grades 5–8 history and social studies textbooks. Section 9305 of the State Education Code required that, to be adopted, textbooks must "correctly portray the role and contributions of the Negro and other ethnic groups." The retrospectively bizarre wording of that Education Code provision should qualify it for inclusion in a time capsule tracing the development of thinking about diversity and education.

According to the adoption process, textbooks submitted by publishers were exhibited at numerous locations around the state so that the public could read and comment upon their contents. Most Californians had no idea that this process was taking place. However, the Los Angeles Unified School District's Black and Mexican American Education Commissions did know and, furthermore, did something about it. They actually read the books, and what they read they did not like. In testimony before the State Board of Education, they made a compelling argument that most of the submitted books failed to meet the state education code's provision on the treatment of ethnic groups and, for that reason, could not legally be adopted.

Caught between the state education code, the tight textbook adoption timeline, the two determined commissions, and frantic publishers eager not to lose out on the lucrative California textbook market, amounting to one-tenth of the nation, the state board did what beleaguered governmental entities often do. It established a task force to review the textbooks. In response to the statewide call for nominations for the task force, some who had heard my "soul course" talk recommended me. I became one of thirteen people chosen—twelve from throughout California and one outsider, a young education professor from the University of Washington named James Banks.

So in October of 1971 the task force began to meet. For me it turned out to be like taking a postgraduate seminar, as I listened to twelve other scholars and community leaders of different backgrounds voicing their concerns about textbook treatment of various groups and providing insights and suggestions about textbook revisions. (A little sidelight: Early in the review process we asked if we could also evaluate the treatment of women, but were informed that we were to stick to ethnic groups. Since they were not covered by the education code, women were none of our business.)

After more than a month of meetings, the task force submitted its report, generally supporting the Los Angeles groups' criticisms. We recommended changes—sometimes extensive ones—for most of the submitted books. The state board seemed nonplussed by the scope of our recommendations (which today would appear rather modest) and by what they may have perceived as the militancy of our position.

Whatever their reasons, the board thanked us for our work and then dissolved the unexpectedly troublesome task force. Instead it chose *one* of our members (not *our representative*, as we were excluded from the selection process) to serve on a new committee, made up primarily of board members, to determine what changes should be required. Changes were made, but not nearly as extensively as we had recommended. In contemporary terms they might well be categorized as classic examples of "tokenism." (I remember one of the suggested revisions, not one from our report: to remove a photo of the Bank of America from one of the social studies textbooks and replace it with a photo of the Bank of Puerto Rico. Now that's progress!)

The textbook controversy received considerable publicity. As one of the few southern California academics on the task force, I began receiving invitations to speak at school districts, universities, and education conferences about the adoption process and the treatment of ethnic groups in textbooks. As with Chicano history, for the second time fate was yanking me into becoming an "instant expert," this time because of my participation on the task force. No longer was I being called upon just to contribute my budding expertise on Chicano history, but also to offer advice on K–12 educational materials and Chicano curricular inclusion in general, although I had never previously taught at either the elementary or secondary level. The demand for ethnic studies "experts" was enormous; the supply was minimal. Learning on the run had taken on new dimensions.

TEACHING ABOUT CHICANOS

Demonstrating the leadership that would make him a global figure in multicultural education, Jim Banks asked a number of scholars, including some of the task force members, to write chapters for a book he was editing for the National Council for the Social Studies, *Teaching Ethnic Studies: Concepts and Strategies* (1973). The book title itself reflects that era's vocabulary—ethnic studies, not multicultural education, not even multiethnic education. Those other labels would emerge later.

The book became widely read. I include my article "Teaching the Chicano Experience" (Selection 2) because even to this day I encounter people who have drawn from it and, in some cases, still find it useful. The article introduced themes that I would develop in other writings as well as ideas that would later blossom into full-scale research endeavors: textbook failings in the treatment of Mexican Americans; the inadequacy of traditional historical frames of reference; and particularly the role of the media in fostering ethnic stereotypes.

Even though dated, my recommendations generally remain valid, some having become standard, noncontroversial elements of most social studies and U.S. history textbooks: the need to address the uniqueness of the Chicano experience rather than treating it as merely a variation of the experiences of African Americans, Native Americans, or other immigrant groups; the importance of engaging what Chicanos have done, not just what was done to them; the imperative of exploring the diversity of Chicano experiences (including drawing upon local community resources, such as oral history) rather than merely highlighting a few heroes and success stories; and, of course, the need to challenge the east-to-west conceptual straitjacket, an issue raised in *Northwest from Tumacácori.*

I am not claiming that my article in particular had a great deal to do with future textbook revisions, although the book as a whole probably had considerable impact. Yet over the next two decades textbook publishers, curriculum developers, and state education departments throughout the country would arrive at conclusions similar to those I and others proposed in the book. For that reason my article, as a historical document, embodies some of that era's challenges to the traditional U.S. history curriculum, as well as suggestions for making it more inclusive, at least from a Chicano perspective. Along with the "soul course," it also launched me on the quest for multicultural curricular reform. I had become part of the struggle for a more equitable, inclusive education.

The corresponding Selection for this Chapter can be found on pg. 80.

CHAPTER 3

FROM ETHNIC STUDIES CHAIR TO MULTICULTURAL EDUCATION SPECIALIST

A T THIS TIME IN HISTORY—THE EARLY 1970s—NOBODY PUR-
sued a graduate specialty in multicultural education,
because the concept had not yet come into existence. Rather,
multicultural education pioneers came from a variety of origins. Most began in other fields of education, such as curriculum and instruction or the social foundations of education.
Some started in new ethnic studies programs, usually concentrating on a single racial or ethnic group. A few, like myself,
began in traditional disciplines, mainly in the arts, humanities,
and social sciences.

My roots lay first in Latin American history, to which I had
added an interest in Chicano studies before later entering the
arena of K–12 education. Along the way I had also become
somewhat involved in the bicultural aspects of the comparably infant field of bilingual, bicultural education. Bicultural usually meant that students would be taught about their own special ethnic cultures and heritages as well as being prepared to
function in the American mainstream.

From that era's burgeoning interest in the bicultural paradigm I had derived the title and perspective for my inaugural
educational article, "Revising the 'All-American Soul Course': A
Bicultural Avenue to Educational Reform." Moreover, the concept of biculturalism also informed my other early Chicano-
based education articles. For example, as a companion piece to
the article on our film, I incorporated my south-to-north perspective into my "Need for a Geo-Cultural Perspective in the
Bicentennial" (1976), which appeared in *Educational Leadership*.

But even as I championed Chicano biculturalism in
speeches, workshops, and articles, I was already undergoing

yet a third transformation—the broadening of my frame of reference into something that would ultimately be referred to as multicultural education. Ironically, the California textbook task force, which had afforded me a broader and more powerful bicultural voice, also became the crucible in which my multicultural thinking had begun to take shape.

MOVING TOWARD MULTICULTURALISM

In early 1974, shortly after the publication of Jim Banks' *Teaching Ethnic Studies*, I received my first three invitations—one from the Los Angeles Unified School District, one from the Association of California School Administrators, and one from the University of Houston—to speak not just about including Chicanos in the curriculum but more broadly about multi-ethnic curricular integration. By that time I had developed a rule-of-thumb for dealing with the growing number of requests: when in doubt, say yes. If the stretch was not too outlandish, go for it.

I did, even though this stretch was truly daunting. Although now relatively well grounded on Chicanos, my knowledge of other ethnic groups was far more limited—not unusual given the infancy of ethnic studies. Moreover, as I mentioned before, I had no K–12 classroom experience.

In preparation for this new endeavor I immersed myself in books and articles on African Americans, Asian Americans, Native Americans, and European immigration. In addition, I painstakingly re-read *Teaching Ethnic Studies*, drawing ideas from each chapter, then trying to incorporate the authors' varied suggestions into an integrated, more meaningful whole. It worked. The presentations not only received enthusiastic responses but also initiated what would become more than a quarter-century of presentations on multicultural education and, later, education in a multicultural society.

In making that stretch from biculturalism to multiculturalism, my career paralleled the professional trajectories of many other scholars who began by specializing in a specific racial, ethnic, or religious group (later on women, gays, the disabled, or other types of groups) and later spread their wings multiculturally. Still there are those, I should add, who have declined to make that stretch and have remained in their single-group scholarly comfort zones. I say this not as a criticism, because many of those group-focused scholars have provided valuable research and insights upon which multicultural generalists like myself have been able to draw. Rather I mention this to suggest the diverse paths followed by those who became caught up in the scholarly and pedagogical crusade to make America, particularly teaching about the United States, more multiculturally inclusive.

Choices often bring both gains and losses. In becoming more of a multicultural generalist and less of a bicultural ethnic specialist, along with reorienting my career to emphasize K–12 education as well as academic history, I had accepted the challenge of grounding myself in a much broader range of scholarship than I could have imagined five years earlier. With each multicultural yes, Latin American history, Chicano studies, and biculturalism became less central to my professional life, although still within my range of interests.

CONCEPTS AND STRATEGIES

Another yes came in response to two invitations from the Social Science Education Consortium: to write a short article on multiethnic education for its November 1975 newsletter; and to coauthor a monograph, *Understanding You and Them: Tips for Teaching about Ethnicity* (1976). The titles of some of my articles suggest not only my evolving views but also the conceptual changes and contending labels in the field itself: "Concepts and Strategies for *Multiethnic* Education" (1975); "New Perspectives on *Multicultural* Education" (1978); "Dealing with the Density of *Diversity:* Groupness and Individuality in the California History/Social Science Framework" (1981); "*Multicultural* Education: A Curricular Basic for Our *Multiethnic* Future" (1990); and "Education in a *Multicultural* Society" (1995).

The development of my personal thinking about diversity and education was occurring within a context in which the field itself was also undergoing a transformation in both content and terminology. For example, in 1975 the National Council for the Social Studies invited me to serve on its Task Force on Ethnic Studies Curriculum Guidelines. Yet, despite our task force's "ethnic studies" designation, we titled our 1976 publication *Curriculum Guidelines for Multiethnic Education*. Time marches on. When Jim Banks, the task force chair, revised the document in 1991, he retitled it *Curriculum Guidelines for Multicultural Education*.

In my case, the 1975 article, "Concepts and Strategies for Multiethnic Education" (Selection 3), my first effort to examine what was then evolving into multicultural education, illustrated my thinking at that time. Some of my multicultural ideas were elaborations of concepts I had proposed for teaching about Chicanos: comparing ethnic experiences rather than forcing them into some "just like" model; emphasizing ethnic activity rather than simply treating ethnic people as passive victims of oppression and discrimination; and avoiding a fixation on heroes and success stories.

I expanded my bicultural *south-to-north* proposal for including Hispano-Mexican dimensions of the U.S. experience into an argument for a *multidirectional* curricular model that called for a more thorough inclusion of African, Asian, and Native American dimensions of the formation and development of the United States. The *bicultural* perspective I had championed in my writings on Chicanos now bloomed into an appeal for the inclusion of *multiethnic* perspectives on U.S. history and society.

However, although I was moving beyond "bi" to "multi," I was still writing mainly about race and ethnicity. While I did touch upon such issues as gender diversity within the various ethnic experiences, a full-scale attempt to stretch out further to grapple in my writing with other aspects of diversity—such as religion, disability, and sexual orientation—was yet to come.

Three transformations down. One more to go. Like the others, its genesis came serendipitously. In this case it also came suddenly, in the person of the Gypsies.

The corresponding Selection for this Chapter can be found on pg. 94.

CHAPTER 4

FROM SCHOOL CURRICULUM CRITIC
TO SOCIETAL CURRICULUM ANALYST

IN SPRING OF 1975 I WAS INVITED BY A LARGE URBAN SCHOOL district to team-teach a year-long (1975–1976) multicultural education institute for some seventy teachers and administrators. The two-day (Friday–Saturday) institute met once a month. During the weeks between meetings, participants would experiment with new multicultural approaches in their classrooms or administrative work, so that we could discuss and critique the results at the next institute session.

One fourth-grade teacher conducted a curricular experiment that turned out to be one of my personal "eureka" moments. It also propelled me in a research direction that ultimately would become central to my multicultural vocation, influence my university teaching, and provide the driving force for much of my subsequent scholarship, drawing me into a special niche at the intersection of history and education.

THE GYPSIES

That fourth-grade teacher decided to present a curricular unit on Gypsies (known more accurately as Rom). The city had a sizable, concentrated Gypsy community, although distant from her suburban school, which had no Gypsy students. Because, as far as she knew, her students had never before studied Gypsies in school, she felt they would provide the proverbial blank slates onto which she could etch new Gypsy knowledge and initiate the process of Gypsy-related intergroup understanding.

To do this she planned to draw upon a number of still-popular multicultural sources for teaching about "other" cultures—documents, stories, maps, movies, photographs . . . even a field trip to the local Gypsy community. (This was long before the Internet, so students could not visit Gypsy web sites, download Gypsies, or engage in cyberspace intercultural dialogues.)

But we also decided that she should do one more thing. To begin the unit, to make certain that student mental slates were, indeed, blank, and to detect any "contaminating" prior knowledge, she would first ask the students what, if anything, they knew about Gypsies. It turned out that they—these nine- and ten-year-old students—knew plenty.

For starters, according to her students, Gypsies were weird and dirty. They dressed strangely, moved around a lot, told fortunes, sang, danced, stole, and kidnapped children. This brief warm-up exercise quickly demonstrated that, where Gypsies were concerned, the teacher's expected multicultural blank slates simply did not exist.

That discovery necessitated the switching of pedagogical gears. In line with the Mark Twain adage, "Education consists mainly in what we have unlearned," she now had to help her students "unlearn" much of what they already "knew" about Gypsies. But first we needed more information about how they knew it.

To secure this the teacher asked her students where they had learned about Gypsies. Answers ranged from parents, other relatives, and friends to incidental personal contact with Gypsies, usually accompanied by parental warnings.

Yet closely following parents, students most commonly cited the media, mainly television, as their main source of Gypsy knowledge. When asked to be more specific, students responded with answers ranging from children's cartoons to local TV newscasts to horror movies. (Many students clearly recalled the Gypsy camp scenes from the 1941 Lon Chaney, Jr., classic, *The Wolf Man*, which played regularly along with Frankenstein and Dracula movies on Saturday afternoon TV horrorthons.)

The teacher's presentation at the institute touched a "hot button," igniting an outburst of educational war stories. Other teachers hastened to share their own struggles with their students' media-based multicultural beliefs and perceptions about race, ethnicity, culture, gender, religion, and other diversity-related topics.

THE SOCIETAL CURRICULUM

In previous writings, lectures, and workshops I had touched upon the issue of the media treatment of diversity, usually focusing on the issue of stereotyping. Yet that night, following the provocative institute discussion, a broader idea began to take shape.

Seemingly out of nowhere three words obtruded in my head—"the societal curriculum," the curriculum presented by society at large rather than by schools. It seemed to be a perfect label for what the teachers had reported—a nonschool curriculum from which students learn about myriad topics, including diversity. A curriculum that operates regardless of the plans or strategies, desires or concerns, decisions or actions, hopes or fears of teachers, administrators, and school boards. An informal curriculum that functions irrespective of the intentions or awareness of its nonschool developers and disseminators, be they parents, peers, religious leaders, heads of youth organizations, or creators of media.

The next day I tried out my "societal curriculum" idea on institute participants, with astonishing results. Not only did it lead to what I considered to be the most intense discussion of the entire institute, but it eventually inspired me to write an exploratory article, "The Societal Curriculum and the School Curriculum: Allies or Antagonists?" (1979). Of the more than 100 articles I have written, few have equaled this five-page think-piece as far as eliciting letters and phone calls.

Not that I had said anything profound—obviously people, including students, learn outside of school. What had struck home was the packaging and labeling. "The societal curriculum" seemed to reverberate because it educationally framed the obvious, employing a dual curricular construct, with nonschool and school teaching as sometimes parallel, sometimes intersecting, inevitably interacting, at times reinforcing, but often competing forces.

Two years later, in a follow-up article, "The Societal Curriculum: Implications for Multiethnic Education" (1981) (Selection 4), I defined the societal curriculum as "that massive, ongoing, informal curriculum of families, peer groups, neighborhoods, churches, organizations, institutions, mass media, and other socializing forces that educate all of us throughout our lives" (p. 24). I also subdivided the societal curriculum into four intersecting categories: the immediate curriculum (family, peers, and community); the institutional curriculum (like religious institutions and youth organizations); the serendipitous curriculum (individual, sometimes incidental, diversity experiences); and the media curriculum (from print and radio to television and motion pictures). Beyond that I suggested strategies for incorporating the societal curriculum into the school curriculum—for example, analyzing the media treatment of ethnicity and studying the local community (a theme I had broached in earlier articles). Since that time much of my research has involved the societal curriculum—particularly the mass media—which also became a regular feature of my workshops, lectures, and university teaching.

TRANSFORMATIONS

Within less than a decade, four major personal transformations had occurred. I had moved from concentrating totally on Latin America to also addressing the Chicano/U.S. Latino experience; from engaging solely in academic history to also working with the K–12 curriculum; from appealing for a Chicano studies–based curricular biculturalism to championing multicultural education; and from focusing narrowly on the school curriculum to broadly incorporating informal teaching aspects of the multicultural societal curriculum, particularly the mass media. As was common among the first wave of multicultural educators, my professional and personal life had become a continuous process of mind-bending experiences, career-altering challenges, and life-affirming transformations.

The corresponding Selection for this Chapter can be found on pg. 103.

CHAPTER 5

CONNECTING MULTICULTURAL TO GLOBAL EDUCATION

DURING MY FIRST DECADE AS A PROFESSOR, PERSONAL AND PRO-fessional transformations had drawn me into a sort of career limbo. Although I continued to teach and write about Latin America, my graduate research interest in Brazil was declining. Although I would teach Chicano history for more than twenty years, chair UCR's Chicano Studies Program for seven-and-one-half years, and write a number of articles in that field, I felt little impetus to develop this into a full-scale research area.

Education, particularly K–12 education, had become my primary concern—make that obsession—as I dedicated myself to social reform via educational change. Yet I had never taken an education course nor had I ever taught at the K–12 level, although this did not seem to restrict the increasing flow of speaking and workshop invitations. Nor did it temper my willingness to accept them, while balancing them with my ongoing university responsibilities.

Sometimes these requests were to address Chicanos, race and ethnicity, or multicultural education per se. But, at other times, I was asked to explore the relationship of multiculturalism to other educational areas, like history, social studies, literature, citizenship, reading, geography, foreign languages, the arts, and occasionally even science and mathematics.

ETHNIC AND AREA STUDIES

Maybe the most natural connection—at least at first glance—seemed to be that between ethnic studies/multicultural education and foreign area studies. After all, they both dealt with issues of diversity. Moreover, I already had one foot in each

21

field—a graduate and academic specialty in Latin America and an added vocation in Chicano studies and multicultural education.

Yet this connection turned out to be both complex and contested. I soon came to recognize how the development of ethnic studies and multicultural education had created tensions for many involved in the study and teaching of foreign areas and cultures. And, in some respects, the existence of foreign area studies had created complications for ethnic studies and multicultural education advocates.

At the university level the tensions involved such classic academic issues as turfdom and resource allocation. Some foreign area specialists saw ethnic studies as poaching on their academic turf of studying and teaching about cultural "otherness." Conversely, some ethnic studies advocates, struggling for an academic foothold, feared that foreign area specialists might highjack their inchoate bandwagon, purloin its newly allocated resources, and relegate ethnic studies into permanently marginal status as a minor subset of international studies. (At a mid-1970s historical conference one retread Mexicanist, who had been pressured into teaching a course on Chicano history, cynically remarked that he spent as much time as he could on Mexico and, then, during the last few weeks of the class, grudgingly got around to talking about Mexican-descent people in the United States.)

But it was not all conflict. At times ethnic studies and foreign area advocates developed good, academically sound, intellectually provocative, and pedagogically valid working relationships, with the sharing of insights and occasionally the creation of joint research agendas. At other times they formed transitory alliances of pragmatic convenience.

On my campus, for example, ethnic studies and foreign area supporters (including the entire foreign language faculty) created an alliance to establish an ethnic and area studies requirement for the College of Humanities and Social Sciences. This requirement mandated that all students take any two courses about ethnic groups and/or foreign areas, to be chosen from a list compiled by the college from department and program offerings. Although hardly qualifying as a painstakingly crafted way of introducing students to the topic of diversity, it was the best that our fragile alliance could achieve in the face of determined opposition to even this modest mandating of a curricular engagement with cultural "otherness." (Two decades later UCR would adopt a *campuswide* one-course ethnicity requirement to accompany its long-extant world history requirement.)

FOREIGN ESCAPISM

Tensions at the K–12 level generally took on a different hue. Multicultural education had arisen from the quest for curricular inclusiveness, educational equity, and social justice. This included the curricular integration of ethnic cultures, voices, and experiences along with the examination of historical and contemporary racism (later adding other "isms"), discrimination, and inequality. The focus was mainly internal; that is, on ethnic groups *within* the United States.

Yet, with the major exception of most American Indians, all ethnic groups had origins that stretched beyond today's U.S. borders. Thus their foreign heritages could not be ignored. This raised the question, To what extent and how should external "foreignness" be included in multicultural education without detracting from the internal focus on U.S. ethnic diversity?

Unfortunately, the consideration of "foreignness" sometimes became a clear and present danger to the establishment and maintenance of internally focused K–12 multicultural education. Particularly as I worked with elementary school teachers and classrooms, I often found multicultural education taking the form of "foreign escapism," in which the long ago and far away became the "safe" substitute for the temporally and physically near at hand.

Some teachers felt more comfortable describing Japanese tea services than discussing Japanese American World War II internment. African art could be admired while avoiding the discussion of racism faced by African Americans. Mexican fiestas and Cinco de Mayo celebrations raised fewer hackles than discussing the plight of Mexican farmworkers. In many schools and districts, what was called multicultural education became dominated by food, fashions, and festivals, with a few famous people tossed in. In the process, ethnic experiences, particularly the real problems and obstacles that ethnic people had historically faced and continue to encounter, often became marginalized, sanitized, or avoided altogether.

However, curricular bridges *could* be built. My participation in that bridge-building process drew me into the arena of global education, a field I barely knew existed.

GLOBAL EDUCATION

My first "official" encounter with global education came in 1975 when George Otero and Andy Smith of the University of Denver's Center for Teaching International Relations asked me to speak. Global education, I soon learned, was not simply old wine in new bottles, not just another label for classic foreign area studies. Rather it addressed global phenomena in a thematic, comparative, cross-national way. As such it sometimes found itself in competition—both conceptually and for resources—with those who had dedicated their careers to studying specific foreign areas.

The Denver Center was then launching a "transnational linkages" project for comparatively examining the relationship between American ethnic groups and their foreign root cultures. Asked to prepare a piece on my ethnic/area specialty, I wrote an exploratory monograph, *Mexico in the Study of Mexican Americans: An Analysis of Transnational Linkages* (1976). (Other project monographs addressed transnational linkages of Arab Americans, African Americans, and Irish Americans). George and Andy wrote an introductory global education conceptual framework. Transnational linkages would ultimately become a core theme of global education.

In April of 1977, when UCLA held a multicultural education conference with a global thrust, I was asked to give the keynote address. My conference proceedings article, "Multicultural Education: A Global Perspective," became my first written attempt to dissect the multicultural–global education relationship. Other global education speaking and writing invitations followed, including a chapter for a 1979 Research for Better Schools publication, *Curricular Dimensions of Global Education.*

Having joined New York's Global Perspectives on Education (later renamed the American Forum on Global Education), Andy Smith asked me to adapt and synthesize that 1979 chapter as a special feature section for its periodical, *Global Perspectives: Education for a World in Change.* Possibly that short 1980 piece, entitled "Global Perspectives and Multicultural Education" (Selection 5), best reflects my early thinking about ways to bridge the two fields. In that article I posited four common areas of concern: an understanding of the significance of groups, globally as well as nationally; an understanding of global interrelatedness; the development of skills (including intercultural communication) for living in a world of diversity; and, as had become a theme in nearly all of my speaking and writing, an understanding of the formation of intergroup images, including through the societal curriculum, and how schools could address this issue.

While, in retrospect, the article exudes an optimism for cooperation between the two fields that has not always occurred, it still continues to offer avenues for integrating both ethnic and global concerns into the curriculum without marginalizing or cannibalizing each other. Moreover, these premises served as bases upon which I would build and expand in future lectures and articles, most recently in my 1998 "Global Education and Multicultural Education: Toward a 21st-Century Intersection."

Maybe most suggestive of my evolving multicultural/global focus was the inclusion of image-formation as one of the four fundamental common areas of concern. The creation, reinforcement, and modification of intercultural images—whether arising from schools or emanating from society at large, disseminated by textbooks or the media, or involving intergroup or international perceptions—had become central to my scholarly and pedagogical orientation. Ultimately this led to the comparative examination of this theme in *Images and Realities of Four World Regions,* the September

1986 special issue of *Social Education*, which I coedited with Dan Fleming of Virginia State Polytechnic University.

Although the fit was not always seamless, global education had taken its place alongside and become intertwined with my multicultural education concerns. It had provided me with a conceptually richer way to connect my foreign area (particularly Latin American) scholarly grounding with my multicultural interests, with a special emphasis on image formation. My lectures on "education in a multicultural society" were sometimes expanded to include "and a shrinking world." Out of my transformations was emerging a professionally more coherent vision and personally more compelling worldview.

The corresponding Selection for this Chapter can be found on pg. 111.

CHAPTER 6

CONNECTING MULTICULTURAL TO OTHER EDUCATIONAL CONCERNS

S LIDING INTO GLOBAL EDUCATION PROVED TO BE A FAIRLY NATU-
ral extension of my multicultural education, Latin
American, and ethnic studies interests. Other invitations, however, created far more challenging situations. While offering
me opportunities to explore a greater variety of intersections,
these invitations also created additional obligations, particularly demands on my time to study, consider, and integrate
scholarship from each new field.

Sometimes these side trips turned out to be term-limited
career interludes, time-consuming detours that ended as
abruptly as they had begun. In other cases these invitations
propelled me down avenues that would become permanent
parts of my multiculturalist career trajectory. Accompany me
on brief overviews of two of these journeys, which illustrate
the contrasting scenarios.

LAW-RELATED EDUCATION

One day in the fall of 1977 I received a call from Lynda Carl
Falkenstein, codirector of a new law-related education project
sponsored by the American Bar Association. The ABA was
planning a national conference in Chicago to kick off its project. Would I be willing to write an article on the relationship
of multicultural education to law-related education (LRE to
insiders)? Of course, I answered, but only if she would first
explain law-related education, a term I had not previously
encountered. Concurring that this would be a pretty good idea,
Lynda agreed to send me some LRE introductory material.
Some material. . . ? An enormous box of books and articles
landed in my office. Before I could even begin thinking about

my article, I faced weeks of concentrated reading about this previously unknown (to me) field.

The Chicago conference in May of 1978 led to an edited collection, *Daring to Dream: Law and the Humanities for Elementary Schools* (1980). My article, "Multicultural Law and Humanities Education: Preparing Young People for a Future of Constructive Pluralism," brought me instant LRE visibility. Foremost—and most involving—it led to a 1980 appointment to the ABA Advisory Commission on Youth Education for Citizenship. This meant six years of meetings and conferences as well as an opportunity to try to make diversity a more significant dimension of LRE initiatives and discussions.

Then, as abruptly as it had begun, my LRE participation ceased. Once my commission appointment ended, I disappeared from the LRE radar screen. Although a fascinating and intellectually rewarding experience, my LRE interlude also turned out to be a time-consuming career detour. I can only hope that it left something of long-range multicultural value to the LRE field.

LANGUAGE MINORITY STUDENTS

Contrast this LRE experience with another journey, which had far more lasting ramifications for my multiculturalist's trajectory. This 1984 phone call came from the California Department of Education's Bilingual Education Office. Over the years that office had facilitated the publication of a series of edited collections on various aspects of the education of what were then being referred to as "language minority students." (Over the years that student cohort has lurched from one label to another, most recently morphing into "English language learners.")

While its previous publications had focused on language learning per se, the office had now decided to coordinate an investigation into the broader issue of how social and cultural factors, not just linguistic ones, influenced the education of those students. The office began in 1983 by commissioning papers by a number of California scholars with track records of dealing with facets of the topic. After critiquing the papers and receiving revised— sometimes multiply revised—versions, the office decided that the papers were ready for "external review" prior to the publication of the collection. Because the papers as a whole addressed the intersections of language with history, culture, and society, the office invited two commentators to provide divergent perspectives in their critiques: Mary McGroarty of UCLA's Teaching English as a Second Language/Applied Linguistics Program and me. Of course I said yes. Imagine me saying no?

In October of 1984, the paper authors, department representatives, and we two commentators met for two days in Sacramento. As we had been asked to do (and as academics are socialized to do), Mary and I carefully read and seriously—sometimes sharply—criticized the papers. Yet we were unprepared for the unusual vigor with which the authors challenged our critiques, fueled both by belief in their own research and, maybe even more, by their concerns about the implications of their research for the lives of young people. The latter concerns provided the bond that held us together that first day, even as our sometimes heated exchanges occasionally threatened to blow us apart.

A casual Chinese dinner and a good night's sleep helped calm frayed egos and refocus both criticizers and criticized on their common purpose—to try to produce a valuable document that could benefit K–12 students. By the end of the second day, two decisions had been reached. First, the writers agreed to once again revise their papers in light of our critiques. Second, the group concluded that the collection needed two more chapters—make that bookends: an introduction providing a conceptual framework for integrating the myriad perspectives presented in the individual papers; and a concluding set of practical recommendations for parents, teachers, administrators, and trainers.

But who should write these chapters? When that question surfaced, all eyes (save two pairs, of course) turned to Mary and me. We had just spent two days critiquing others. Now it was our turn to put ourselves on the line. Peer pressure proved powerful, especially after our extended grappling with the issue of educational equity. Mary agreed to write the concluding practical recommendations; I committed myself to the conceptual introduction about the education of language minority students. As with law-related education, this was a subject about which I fell far short of being an expert, although I had written about the bicultural dimensions of bilingual education. Circumstances had once again dealt me a new challenge.

A MODEL EMERGES

Preparing that introductory chapter turned out to be one of the most arduous scholarly tasks I had ever undertaken. Before I could try to develop a framework embracing the disparate papers, I had to immerse myself in the exploding, conflicting scholarship (and sometimes breathtaking jargon) on language minority education, including the embattled frontier of theories of second-language learning.

Fortunately, I hasten to add, I had wonderful support on this journey. Daniel Holt and Dennis Parker of the State Bilingual Education Office provided continual advice, insightful criticism, and vital encouragement as I waded into this inchoate, controversial field. In particular they helped me develop what ultimately became labeled and widely disseminated as "my" Contextual Interaction Model for the Education of Language Minority

Students. As had now become de rigueur, I incorporated my own concept of the societal curriculum into the model. Moreover, Dan and Dennis showed me how I could also integrate elements from the Bilingual Education Office's *Interaction Model for Language Minority Students* (1981), based on the work of James Cummins. The result was the book's opening chapter "The Education of Language Minority Students: A Contextual Interaction Model" (Selection 6), which posited a framework for helping school educators more clearly conceptualize and more effectively address the ways in which non-school societal factors (including families and the media) affect the process of schooling.

The book, *Beyond Language: Social and Cultural Factors in Schooling Language Minority Students,* was unveiled in January 1986 at a major session of the California Association for Bilingual Education Conference in San Francisco. As the accidental author of the introductory conceptual chapter, I was anointed to be the featured speaker, describing the book's genesis, highlighting the importance of the individual studies, and, of course, unveiling "my" model.

UNINTENDED CONSEQUENCES

Then the aftermath, the law of unintended consequences in full flower. What I assumed would be the end of the project instead became the beginning of a new dimension of my career. The Contextual Interaction Model soon took on a life of its own, divorced from its tortuous origins. It began being referred to and cited by others, garnered me requests to write follow-up pieces, and led to conference and workshop invitations to speak about the "beyond language" idea and to help teachers implement my model.

From Latin American historian, ethnic studies advocate, and multicultural educator, I had accreted a new diversity badge of honor: second-language education analyst. I was introduced at conferences as the progenitor of the Contextual Interaction Model, which I proudly displayed on an overhead. Before one talk one national educational leader even described me as a major "theorist" of second-language learning!

To be honest, although I regularly take pains to disclaim sole authorship and wish I could retrospectively bowdlerize its sometimes obscurantist jargon, I am still proud of the model. Despite the heated, ongoing controversy over bilingual education, this "beyond language" model continues to be of value to educators on various sides of that educational conflict and is still being widely used in teacher training. (My niece, Natalie, once called to tell me that one of my articles, derived partially from my model, was required reading in one of her education graduate courses at Vanderbilt University.) Over the years I have modified the model (and, I hope, improved it), particularly by making it more generic and applicable to other facets of education, by enlarging the role of the societal curriculum, and by eliminating much of the original jargon, thereby rendering it more accessible to the educated public, not just the second-language in-crowd.

Moreover, speaking and writing about issues related to language—not just the Contextual Interaction Model—have become ongoing aspects of my career. Nearly two decades later I still receive invitations to speak not only about the education of language minority students, but also about related topics like American and global multilingualism, the history of bilingual education and U.S. language policy, the intersection of language and culture, two-way bilingual immersion programs, and such "hot button" issues as official English and language use in the workplace.

Starting with that simple invitation to comment on papers for a California Department of Education project, I have become a major speaker at language conferences ranging from the 1992 International Conference of Teachers of English to Speakers of Other Languages in Vancouver to the 2000 National Conference of the Korean Association of Teachers of English in Seoul. Once again, serendipity had opened intellectual doors, altered the course of my professional career, expanded my range of social activism, and drawn me more deeply into yet another multicultural struggle for educational equity, this time with far greater long-range personal and career implications than had my LRE episode.

The corresponding Selection for this Chapter can be found on pg. 118.

CHAPTER 7

CONNECTING SCHOOLS TO
MEDIA IMAGES

M Y TRANSFORMATION INTO A MULTICULTURALIST, PARTICULARLY
with the ensuing opening of doors to other educational intersections and my relentless pursuit of these new avenues, had become a driving force of my professional life. It was exciting, invigorating, challenging, sometimes inspiring. Above all, it provided me with the opportunity to participate in my own way in the struggle for social justice and equity— building on my academic foundations, drawing upon my personal strengths, and applying them within the educational arena.

It was nirvana, but it came with a cost. I had dedicated myself "unofficially" to a professional life of scholarly driven multicultural educational activism, but I also led an "official" life, that of a historian at the University of California, Riverside.

Through a combination of choice, serendipity, and personal commitment, my multiculturalist career had inexorably drawn me into areas sometimes tangential to—occasionally even distant from—my historical vocation. The tensions between these two trajectories were slowly developing into a major problem both for me and for my department.

THE ACADEMIC GANTLET

The University of California is a classic publish-or-perish institution. It has the traditional academic hierarchy of ranks—assistant, associate, and full professor—but it also has designated merit increase "steps" within each rank. To move up the professorial ladder, faculty members are evaluated by their department peers for each "step" advancement, usually once every two or three years. While teaching and service (professional, public, and campus) "count" in those evaluations, the emphasis is clearly on research, usually expected to be demonstrated by publications *since* the previous advance. (This has given rise to the sardonic joke, voiced often during my three years as a member of the campuswide Academic Personnel Committee, "That's swell, Mr. Einstein, but what have you published *since* your last advance.") During my personnel evaluations, the emphasis was on research performance, particularly publications, as a historian, not as a multiculturalist or as an analyst of education.

Let truth be told. Both UCR and my departmental colleagues demonstrated some flexibility in assessing my nontraditional career and did recognize my overall accomplishments at evaluation time. I had more than met my campus responsibilities. I chaired for more than half of my UCR career, first Latin American studies (1969–1971), then Chicano studies (1972–1979), and, finally, history (1982–1986), while often teaching course overloads and also serving on some of UCR's and systemwide UC's most time-consuming committees. I received both UCR's Distinguished Teaching Award and its Faculty Public Service Award. Recognition also came from beyond campus, such as being selected by the California Council for the Humanities for its Distinguished California Humanist Award and being named a Smithsonian Institution Public Lecturer.

Well and good. But still my research presented a dilemma. Although widely published, during personnel evaluations I increasingly faced the question, How much of what I was doing was really history? I had received prizes for my published scholarship, including for *Gaúcho Politics in Brazil.* My record also included numerous articles on Latin American, Chicano, and U.S. Latino history, as well as on the intersection of history and education. However, some of my writing fell into areas of education and diversity writ large rather than history as traditionally defined. It had become increasingly clear that I needed to develop a more "acceptable" history research agenda, particularly as I moved up the faculty ladder toward its higher echelons.

Yet I remained committed to the field of multicultural education. Somehow I had to build yet another, more clearly discernible, bridge, this one between my official, anointed role as an academic historian and my unofficial, chosen role as a multicultural education specialist. In this case, history, my personal history, came to the rescue.

THE MEDIA GAMBIT

Before becoming a historian I had pursued a brief career in the mass media. After earning a B.A. in Communications and Public Policy at the University of California, Berkeley, and an M.S. in Journalism at Columbia University, I had spent five years in various media endeavors. Maybe this early formation had somehow laid the groundwork for the 1976 workshop-generated, media-based genesis of my societal curriculum concept. In any respect, that concept ultimately provided me with a more coherent way of bridging history and multicultural education.

After a couple of brief articles exploring the idea of the societal curriculum—particularly its media dimensions—I moved on to the logical next question. Since there is a media curriculum on diversity that parallels the school curriculum, what does that curriculum actually teach? Or in a more historical framing, what has that media curriculum taught about diversity *over time?* This question became central to my efforts to build a bridge between—in some respects merge—my two professional lives.

Trying to carefully analyze the entire media curriculum over an extended period of time was obviously too audacious a research task. Therefore I decided to focus on one dimension of the media, motion pictures—the historical process by which American movies had been teaching about race and ethnicity. This also intersected with my UCR teaching trajectory. Since the mid-1970s I had been offering a variety of film-and-history courses and had coedited a series of film-and-history monographs. With my expanding interests, I had also developed a History of the Mass Media course, which I taught annually until I retired.

As with my forays into various facets of education, a serious effort to systematically examine the movies' historical treatment of race and ethnicity meant delving into a whole new scholarly literature, particularly myriad books and articles on the movie treatment of individual racial and ethnic groups. Then, of course, came the incredibly time-consuming, admittedly pleasurable, challenge of watching and taking notes on hundreds—make that thousands—of movies spanning the twentieth century. It was a research agenda without end, as hundreds of American movies are produced every year.

Almost predictably my first research article on the media treatment of diversity dealt with Mexican Americans. Entitled "*The Greaser's Revenge* to *Boulevard Nights*: The Mass Media Curriculum on Chicanos," it appeared in the 1983 proceedings of a National Association for Chicano Studies Conference.

From then on it was full steam ahead, with articles, lectures, and workshops on the historical evolution of movie images of various ethnic groups, foreign nations, culture areas, and cross-cultural diversity-related themes, as well as examinations of my film-and-history research methodology and pedagogy. In addition, for five years (1985–1990) I wrote a column on diversity for *Media & Values: A Quarterly Review of Media Issues and Trends.*

As my research developed, I attempted to tease out decades-spanning themes that embodied the continuities and changes in Hollywood's public curriculum on diversity. Two movie themes that emerged as particularly revealing were immigration and interracial love. The latter theme also provided me with an avenue for combining my analysis of race and ethnicity with an examination of the movie treatment of gender.

For example, in my 1991 article, "Hollywood Interracial Love: Social Taboo as Screen Titillation" (Selection 7), I compared how Hollywood has portrayed (or avoided) different interracial love combinations and demonstrated how the industry-codified screen taboo against showing interracial love has not been absolute and rigid. Rather it has changed over time and has varied, in part, based on the specific racial/ethnic combinations involved, the intersection of race and gender, the racial/ethnic identity of the actors, the era portrayed by the film, and the geographical locale (particularly whether the relationship occurs within or outside of the United States).

As my historical movie research progressed, within multicultural education I increasingly emphasized the implications of my media analysis for pedagogy and curriculum development. For example, because movies functioned as omnipresent informal public textbooks on diversity, I continuously worked with teachers on how to draw upon this media curriculum for their teaching about diversity.

The concept of Hollywood movies as a public multicultural curriculum struck a responsive chord, at least with a limited audience. Beyond articles there came invitations to do workshops, give public lectures, participate in panel discussions, and appear on television talk shows concerning the media. By combining history, the mass media, and education, I had succeeded in carving out a special scholarly, pedagogical, and activist niche.

Yet two questions remained. How much broad-scale impact would my media research have on multicultural education? And, of course, how well would this bridge-building research endeavor satisfy my university colleagues?

The corresponding Selection for this Chapter can be found on pg. 129.

CHAPTER 8

DIVERSITY AND SOCIETY: BEYOND CELEBRATION TO CONTEMPLATION

L IKE ALL REFORM MOVEMENTS, MULTICULTURAL EDUCATION HAS had its flaws. Or put another way, while multicultural education has provided long overdue critical perspectives on and correctives to traditional U.S. educational practices, the implementation of multicultural education has sometimes fallen short of its ideals.

My participation in the multicultural education movement generated a sense of personal euphoria, of accomplishment and contribution, and of growth and transformation. I reveled in being part of the movement and eagerly engaged such critics as Linda Chávez and Arthur Schlesinger, Jr., in public debate. Yet over the years I developed concerns about certain dimensions of multicultural education: foreign escapism; school-level superficiality (as represented by the over-emphasis on "foods, fashions, festivals, and famous people" approaches); and a tendency to ignore substance while relying on platitudes ("celebrating diversity").

COMMONALITY WITHIN DIVERSITY

Yet even more upsetting was a 1978 experience during a day-long multicultural education workshop for a major urban school district. Organized in a relatively traditional manner, the workshop began with my keynote address, followed by smaller "break-out" sessions conducted by other consultants and district personnel. During that time I dropped in on various sessions in preparation for my day-ending wrap-up address.

In one session I listened as the presenter repeated, over and over, that teachers should focus on difference. "Difference,

difference, difference. That's the important thing," he said. When one of the participants asked if it wasn't also important to look for things that people had in common, the presenter retorted even more emphatically that "difference" was what counted.

The response left me gasping. I'm sure I hadn't implied that in my keynote address. Nor, as far as I was concerned, was this a goal of the multicultural movement.

Certainly differences are important. If all people and cultures were exactly alike, we probably wouldn't need multicultural education or, for that matter, such fields as anthropology, sociology, psychology, history, cultural geography, religious studies, comparative literature, or sociobiology.

But similarities are important, too. Stressing differences while ignoring similarities (or vice versa) does injustice to our understanding of the human condition. Maybe even worse, an educational process that does not simultaneously build a respect for diversity *and* forge bonds of commonality can undermine the social fabric. So concerned was I with that session presenter's relentless hammering on differences that, in my wrap-up, I placed more than my normal emphasis on the importance of addressing *both* similarities and differences, diversity and commonality.

"Celebrating Diversity" had become a clarion call, at times a knee-jerk affirmation, of the multicultural education movement. In truth, I have carved out a minicareer speaking at "celebrating diversity" conferences, for which I offer no apologies. Diversity *is* worth celebrating. But equally worthy of celebration are bonds of human and societal commonality.

CONFRONTING DILEMMAS

Events such as that school district workshop, as well as writings of some scholars whose emphasis on differences seemed to relegate similarities to the garbage dump of societal ideas, struck me as a distortion, maybe even a parody, of the multicultural education in which I believed. I rededicated myself to moving further beyond mere celebration—without giving up celebrating—by undertaking a more serious contemplation of the complexities, complications, and conflicts inherent in both multiculturalism and multicultural education.

Over time I identified a set of issues—call them dilemmas—that I felt lay at the heart of the opportunities and challenges of multicultural living and educating. Among these lay the tenuous, unstable, triangular relationship involving the issues of equity, balance, and limits.

How can we achieve a socially healthy *balance* between diversity and commonality? That is, how can we build common ground upon which we can further a just community while also recognizing that group differences, not merely individual ones, are real, that group-based inequality exists, and that a truly democratic society must seek to reduce inequities related to those differences?

In order to address this delicate balancing act, we also need the contemplation, compassion, clarity, and courage to set *limits* on both conformity and diversity. That is, we need to restrain pressures for a lockstep conformity that penalizes diversity or restricts the rights of those who are different. At the same time we need to recognize that anarchic diversity can undermine the societal and organizational common ties that bind.

Finally, how can we engage in both balancing and limiting while at the same time striving for greater societal justice and equality, including the consideration of such factors as privilege and power? Those three imperatives— striving for equality, balancing unity and diversity, and setting limits—have remained central to my thinking, speaking, and writing since the mid-1980s.

Probably the nonschool article that most directly addressed my triangular dilemmas was my 1994 "Limits to *Pluribus,* Limits to *Unum:* Unity, Diversity, and the Great American Balancing Act" (Selection 8). In that exploratory piece I applied the "balancing act" concept to American life while criticizing both *pluribus* and *unum* extremism. In particular I focused on the complexities of two balancing-act issues: language and ethnicity-based religion. Although brief, this article suggests some of the ways in which I have been grappling in lectures and workshops with the three inevitably intersecting imperatives—balance, limits, and equity.

Yet even as I struggled with these dilemmas, another phone call would yank me from ivory tower contemplation and even from the groves of K–12 education. That call would challenge me to make yet another multicultural leap, this time a giant one, from theory to practice. I would be asked to address these perplexing concerns in what would be for me a new reality, the pragmatic world of private enterprise.

M & M

The 1979 call came from the educational director of M&M, formerly the Los Angeles Merchants and Manufacturers Association. M&M, which provided training programs for member organizations, was planning to launch a series of day-long seminars on Mexican Americans. They needed a presenter. Some of the M&M leaders had heard me lecture or give workshops on Latinos—I can't recall exactly which—and liked what I had to say. Would I be willing to give this new program a try, applying my Latino cultural knowledge and educational experiences to the workplace?

"Try" was the operative word. I had not been involved in the workplace, other than the educational workplace, since I had entered graduate school in 1962. Possibly more than any other invitation I would ever receive, this one truly jerked me out of my professional comfort zone. Yet I had been teaching and lecturing about Chicanos, Latinos, and diversity for more than a decade and figured that I had a day's worth of valuable information to dole out. So, as usual, I said "yes."

My first workshop involved probably my biggest career leap of faith in myself. I will not claim that the workshop was good, only that it might not have been *too* bad. Let's put it this way: It went well enough that I was invited to give a second workshop. And a third. And many more, intermittently, for nearly a decade, as M&M decided to expand the theme of my workshops from Mexican Americans to Hispanics as a whole, with an emphasis on the workplace and marketplace.

Talk about on-the-job training. Participants may have gained something of value from me, but I learned even more from them—their tales of ongoing struggles to operate companies while grappling with the growing racial, ethnic, religious, gender, and linguistic diversity of both employees and clientele. Grounded in theories, models, and paradigms of ivory-tower multiculturalism and conversant with issues of diversity and education, I watched as my academic and K–12 knowledge, muted by private business inexperience, collided with the challenges and dilemmas of day-to-day practice.

Ranging from factory "lead people" to company presidents, most participants came neither to celebrate nor to condemn diversity but to learn how to function more successfully in an increasingly multicultural world of work. They shared accomplishments and failures while asking tough questions, which I answered as well as I could by drawing upon and trying to apply insights from educational research, multicultural scholarship, and personal experiences.

My early day-long M&M workshops literally wiped me out, not to mention making me hyper-aware of my limitations outside of the academic and educational arenas. T. S. Eliot once wrote, "We had the experience but missed the meaning." In those workshops I had plenty of experiences and, over time, with them came new meaning and better participant responses, good enough that my activities grew in scope.

I began being asked by companies to make site visits, do in-house workshops, conduct cross-cultural evaluations, and make recommendations, not merely regarding Hispanics but about how to *multiculturally* improve their organizations. The institutions with which I worked became more diverse— factories, offices, hospitals, mental health services, nonprofits, youth organizations, religious institutions, government agencies, and professional associations. Inevitably came offers to speak at conferences on the organizational and societal implications of diversity. Far from inevitable was being honored, years later, by the American Society for Training and Development as its Multicultural Trainer of the Year.

Of course the M&M-incubated experiences also necessitated another extensive intellectual detour. I had to immerse myself in the scholarly literature on management, leadership, change, and organizational psychology. With diversity training taking off as a field, I read about various training practices and observed other trainers, with both delight and dismay. Sometimes these trainers addressed diversity impressively, with nuance, insight, and depth of knowledge. Other times diversity workshops reeked of dogmatism, polarizing guilt trips, or superficial gimmickry.

My educational experiences had helped me start down this new professional avenue. Conversely, my private business and other organizational experiences also gave me a nonschool opportunity to "ground" and re-examine my ideas about diversity, including the triangular dilemmas of seeking greater equity, striving for balance, and setting limits. Much as my branching out in different directions within K–12 education had provided a healthy corrective to higher education ivory-towerism, struggling with day-to-day workplace and organizational realities forced me to challenge and rethink canonical multicultural paradigms, propositions, and platitudes. The process of personal multicultural remaking—as a scholar, as a teacher, as an activist, and as a person—was in full swing.

The corresponding Selection for this Chapter can be found on pg. 145.

CHAPTER 9

DIVERSITY AND HIGHER EDUCATION:
BEYOND ACTIVISM TO ANALYSIS

A FTER THE CHALLENGING, CAREER-ALTERING EXPERIENCES THAT resulted from the M&M phone call, a 1990 invitation I received from the Harvard Graduate School of Education seemed almost benign. Would I be willing to teach about diversity in its summer institutes for college and university administrators?

As with so many other multicultural surprises, this one came through serendipity. William Vega, a California community college president who had heard me speak on several occasions, happened to serve on the advisory board for Harvard's Management of Lifelong Education (MLE) program, a two-week summer institute focused at that point on lifelong learning (later on fostering institutional change). He recommended me to serve on its faculty. As it turned out, MLE was already set for that summer (1990), but one of its companion higher education institutes, the Management Development Program (MDP), needed someone to give a few sessions on diversity, so I was asked to do so. Given my penchant for saying yes to most new endeavors unless there was some compelling reason not to, I answered in the affirmative.

Admittedly, I had done little scholarly research about higher education and had written just one accidental article on the topic. Back in the early 1970s a casual luncheon with another UCR colleague, a young psychologist named Roy Goldman, had led to a collaborative research effort to develop an alternative approach both to increasing the minority presence in professional schools and to providing more effective services to minority communities. Roy's sudden death briefly derailed the project, but one of his doctoral students, Barbara Newlin Hewitt, picked up the slack. Our collaboration resulted in a 1977 article, "To Serve Society: An Alternative Model for the Selection of Professional School Students." One of our major recommendations—visionary, we thought, for the time—was that community service should be considered a more significant factor in professional school admissions decisions. Today such consideration has become a widespread, although not universal, practice. While I certainly do not claim any causative relationship, let's just say that our article may have been slightly ahead of the admissions debate curve.

Yet although I was no higher education scholar, how difficult could it be to teach in the Harvard institutes? Compared with other new initiatives I had undertaken, such as my foray into language acquisition and especially my M&M adventure, Harvard looked to be a stroll in the park. After all, this was home territory. I had been a university professor for twenty-two years. I was a veteran department chair and an experienced campuswide and systemwide committee member. I had lectured and given diversity workshops at myriad colleges, universities, and higher education conferences, and had even broken into the commencement-and-convocation address circuit.

HARVARD DEBUT

Talk about misplaced confidence! My summer, 1990, teaching for MDP, turned out to be an unexpected disaster, worse than my first try at corporate training for M&M. Neither years of higher education lectures and workshops nor my UCR experience had prepared me for conducting 90-minute, high-tension discussions involving eighty to one hundred college administrators using the case study method emphasized by the Harvard institutes. This called for a whole new set of teaching skills and mental muscles, quite unlike those I had honed at UCR and on the multicultural lecture/workshop circuit. I was like a professional football player suddenly making my debut in major league baseball. I struck out.

Fortunately, some of the institute leaders spotted potential rather than merely writing me off. I was invited back and, in fact, became a regular in Harvard's higher education institutes. My success was greatly a result of a number of Harvard faculty who, bless their hearts, had the patience to work with me on using the case study teaching approach. As of 2002, I have been teaching at Harvard for thirteen summers.

As with my other multicultural experiences, I also learned as well as taught, in this case from both classroom and informal interactions with administrators from around the country and, to a degree, the world. Those Harvard institutes have become my annual "refresher course" on diversity and higher education, continuously updating me on new challenges and changing complexities. Moreover, this has led to increasing numbers of visits to individual campuses to help them address a range of diversity issues, from curricular integration to student affairs challenges, from the creation of single-group and multicultural centers to improving intergroup relations within residence life, and from community outreach to working with K–12 education.

AMERICAN COMMITMENTS

Teaching at Harvard also contributed to yet another phone call, this time from one of my neighbors, Frank Wong, provost and vice president for Academic Affairs at nearby University of Redlands. One of the preeminent thinkers about diversity in higher education, Frank asked me to participate on a panel being established by the Association of American Colleges (later the Association of American Colleges and Universities, AAC&U). The panel was about to undertake a multiyear project, American Commitments: Diversity, Democracy, and Liberal Learning, leading to the publication of a series of monographs on that topic. How could I say no? I didn't.

The American Commitments Panel began meeting in spring of 1993. If Harvard presented me with the opportunity to observe the interplay of ideas about diversity from *across* the higher education spectrum, the American Commitments Panel gave me the opportunity to observe the equally provocative interplay of ideas *within* the multicultural movement. Panel meetings became vivid demonstrations of the fact that, notwithstanding the hyperbole of antidiversity academics and pundits, multiculturalists do not all think alike. Far from the "political correctness" stereotype perpetrated by sometimes hyperventilating columnists, talk show provocateurs, and professional PCologists, the panel became a scintillating forum, an arena, sometimes a battleground of both divergent and convergent ideas and perspectives about diversity, as suggested in our panel's series of publications.

COMMUNITY AND COMMUNITIES

The Harvard and AAC&U experiences, along with my continued participation in higher education conferences and regular visits to speak and do workshops at college campuses, helped to further my thinking. In the process I became fascinated by one of higher education's tantalizing diversity-related issues—the tension between striving for a sense of community while responding to the inevitable existence of multiple campus communities, a corollary to my equity-balance-limits triangulation.

Diversity and community became a core theme of my Harvard institute sessions, as well as a topic that I addressed more and more at campuses and conferences. One investigation of this topic was my 1999 article, "Building Community from Communities: Diversity and the Future of Higher

Education" (Selection 9), which appeared in a special issue of *Metropolitan Universities*. Drawing on both published scholarship and my own experiences working with myriad colleges and universities, I addressed four areas in which community–communities tensions play out: the inevitable proliferation of campus affinity groups, often in the form of student organizations and centers; the challenge of facilitating constructive intergroup relations; the emergence and modification of personal and group identities, particularly mixed race and sexual orientation; and the restructuring of college curricula through both the creation of new programs and the modification of traditional disciplines.

Although not exactly a microcosm of U.S. society, American colleges and universities nonetheless find themselves grappling with some of the same diversity-related issues as society at large: balance and limits, community and communities, pluribus and unum, group attachments and intergroup relations, and the quest for equity. In a sense, my Harvard, AAC&U, and related higher educational experiences provided a complement to my work with M&M and private enterprise, affording me additional prisms through which to examine issues of diversity. Moreover, they helped me develop a firmer, more nuanced grasp of multiculturalism, particularly the opportunities and challenges that inevitably arise from living in a world replete with individual and group differences and similarities.

The corresponding Selection for this Chapter can be found on pg. 150.

CHAPTER 10

DIVERSITY AND BOUNDARIES:
BEYOND BEING TO BORDERING

SINCE THE BEGINNING OF MY INVOLVEMENT IN ETHNIC STUDIES and multicultural education, the theme of borders and boundaries had been a subtext of my thinking, teaching, speaking, and writing. Occasionally my articles had addressed that topic explicitly.

In a 1980 article, "The Chicanos—A Frontier People," I had explored the role of borders in Chicano experience and identity. Four years later, my 1984 piece, "Searching for Imaginative Responses to Inevitable Challenges," had appeared in *Border Perspectives on the U.S./Mexico Relationship*, a special issue of *New Scholar*, which had grown out of a San Diego conference on that topic. When Paul Loukides and Linda Fuller invited me to contribute to their 1993 book, *Locales in American Popular Film*, I returned to that theme with an article entitled "International Borders in American Films: Penetration, Protection, and Perspective."

ALANA

Yet the impetus for delving more deeply into the borders and boundaries issue came not from my professional life but from my daughter, Alana. The request was deceptively simple. For years I had been telling her stories about our family. Could I write them down for her? Well, to be honest, the request was not quite that simple. In actuality, for a number of years she had been bugging me rather incessantly despite my rejoinders of being too busy.

Finally I began writing. First came lengthy biographical sketches of family members: my mother and father; my grandparents; my brother; and my folks' two extended families. Then came vignettes about my own life, including the roles that ethnicity and religion had played in it.

Alana delighted in them. Yet as I read them to her she had to stop me constantly with questions, attempting to clarify the temporal relationships among the decades-spanning biographical sketches, trying to make sequential sense of the chaotic mosaic of family members, events, and recollections. The parallel, overlapping, and intersecting time lines of the sketches made it impossible for her to keep things straight. So I deconstructed the sketches and reconstructed their contents in roughly chronological fashion, filling in the temporal blanks with other material. In the process I became the center of the narrative, a participant observer of a family saga.

Academic writing tends to decimate personal voice. Relatively few academic scholars successfully challenge the professional pressures for detachment, the mystical supremacy of objectivity, and the sanctity of the "third person." This becomes most apparent in much social science writing where "I" is almost a four-letter word, seldom appearing while usually being obscured by such traditional, evasive phrases like "It was concluded" or "It was determined," without explicit reference to who did the concluding or determining.

Free from such constraints, I could now indulge myself in writing my family story from a first-person perspective. The result was an evolving family history as framed by my own experiences and discoveries, beginning as a young boy growing up in Kansas City, Missouri, and ending as a historian and multiculturalist ensconced in California, yet regularly dipping into my family's ongoing drama. The written format became a series of letters from me to Alana, chronologically explaining both my family's story and the process of my discovery of that story, particularly as it affected the trajectory of my own life. Almost without intention, my individual sketches had evolved into a full-scale family autobiography, the (hopefully) forthcoming *Letters to Alana*.

LOOKING FROM THE MARGINS

The process of writing *Letters to Alana* also revealed something that had remained latent, submerged, maybe even repressed. I had lived most of my life straddling a series of borders, most cogently growing up multiculturally, the son of a Mexican Catholic immigrant father and a U.S.-born Jewish mother of Austrian and Russian immigrant parents. As I wrote I began to develop a clearer understanding—an understanding still in process—of why I had never felt comfortable being pigeonholed into a single-group identity.

The way I was reared and experienced life, with different dimensions of my heritage playing important roles, sometimes conflicting ones, at different times and in different circumstances, had influenced my personal development, my worldview, and my cognitive and emotional reactions to life's experiences. As absurd as it may seem, my attempt to satisfy a daughter's curiosity had led me not only to confronting and better understanding myself but also to once again rethinking multiculturalism and multicultural education, now through the eyes of a "multi," a person of mixed heritage. And much of what I saw I did not like.

Upon revisiting multicultural education literature and now-canonical suggested practices, I found it brutally clear that single-group racial (and, to a lesser extent, ethnic) identity had become the virtually unexamined "default function" of most multicultural thinking. Such single-race assumptions dominated group studies, curricular integration, diversity training, culturally responsive pedagogy, and models of identity development. Although ethnic studies and multiculturalist scholars seldom made that assumption explicit, the underlying, uncritical acceptance of single-group identity as the diversity lodestone had fueled and entrapped much of multicultural education writing.

In truth many—maybe most—Americans live with single-race identities, whether self-selected or imposed by the larger society. But a rapidly growing number of Americans do not. I became increasingly chagrined that, by ignoring "multis" like me, multicultural education had marginalized, even vaporized us. Because we "multis" did not fit cleanly into most of the reigning schemes of American racial and ethnic categorization, including those models, paradigms, and practices devised, disseminated, and championed by many multiculturalists, we "multis" did not exist. Except that here I was.

LIFE AS A "MULTI"

My chagrin fueled so much determination to challenge those dogmas that when the next phone call came, this one from Alan Blankstein, Senior Editor of the National Educational Service, asking me to contribute an article to "Building Cultural Bridges," the special Winter 1999 issue of *Reaching Today's Youth,* I decided to address my concern about the neglect and marginalization of "multis." My article, "Mixed-Race Children: Building Bridges to New Identities" (Selection 10), became a historian's effort to retrospectively examine the issue of identity and its relationship to heritage. Where psychologists, sociologists, and educational social scientists might have approached this topic using interviews, focus groups, surveys, or observation, I decided to adopt what is sometimes referred to as "unobtrusive empiricism." Rather than obtruding into my subjects' lives, I based my research on what multiple-heritage people *had previously said* or *written* about themselves and their identities, using such sources as autobiographies and published interviews.

What I concluded through this collective biography approach was that "multis" have tended to develop five types of (often transitory) racial identities, only one of which is single-race, that is, identification with only one dimension of their racial heritages. In addition, I discussed the implications of these different types of "multi" identities for interpersonal relations, student organizations, and school curricula. In a subsequent article, "The Diversity Within: Intermarriage, Identity, and Campus Community," published the following year in *About Campus*, I revisited that topic and suggested the college-level ramifications of these different kinds of racial identities.

While not disagreeing with my conclusions, several psychologists and counselors who have read the articles have suggested that my findings would be more relevant, scientific, important, and applicable to educational and counseling practice if I could determine if "multis" followed some *pattern* of racial identity transformation or development as they passed through stages of their lives. Point well taken. Maybe they do, but I think not. My autobiographical readings suggest that no single developmental pattern exists. Rather, there seem to be a variety of patterns that "multis" tend to follow, influenced by diverse individual, group, and socioenvironmental factors.

The discussion of increasing intermarriage, the growing number of "multis," and the resulting societal and educational implications have now become part of most of my multicultural writings, lectures, and workshops, with an unexpected but rewarding result. By my raising and legitimizing this topic, some participants seem to feel liberated to talk about their own multiple ancestries, their intermarriages, and their children's mixed identities and cross-cultural love relationships. They thank me for addressing the issue and providing them with space to voice their personal stories, free from the tyranny of single-race (sometimes single-ethnic or single-religion) multicultural dogma.

Fortunately I have not been alone in my quest for the recognition of "multis." Other scholars are now addressing this issue, while national organizations of multiracial and multiethnic Americans, as well as the federal decision to permit Americans to check as many racial boxes as they wished in the year 2000 census, suggest that the time of the "multi" may have arrived. This may prove a challenge for administrative record keepers, social scientists who thrive on categorically clean, comparable longitudinal data, and resistant multicultural education advocates wedded to single-race models and practices. Yet as a "multi" and one who views multicultural education as a liberating movement, not a constricting orthodoxy, I need to thank my daughter, Alana, for insisting that I write our family history.

The corresponding Selection for this Chapter can be found on pg. 159.

CHAPTER 11

DIVERSITY AND THE MASS MEDIA:
BEYOND IMAGES TO INTROSPECTION

IN 1994 MY REMAKING AS A MULTICULTURALIST INTERSECTED IN A new way with my remaking as a professional. I took early retirement from the University of California, Riverside, the result of a confluence of factors.

In Chapter 7 I mentioned that my promotion and merit increase evaluations were becoming increasingly conflictive. Partly to address growing concerns by some departmental colleagues that I was not really "doing history" and partly because of my desire to pursue the deeper analysis of the mass media as a long-standing public multicultural curriculum, I had dedicated myself to research on the historical development of the movie treatment of race and ethnicity. The results, in terms of reception, were mixed.

Within the field of multicultural education I had hacked out a special historian's niche, focusing on the media aspects of the societal curriculum. Within my department, too, my numerous articles on the media received "credit" (in University of California parlance) as historical contributions, at least from most of my colleagues. But by the late 1980s contentiousness and predictably split votes had become the norm in my personnel cases.

My multiple loyalties had taken their toll. On the one hand there was my deep, visceral, equity-driven commitment to multicultural education and personal engagement with diversity-related dimensions of American life; on the other was the awareness that my departmental life, particularly when it came to personnel evaluations, had become a source of personal discomfort, time-consuming struggles, and emotionally draining tensions. (I need to point out, however, that my *personal* relations with most of my colleagues remained good. After I retired I continued to serve on committees and supervise doctoral dissertations, even accepting the dean's request to return for two years, from 1998 to 2000, as vice chair during a period of departmental turbulence.)

ADVANCING TO EMERITUS

Nonetheless my capacity to continue in this state of continual career tension had its psychological term limits. Fortunately, the University of California came to the rescue with a generous early retirement offer to all older faculty and staff. The offer arrived in the nick of time, like in the movies when the hero rides up at the moment of greatest peril. Yet I hesitated, maybe because I could not quite envision myself becoming labeled an emeritus, having just turned sixty.

But my wife, Laurel, as usual a crystalline thinker, pointed out the advantages of freedom from class schedules, department meetings, committee responsibilities, and other university duties, not to mention the nightmare of personnel evaluations. She was right. So I accepted the university's offer and, on July 1, 1994, became a professor emeritus.

Of course Laurel was right. Freedom gave me the opportunity to more fully pursue my passions—multicultural education and the societal implications of diversity. It also came precisely at a time when I was seriously reconsidering the relationship between the media, diversity, and education.

In the first decade of my media-and-diversity research I had pursued what had become the standard, nearly clichéd approach to that topic—the study of media images, sometimes stereotypes. With the burgeoning interest in diversity, scholars and journalists were now churning out books and articles on media images and stereotypes of different groups—racial, ethnic, gender, religious, cultural, national, sexual orientation, and disability. Name the group, and you can probably find "images of" articles, maybe even books, sometimes by the dozens.

This is not to downgrade the importance of that work, although the quality of such scholarship has varied wildly. After all, I had written my share of "images" articles. Moreover, my major book project was to be the granddaddy of all "images" books, tentatively titled *Hollywood's Multicultural Curriculum: A History of the Treatment of Race and Ethnicity in American Motion Pictures*. In fact I had nearly completed a four-hundred-page manuscript. All that remained was to finish revising the introductory, conceptual chapter. Yet it was precisely that introduction that drew me away from thinking merely about images into personal introspection as to the larger significance of what I was doing. Three other invitations set me off on paths that would converge in my new approach to the topic of media and diversity.

TALKING WITH TJ

The first invitation came in 1991 when Karen Bartz, then director of the Hallmark Corporate Foundation's Child Development Philanthropy Program, asked me to serve on the advisory committee for a new youth conflict resolution project. The committee consisted primarily of a small group of scholars, mainly psychologists and sociologists, as well as leaders of several major national youth organizations. We soon decided that the basis of the program should be a series of videotape conflict dilemmas, which young people would be asked to attempt to resolve.

Once again I found myself back on the other side of the barricades, not as a media analyst and critic but as a participant in the media creative process. This is not the place for a detailed discussion of our multiyear project—analyzing myriad scripts, reacting to formative research on young people's responses to various scenarios that were read to them, and debating the messages we wanted to send versus the ways that young people were interpreting them. Let's put it this way: Participating in that five-year project, which led to the six-episode videotape series, *Talking with TJ*, was like taking another postgraduate seminar. More than any academic media conferences I had attended or scholarship I had read, more than any of the numerous other media projects in which I had been involved, the TJ process increased my understanding of the complexities of the visual media, particularly the sometimes perplexing disconnects between media creation, content, and impact.

RETHINKING MEDIA

Parallel with my work on the Hallmark project came a second request, this time from James Lynch, a United Kingdom professor, to write a chapter for his book *Prejudice, Polemic or Progress?* Actually, he asked me to address language and culture, a hangover from my Contextual Interaction Model reputation, but I countered with a recommendation for a chapter on the mass media. When he accepted, I decided to try to develop a new, more integrative conceptual framework for my work on media and multicultural education.

That 1992 article, "Pride, Prejudice and Power: The Mass Media as Societal Educator on Diversity" (Selection 11), became one of my analytical benchmarks. Moving beyond content and "images of," I also wrestled with the elusive issue of audience reception and media impact. In addition, I extended my analysis beyond movies to seriously considering other mass media—television, radio, and print. For the first time I posited in writing what would become my five basic analytical categories for the ways that media teach about diversity: provide information; organize information and ideas; transmit values; create and reinforce expectations; and model behavior.

That categorical framing, in fact the article itself, became my baseline for the third request, when Jim and Cherry Banks asked me to write an article on mass media and knowledge construction for their 1995 *Handbook of Research on Multicultural Education*. Moreover, it provided the impetus for again rethinking the introduction to my movie book, an introduction that had been causing me problems. As it turned out, too good an impetus.

As I wrote and rewrote the book introduction, it kept getting bigger and bigger . . . and bigger. . . . Before long, it had become nearly one fifth of the manuscript. The grain was devouring the cattle.

Once more serendipity struck, again in the form of Jim Banks, this time accompanied by Brian Ellerbeck, then senior acquisitions editor of Teachers College Press. Would I consider expanding my *Handbook* article into a book? Would I! That query came at the perfect time. Early retirement had just liberated me from the tyranny of academic personnel evaluations and the pressures to demonstrate that, indeed, I was "doing history." I could write *my book my way* without being concerned about my colleagues' judgment.

The rest is, as they say, history. In March of 2000, Teachers College Press published the book, *The Children Are Watching: How the Media Teach about Diversity*. I had completed my odyssey from Latin American historian to ethnic studies advocate to multicultural education specialist to movie image analyst to . . . well, I'm not quite sure how to categorize myself now. Let's just leave at this. I am a multiculturalist, still in the ongoing process of continuous remaking.

The corresponding Selection for this Chapter can be found on pg. 166.

CHAPTER 12

GROWING WITH GRANDFATHERHOOD

T HE BIRTH OF ONE'S CHILD IS EXCITING. THE BIRTH OF ONE'S grandchild is metaphysical because it projects the significance of your lifetime far into the future, long after your own death. The world you help make will be the world in which they will live, although you won't be around to see all of the results. That is why the birth of my first granddaughter, Holly, on October 8, 1992, became such an important part of the continuous process of my remaking as a multiculturalist.

The immediate impact was tangible. My wife, Laurel, took early retirement in November of that year in order to be able to take care of Holly during the day. But soon I found that Holly's presence had a more profound meaning for me, influencing my thinking about the world, the future, and, inevitably, multiculturalism.

When Kappa Delta Pi asked me to write a short piece for its 1994 special publication, *Insights on Diversity,* I built it around my dreams—"A Better World for Holly." Two granddaughters later another invitation, to write an article for the Texas Elementary Principals and Supervisors Association publication, *Instructional Leader,* led to "A Better Multicultural Future for Holly, Melissa, and Kai." The importance of these three little girls in my life had forced me to rethink basic issues, including multicultural ones, as well as the way that I would orient my remaining productive years. For me, multicultural education had never before been so real, so important, or so personally relevant.

But Holly and Melissa did something else. Because they spent many days and nights in our home, I could observe them in many settings—playing in the yard, learning to draw and build, speaking, reading, and writing. And at times watching television or movie videotapes.

LEARNING FROM HOLLY AND MELISSA

Before long I observed them learning from the TV set, including about diversity. Multicultural education was occurring regularly before my very eyes. Research studies on media images and media impact had become personified in my two little preschool girls.

I watched and contemplated. Sometimes their learning about diversity was predictable. Other times it was surprising, even jolting, particularly to an "expert" like me who had been immersed in the topic. Maybe most illuminating was how often their interpretations of a specific show or movie clashed with dogmatic, published scholarly assertions about what kids must be learning from that source.

My observations of Holly and Melissa paralleled my writing of *The Children Are Watching.* Then I realized that these observations belonged in the book. Better yet, they should open the book. Chapter 1 became "Holly and Melissa's Multicultural Curriculum" (Selection 12), a series of vignettes about how these two little girls were learning about diversity—from such sources as *Cinderella, Pocahontas, The Lion King, The Karen Carpenter Story,* and Shirley Temple movies—before they ever set foot in a classroom where, in theory, multicultural education might "officially" begin.

TOUCHING LIVES

If I were restricted to preserving for posterity just one of my articles or chapters, it might be that one. Not that it's the *best* thing I have ever written. Certainly it is not the most scholarly contribution, not even the most scholarly chapter, in that book. But it is the piece that seems to have drawn the most intense and heartfelt responses.

Letters from cyberspace. Thanks from people at book signings, because the chapter has caused them to rethink the way to raise their children and relate to their grandchildren. People buying copies to give to their grown daughters and sons who had children. Teachers who work with young people, products of the media curriculum. Early childhood educators who said that they now viewed their tasks differently.

Holly and Melissa not only caused me to rethink the world and my role in helping to shape it, they also forced me to once again rethink my conclusions about the mass media and about multicultural education itself. These two little girls had become part of my remaking as a multiculturalist.

The corresponding Selection for this Chapter can be found on pg. 183.

CHAPTER 13

FACING THE FUTURE

A ND SO IT GOES. NOW THAT WE HAVE CROSSED THE PROVER-
bial bridge into the twenty-first century, my life as a
multiculturalist, with its constant remaking, continues.

In some respects the approach and advent of the new millennium have brought extensions of the past—lectures and workshops, committees and task forces, consulting and commence-
ment addresses, books and articles; sometimes wall-to-wall visits
to colleges, universities, school districts, businesses, government
agencies, mass media, communities, and conferences.

Yet, in other respects, changes in the world continually
force me to rethink multiculturalism. Little Jake has joined my
three granddaughters, now in elementary school, which means
a new dedication in some future article. The information technology revolution has spurred me into developing a presentation on its social and cultural implications. I have plunged
into futurism, with lectures on such topics as diversity and the
American future, the changing face of America, and the challenge of leadership in a multicultural society.

And the tragedy of September 11, 2001, has inevitably
raised the stakes for both multicultural and global education.
It has dramatized the increasingly interconnected nature of our
shrinking world. Moreover, it has foregrounded the importance
of both unum and pluribus, of cherishing the ties that bind
and of understanding more thoroughly our complex internal
diversity.

More phone calls and chance meetings have brought new
opportunities and challenges, avenues and distractions, constantly compelling me to recast my role as an increasingly public multiculturalist. At the 1991 national conference of the
American Association for Higher Education, where I was on
the plenary panel, I met Milton and Janet Bennett, directors of

the Intercultural Communication Institute in Portland, Oregon. This led first to guest lectures at their Summer Institute for Intercultural Communication and then, beginning in July 1995, to joining the institute faculty. With Milton and Janet's encouragement, support, and advice I created an annual week-long course, "Developing a Multicultural Vision" (later adding "for the New Millennium"). That yearly retreat, which has brought me into regular contact with institute faculty members and other professionals from around the world, leaders in the field of intercultural communication, has added a new, ongoing aspect to my learning and multicultural remaking.

THE POWER OF A TITLE

Then there was my book. Better yet, my book title, which had begun in its first draft as "Mass Media as Multicultural Education." Pursuant to an interchange with Jim Banks, the title morphed into "How the Media Teach about Diversity." Then, after submitting the manuscript, I received a call from my press editor, Brian Ellerbeck, with yet another suggestion, "The Children Are Watching." After further discussion we agreed on the ultimate title, *The Children Are Watching: How the Media Teach about Diversity.*

Much as my opening chapter for *Beyond Language* had drawn me into the language acquisition arena, the new title, combined with other elements of the book, including chapter 1 and the epilogue about Holly and Melissa, vaulted me into the area of early childhood development, with ensuing workshops, presentations, and consulting. For example, another chance meeting at a conference in early 2000, this time with members of the creative team for an upcoming Nickelodeon preschool television series, *Dora the Explorer*, led to my becoming a series consultant.

It was against the backdrop of such serendipitous events that I received a call from Jim Carnes, editor of *Teaching Tolerance*, asking me to be interviewed for his magazine. That interview, "Searching for Patterns: A Conversation with Carlos Cortés" (Selection 13), gave me the opportunity to muse about multiculturalism and my relationship to it—as educator, as media analyst, as an American of mixed ethnic and religious heritage, and as a grandfather.

LOOKING BACKWARD

But even as I continue down the road of multicultural unpredictability, I have had greater occasion and impetus to simultaneously rethink my career and my life. Moving forward has also caused me to look backward, to reconsider my crossroads, dilemmas, opportunities, and challenges, and to reevaluate my decisions and ponder their consequences, sometimes intended, often unintended.

By and large I look back without regret. Participating in the multicultural struggle has allowed me to contribute and to become visible in the quest for educational and societal equity. Yet the very nature of my career—disjointed, segmented, sometimes chaotic, writing and speaking for disparate audiences about disparate topics—has led to one underlying irony. Nobody quite knows how to categorize me as a professional. Most people know only part—or parts—of my career, sometimes reacting with surprise when they discover other areas in which I have been involved.

Maybe I'm happier that way, residing permanently on the categorical margins, operating alone in the penumbra of multiculturalism. To this day I receive calls from people asking me if I am able to speak or write about anything other than Latinos . . . or the media . . . or language . . . or higher education . . . or diversity in the workplace . . . or K–12 curriculum. In June of 2001 I even received a request to translate my 1974 *Gaúcho Politics in Brazil* into Portuguese for publication in Brazil.

I realize, too, that my career trajectory has come at a cost. By extending myself in so many directions, simultaneously following so many avenues, I have probably forfeited the opportunity of rising to a position of eminence in any one area. Yet it's a price that I am happy to have paid.

Maybe this is why I was so moved in the fall of 2000 when I was informed that the National Association of Student Personnel Administrators had selected me to receive its 2001 career award for Outstanding Contribution to Higher Education. It was not just that I had been recognized personally, although clearly I relished the honor. It was that this selection said to me that I *had* made the right decisions, despite their costs, and that maybe I had actually made a difference.

From my Seattle hotel, the night before receiving the award in March 2001, I called Holly and Melissa as I do every night when I am on the road. Some nights they seem to take no heed of my absence. That night, however, Holly (then eight) wanted to talk and asked me imperiously, "Granddad, why do you have to be gone so often?" After listening to my explanation about the award, she asked if it was sort of like when she and Melissa made their school honor roll. When I answered more or less in the affirmative, Holly thought for a time and then announced, "Granddad, I'm proud of you. I think I'm going to give you a B+."

The corresponding Selection for this Chapter can be found on pg. 192.

A selection of the author's works on the issues considered in each chapter. **Boldfaced entries** *are included in Part II: Selected Anthology.*

THEME I
EXPERIENCING TRANSFORMATIONS

CHAPTER 1 – *From Latin Americanist to Chicano Studies Advocate*

CHICOP: A response to the challenge of local Chicano history. *Aztlán, Chicano Journal of the Social Sciences and the Arts, I*(2), (Fall, 1970), 1–14.

The Mexican American. New York: Arno Press, 1974. [Twenty-one volume reprint series.]

Three perspectives on ethnicity: Blacks, Chicanos, and Native Americans (with Arlin I. Ginsburg, Allan W. F. Green, and James A. Joseph). New York: Putnam, 1976.

"Northwest from Tumacácori": A Chicano perspective on the American Revolution bicentennial. In John R. Brumgardt (Ed.), *The revolutionary era: A variety of perspectives.* **Riverside, CA: Historical Commission Press, 1976, pp. 15–26.**

The Chicano heritage. New York: Arno Press, 1976. [Fifty-five-volume reprint series.]

Mexicans. In *Harvard encyclopedia of American ethnic groups.* Cambridge, MA: Harvard University Press, 1980, pp. 697–719.

Hispanics in the United States. New York: Arno Press, 1980. [Thirty-volume reprint series.]

The Chicano heritage: Dual origins of Mexican Americans. In Josina Osorio (Ed.), *A bridge between two peoples: The aftermath.* Moscow, ID: University of Idaho, 1981, pp. 2–4.

The Chicano circumstance. In Josina Osorio (Ed.), *A bridge between two peoples: The aftermath.* Moscow, ID: University of Idaho, 1981, pp. 5–6.

Mexican Americans in twentieth-century California. In *California's Mexican heritage.* Special issue of *Masterkey: Anthropology of the Americas, LX*(2–3), (Summer/Fall, 1986), 36–48.

The Mexican-American press. In Sally M. Miller (Ed.), *The ethnic press in the United States: A historical analysis and handbook.* Westport, CT: Greenwood Press, 1987, pp. 247–260.

The Latino press in American journalism history. In Carolyn Martindale (Ed.), *Pluralizing journalism education: A multicultural handbook.* Westport, CT: Greenwood Press, 1993, pp. 103–111.

CHAPTER 2 — *From Historian to Education Activist*

Revising the "All-American soul course": A bicultural avenue to educational reform. In Alfredo Castañeda, Manuel Ramírez III, Carlos E. Cortés, and Mario Barrera (Eds.), *Mexican Americans and educational change.* Riverside, CA: Mexican American Studies Program, University of California, 1971, pp. 314–339. [Reprinted by Arno Press, New York, 1974.]

Mexican Americans and educational change (coedited with Alfredo Castañeda, Manuel Ramírez III, and Mario Barrera). Riverside, CA: Mexican American Studies Program, University of California, 1971. [Reprinted by Arno Press, New York, 1974.]

Teaching the Chicano experience. In James A. Banks (Ed.), *Teaching ethnic studies: Concepts and strategies*. Washington, D.C: National Council for the Social Studies, 1973, pp. 181–199.

The Mexican-American experience: Its significance for American education. In *Mexican-Americans, education and public policy.* Kansas City: University of Missouri Ethnic Awareness Center, 1975, pp. 23–34.

Need for a geo-cultural perspective in the bicentennial. *Educational Leadership, XXXIII*(4), (January, 1976), 290–292.

Commonalities and diversity in the Latino experience: A conceptual framework for exploring Latino challenges and opportunities. In *Conference Proceedings of the Second Annual Meeting of the International Advisory Panel of the Ibero-American Heritage Curriculum Project, Latinos in the Making of the United States of America: Yesterday, Today,and Tomorrow, October 6–9, 1988.* Albany: University of the State of New York and State Education Department, 1989, pp. 127–137.

CHAPTER 3 — *From Ethnic Studies Chair to Multicultural Education Specialist*

Concepts and strategies for multiethnic education. *Social Science Education Consortium Newsletter, 24* (November, 1975), 1–4.

The role of educational institutions in promoting cultural pluralism. In *School desegregation and cultural pluralism: Perspectives on progress.* San Francisco: Service,

Training and Research in Desegregated Education, Far West Laboratory for Educational Research and Development, 1975, pp. 21–28.

Understanding you and them: Tips for teaching about ethnicity (with Fay Metcalf and Sharryl Hawke). Boulder, CO: ERIC Clearinghouse for Social Studies/Social Science Education and Social Science Education Consortium, 1976.

Multicultural education: Hope for America's third century. In *Compensatory education: Renaissance through the Spirit of '76*. California Association for Compensatory Education, 1976, pp. 5–9.

Curriculum guidelines for multiethnic education (with James A. Banks, Geneva Gay, Ricardo L. García, and Anna S. Ochoa). Arlington, VA: National Council for the Social Studies, 1976.

Nondecision-making and decision-making in multicultural education. In *Multicultural education: The interdisciplinary approach*. Sacramento, CA: Bureau of Intergroup Relations, California Department of Education, 1976, pp. 18–42.

New perspectives on multicultural education. *Thrust for Educational Leadership, VII*(3), (January, 1978), 20–22.

Dealing with the density of diversity: Groupness and individuality in the California history/social science framework." *Social Studies Review, XXI*(1), (Fall, 1981), 12–18.

Toward educational equity for all: A planning guide for integrating multicultural/nonsexist education into the K–12 curriculum (with Anthony V. Codianni and Bruce E. Tipple). Manhattan, KS: Midwest Race and Sex Desegregation Assistance Centers, 1981.

Multicultural education: A curricular basic for our multiethnic future. In *Doubts & Certainties, IV*(7–8), (March-April, 1990), 1–5. [Reprinted in Peter A. Barrett (Ed.), *Doubts & certainties: Working together to restructure schools*. Washington, DC: National Education Association, 1991, pp. 59–69.]

Bone and flesh: Uses and abuses of literature in the teaching of history. In *Humanities and the social studies*. Special issue of *Social Studies Review, XXXI*(2), (Winter, 1992), 45–52.

Education in a multicultural society. *Restructuring Brief,* No. 9 (May, 1995), 1–8.

CHAPTER 4 — *From School Curriculum Critic to Societal Curriculum Analyst*

The societal curriculum and the school curriculum: Allies or antagonists? *Educational Leadership, XXXVI*(7), (April, 1979), 475–479.

Hispanics in the media and the impact on public policy: A humanistic assessment. In Virginia Correa-Jones, Alfredo Benavides, and Miguel A. Terán (Eds.), *The Hispanics: A missing link in public policy*. Des Moines, IA: Spanish Speaking Peoples Commission of Iowa, 1980, pp. 29–35.

The role of media in multicultural education. *Viewpoints in Teaching and Learning, LVI*(1), (Winter, 1980), 38–49.

The societal curriculum: Implications for multiethnic education. In James A. Banks (Ed.), *Education in the 80's: Multiethnic education*. Washington, D.C.: National Education Association, 1981, pp. 24–32.

Historians and the media: Revising the societal curriculum of ethnicity. *Federation Reports, IV*(1), (January-February, 1981), 9–14.

Use—don't be used by—society's curriculum. *Today's Education, LXX*(1), (February–March, 1981), 46–49, 52.

The mass media: Civic education's public curriculum. In *The civic education of the American teacher.* Special issue of the *Journal of Teacher Education, XXXIV*(6), (November–December, 1983), 25–29.

Mass media and public perspectives. In *Proceedings of the First Annual Meeting of the International Advisory Panel of the Ibero-American Heritage Curriculum Project, Latinos in the Making of the United States of America: Yesterday, Today and Tomorrow.* Albany: University of the State of New York and State Education Department, 1988, pp. 99–110.

The media curriculum on ethnicity: Implications for schooling. *Multicultural Leader, I*(3), (Summer, 1988), 1–2.

Uncovering the "societal curriculum." *American Association for Higher Education Bulletin, XLIII*(10), (June, 1991), 3–5.

Mass media as multicultural curriculum: Public competitor to school education. *Multicultural Education, II*(3), (Spring, 1995), 4–7.

The media will teach it, even if we don't. *Civic learning in a diverse democracy.* Special issue of *Peer Review, II*(1), (Fall, 1999), 10–11.

THEME II
BUILDING BRIDGES

CHAPTER 5 — *Connecting Multicultural to Global Education*

Mexico in the study of Mexican Americans: An analysis of transnational linkages. Denver: Center for Teaching International Relations, University of Denver, 1976.

Multicultural education: A global perspective. In William E. Lipsky (Ed.), *Planning for multicultural education: A workshop report.* Los Angeles: Curriculum Inquiry Center, University of California, 1977, pp. 22–37.

Multicultural education and global education: Natural partners in the quest for a better world. In *Curricular dimensions of global education.* Philadelphia: Pennsylvania Department of Education and Research for Better Schools, 1979, pp. 83–97.

Global perspectives and multicultural education. *Global Perspectives: Education for a World in Change,* **Feature Section, (February, 1980), 3–6.**

The dilemma of perspective: Obstacle or avenue to global thinking? *Thresholds in Education, VIII*(4), (November, 1982), 6–9.

Multiethnic and global education: Partners for the eighties? *Phi Delta Kappan, LXIV*(8), (April, 1983), 568–571.

Teaching about human migration in global perspective (Occasional Paper No. 4). New York: Global Perspectives in Education, June, 1983.

Global education and textbooks (with Dan B. Fleming). In Carlos E. Cortés and Dan B. Fleming (Eds.), *Images and realities of four world regions.* Special issue of *Social Education, L*(5), (September, 1986), 340–344.

Changing global perspectives in textbooks (with Dan B. Fleming). In Carlos E. Cortés and Dan B. Fleming (Eds.), *Images and realities of four world regions.* Special issue of *Social Education, L*(5), (September, 1986), 376–384.

Global education and multicultural education: Toward a 21st-century intersection. In Leslie Swartz, Linda Warner, and David L. Grossman (Eds.), *Intersections: A professional development project in multicultural and global education, Asian and Asian American studies.* Boston: Children's Museum, 1998, pp. 109–128.

CHAPTER 6 — *Connecting Multicultural to Other Educational Concerns*

Multicultural law and humanities education: Preparing young people for a future of constructive pluralism. In Lynda Carl Falkenstein and Charlotte C. Anderson (Eds.), *Daring to dream: Law and the humanities for elementary schools.* Chicago: American Bar Association, 1980, pp. 56–61.

"Why in the World": Using television to develop critical thinking skills (with Elinor Richardson). *Phi Delta Kappan, LXIV*(10), (June, 1983), 715–716.

Citizenship education and cultural pluralism: A personal perspective. In *America's changing face: Civic values and the challenges of immigration.* Report of the Fifth Annual Jennings Randolph Forum of the Council for the Advancement of Citizenship, (December, 1986), pp. 33–35.

The education of language minority students: A contextual interaction model. In California State Department of Education, *Beyond language: Social and cultural factors in schooling language minority students***. Los Angeles: Evaluation, Dissemination and Assessment Center, California State University, 1986, pp. 3–33.**

Educating society for equity. In H. Prentice Baptiste, Jr., Hersholt C. Waxman, Judith Walker de Felix, and James E. Anderson (Eds.), *Leadership, equity, and school effectiveness.* Newbury Park, CA: Sage Publications, 1990, pp. 259–272.

Coping with the A words: Acculturation, assimilation, and "adducation." *BEOutreach, IV*(1), (March, 1993), pp. 3–5.

Multiculturation: An educational model for a culturally and linguistically diverse society. In Karen Spangenberg-Urbschat and Robert Pritchard (Eds.), *Kids come in all languages: Reading instruction for ESL students*. Newark, DE: International Reading Association, 1994, pp. 22–35.

Language and culture: Inevitable intersections. *Embracing ELT in the New Millenium: Proceedings of the Summer, 2000, International Conference of the Korea Association of Teachers of English* (June, 2000), pp. 39–44.

CHAPTER 7 – *Connecting Schools to Media Images*

Latin America: A filmic approach (with Leon G. Campbell and Robert Pinger). Riverside, CA: Latin American Studies Program, University of California, 1975.

A filmic approach to the study of historical dilemmas (with Leon G. Campbell and Alan Curl). Riverside, CA: Latin American Studies Program, University of California, 1976.

Film as revolutionary weapon: A pedagogical analysis (with Leon G. Campbell). Riverside, CA: Latin American Studies Program, University of California, 1977.

Race and ethnicity in the history of the Americas: A filmic approach (with Leon G. Campbell). Riverside, CA: Latin American Studies Program, University of California, 1979.

The Greaser's Revenge to *Boulevard Nights:* The mass media curriculum on Chicanos. In National Association for Chicano Studies, *History, culture, and society: Chicano studies in the 1980s*. Ypsilanti, MI: Bilingual Review/Press, 1983, pp. 125–140.

The history of ethnic images in film: The search for a methodology. In *Ethnic images in popular genres and media*. Special issue of *MELUS, The Journal of the Society for the Study of the Multi-Ethnic Literature of the United States, (XI)3* (Fall, 1984), 63–77.

Chicanas in film: History of an image. In Gary D. Keller (Ed.), *Chicano cinema: Research, reviews, and resources*. Binghamton, NY: Bilingual Review/Press, 1985, pp. 94–108.

Italian-Americans in film: From immigrants to icons. In *Italian-American Literature*. Special issue of *MELUS, The Journal of the Society for the Study of the Multi-Ethnic Literature of the United States, XIV(3–4)*, (Fall-Winter, 1987), 107–126.

To view a neighbor: The Hollywood textbook on Mexico. In John H. Coatsworth and Carlos Rico (Eds.), *Images of Mexico in the United States*. La Jolla, CA: Center for U.S.–Mexican Studies, University of California, San Diego, 1989, pp. 91–118.

The immigrant in film: Evolution of an illuminating icon. In Paul Loukides and Linda K. Fuller (Eds.), *Stock characters in American popular film* (Vol. I of *Beyond the Stars*). Bowling Green, OH: Bowling Green State University Popular Press, 1990, pp. 23–34.

Hollywood interracial love: Social taboo as screen titillation. In Paul Loukides and Linda K. Fuller (Eds.), *Plot conventions in American popular film* (Vol. II of *Beyond the Stars*). Bowling Green, OH: Bowling Green State University Popular Press, 1991, pp. 21–35.

The convenient arena: Mexico in U.S. motion pictures. In Paul Ganster and Mario Miranda Pacheco (Eds.), *Imágenes recíprocas: La educación en las relaciones México-Estados Unidos de América/Reciprocal Images: Education in U.S.–Mexican Relations.* Mexico City: ANUIES-PROFMEX, 1991, pp. 235–244.

Harmony and conflict of intercultural images: The treatment of Mexico in U.S. feature films and K–12 textbooks (with Gerald Michael Greenfield). *Mexican Studies/Estudios Mexicanos, VII*(2), (Summer, 1991), 283–301.

Who Is María? What is Juan? Dilemmas of analyzing the Chicano image in U.S. feature films. In Chon A. Noriega (Ed.), *Chicanos and film: Essays on Chicano representation and resistance.* New York: Garland, 1992, pp. 83–104.

Them and us: Immigration as societal barometer and social educator in American film. In Robert Brent Toplin (Ed.), *Hollywood as mirror: Changing views of "outsiders" and "enemies" in American movies.* Westport, CT: Greenwood Press, 1993, pp. 53–73.

Gender gap/gender trap: Hispanic–Anglo love in U.S. motion pictures. In Renate von Bardeleben (Ed.), *Gender, Self, and Society: Proceedings of the IV International Conference on the Hispanic Cultures of the United States.* Frankfurt: Peter Lang, 1993, pp. 257–276.

The Hollywood curriculum on Italian Americans: Evolution of an icon of ethnicity. In Lydio F. Tomasi, Piero Gastaldo, and Thomas Row (Eds.), *The Columbus people: Perspectives in Italian immigration to the Americas and Australia.* Staten Island, NY: Center for Migration Studies, 1994, pp. 89–108.

Media and education in a multicultural society: A historian's perspective. In Diane Carson and Lester D. Friedman (Eds.), *Shared differences: Multicultural media and practical pedagogy.* Urbana, IL: University of Illinois Press, 1995, pp. 110–123.

THEME III
EXPANDING VISIONS

CHAPTER 8 — *Diversity and Society:*
Beyond Celebration to Contemplation

Supreme Court report: The dislike of the unlike (with Van Perkins). *Update on Law-Related Education, IV*(3), (Fall, 1980), 4–8, 58–59.

Ethnic groups and the American dream(s). *Social Education, XLVI*(6), (October, 1982), 401–403.

Cultural pluralism and the humanities. In *Proceedings of the Meeting on the Humanities, Los Angeles, 1984.* Washington, D.C.: Council of Chief State School Officers, 1984, pp. 155–163.

E pluribus unum: Out of many one. In JoAnn Cabello (Ed.), *California perspectives: An anthology from the immigrant students project.* San Francisco: California Tomorrow, 1990, pp. 13–16.

Multicultural education and the challenge of PCology: A multiculturalist's manifesto, *National Association for Multicultural Education News, I*(2), (Winter, 1992), 1–2.

Different strokes. . . . *Fiat Lux,* IV(2), (January, 1994), 62–65.

Limits to *pluribus,* limits to *unum:* Unity, diversity, and the great American balancing act. *National Forum, LXXIV*(1), (Winter, 1994), 6–8.

Official English and the envisioning of America. *Multicultural Education, IV*(2), (Winter, 1996), 1.

CHAPTER 9 – *Diversity and Higher Education: Beyond Activism to Analysis*

To serve society: An alternative model for the selection of professional school students (with Barbara Newlin Hewitt). *Aztlán, International Journal of Chicano Studies Research, VIII* (1977), 201–216.

Pluribus & *unum:* The quest for community amid diversity. In *Change: The Magazine of Higher Learning, XXIII*(5) (September/October, 1991), 8–13.

Diversity workshops: Possibilities and paradoxes. *Diversity Digest,* (Summer, 1997), 12–13.

Building community from communities: Diversity and the future of higher education. *Metropolitan Universities: An International Forum, IX*(4), (Spring, 1999), 11–18.

CHAPTER 10 – *Diversity and Boundaries: Beyond Being to Bordering*

The Chicanos—A frontier people. *Agenda, A Journal of Hispanic Issues, X*(1) (January-February, 1980), 16–20.

Searching for imaginative responses to inevitable challenges. In Joseph Nalven (Ed.), *Border perspectives on the U.S./Mexico relationship.* Special issue of *New Scholar, IX*(1–2), (1984), pp. 39–49.

International borders in American films: Penetration, protection, and perspective. In Paul Loukides and Linda K. Fuller (Eds.), *Locales in American popular film* (Vol. IV of *Beyond the Stars*). Bowling Green, OH: Bowling Green State University Popular Press, 1993, pp. 37–49.

Mixed-race children: Building bridges to new identities. *Reaching Today's Youth, III*(2), (Winter, 1999), 28–31.

The diversity within: Intermarriage, identity, and campus community. *About Campus, V*(1), (March-April, 2000), 5–10.

The liquidity of national borders. *Telemedium, The Journal of Media Literacy, XLVII*(3), (Fall, 2001), 23.

CHAPTER 11 — *Diversity and the Mass Media:*
Beyond Images to Introspection

Challenges of using film and television as socio-cultural documents to teach history. In John E. O'Connor (Ed.), *Image as artifact: The historical analysis of film and television.* Malabar, FL: Robert E. Krieger and the American Historical Association, 1990, pp. 156–168.

Feature films and the teaching of world history (with Tom Thompson). *Social Studies Review, XXIX*(2), (Winter, 1990), 46–53.

Empowerment through media literacy: A multicultural approach. In Christine E. Sleeter (Ed.), *Empowerment through multicultural education.* Albany: State University of New York Press, 1991, pp. 143–157.

Media literacy: An educational basic for the information age. In Catherine Emihovich and Walter Wager (Eds.), *Media culture/school culture: Technology in education.* Special issue of *Education and Urban Society, XXIV*(4), (August, 1992), 489–497.

Pride, prejudice and power: The mass media as societal educator on diversity. In James Lynch, Celia Modgil, and Sohan Modgil (Eds.), *Prejudice, polemic or progress?* (Vol. II of *Cultural diversity and the schools.*) London: Falmer Press, 1992, pp. 367–381.

Power, passivity, and pluralism: Mass media in the development of Latino culture and identity. *Latino Studies Journal, IV*(1), (January, 1993), 3–22.

Knowledge construction and popular culture: The media as multicultural educator. In James A. Banks and Cherry A. McGee Banks (Eds.), *Handbook of research on multicultural education.* New York: Macmillan, 1995, pp. 169–183.

The children are watching: How the media teach about diversity, edited by Carlos E. Cortés. New York: Teachers College Press, 2000.

The mass media as multicultural educators. *Telemedium: The Journal of Media Literacy, XLVII*(2), (November, 2001), 7–9.

THEME IV
GRAPPLING WITH NEW CHALLENGES

CHAPTER 12 — *Growing with Grandfatherhood*

A better world for Holly. *Insights on diversity.* West Lafayette, IN: Kappa Delta Pi, 1994, p. 41.

A better multicultural future for Holly, Melissa, and Kai. *Instructional Leader, VII*(5), (September, 1994), 1–3, 12.

The omnipresent educator: The mass media curriculum on diversity. *Instructional Leader, XIII*(4), (July, 2000), 1–2, 10–12.

Holly and Melissa's Multiculutral Curriculum. In Carlos E. Cortés (Ed.), *The*
children are watching: How the media teach about diversity. **New York:**
Teachers College Press, 2000, pp. 7–16.

CHAPTER 13 – *Facing the Future*

Pluribus, unum, and the American future. *Today, XV*(3), (Spring, 1990), 8–10.

Backing into the future: Columbus, Cleopatra, Custer, & the diversity revolution. In
Higher Education Exchange. Dayton, Ohio: Kettering Foundation, 1994, 6–14.

Beyond affirmative action. *Multicultural Review, V*(1), (March, 1996), 16–21.

Preparing for a multicultural future. *Principal, LXXVI*(1), (September, 1996), 16–20.

From multiculturalism to interculturalism: America's inexorable journey. *SIETAR*
International Communique, No. 10 (1997), 6–7.

The accelerating change of American diversity. *The School Administrator, LVI*(5),
(May, 1999), 12–14.

Searching for patterns: A conversation with Carlos Cortés (with Jim Carnes).
Teaching Tolerance, 16 **(Fall, 1999), 10–15.**

Dr. Carlos Cortés: Writer, lecturer, and consultant to a multicultural society and a
shrinking world (by Joe Beck). *The Hispanic Outlook in Higher Education, XI*(12),
(March 26, 2001), 37–38.

Watch out! An interview with Carlos E. Cortés (by Irvin D. Harrison). *Mirage, XIX*(2),
(Winter, 2001), pp. 18–19.

PART TWO

SELECTED ANTHOLOGY

The following thirteen previously published selections—eleven of my articles, one of my book chapters, and an interview with me—were chosen because of their value as historical artifacts, not because I consider them the best of my writings. Taken individually, each helps to document one of the thirteen related autobiographical essays in the book's first section. Taken as a whole, along with the other entries in the Selected Bibliography of my writings, they suggest the trajectory of my ideas about multicultural education and the development of my thinking about broader issues of unity and diversity.

SELECTION 1

"NORTHWEST FROM TUMACÁCORI": A CHICANO PERSPECTIVE ON THE AMERICAN REVOLUTION BICENTENNIAL

WHAT IS A CHICANO PERSPECTIVE AND WHAT DOES IT HAVE to do with the American Revolution Bicentennial? If this sounds like the title of some pretentiously artsy motion picture, please accept my apology. Yet these two questions need to be asked and answered if we are to deal honestly with the relationship between the current national birthday party and the experience of Mexican Americans, the country's second largest minority.[1]

First, what is a Chicano perspective? Please note—I said *a* Chicano perspective, not *the* Chicano perspective. There is no such thing as *the* Chicano perspective, nor, for that matter *the* Black perspective, *the* Native American perspective, *the* Anglo perspective, or *the* perspective of any group. Not all members of any group think alike or act alike. Unifying historical experiences and cultural patterns, no matter how pervasive and significant, can never obliterate the inevitable and enriching internal diversity of every group.

But Chicano perspectives there are, and they provide important alternatives to traditional perspectives on the American experience. For the most part, the study and presentation of American history has been based on an east-to-west structural framework—the Eurocentric view of the United States as a strictly unidirectional product of civilization which spread from Western Europe across the Atlantic Ocean to the

Source: John R. Brumgardt (Ed.), *The Revolutionary Era: A Variety of Perspectives* (Riverside, CA: Historical Commission Press, 1976), pp. 15–26.

Reprinted by permission of John R. Brumgardt.

east coast of what is today the United States and then west to the Pacific. This ethnocentric vision of our nation's past strait-jackets most thinking and teaching about the American past and dominates American institutions, including the educational system and the mass media.

Representative of such ethnocentric tunnel vision is the recent article, "The Great Frontier Thesis as a Framework for the American History Survey in Secondary Schools," by Raymond Starr.[2] In his article, Professor Starr suggests that teachers organize their U.S. history survey courses around the theme of the advancing frontier, as posited by such scholars as Frederick Jackson Turner and Walter Prescott Webb. Of course, when Professor Starr says "Great Frontier," he means only the east-to-west advancing frontier of the United States. And how would such an approach deal with those people—particularly Mexicans and Native Americans—who happened to be in the way of this advancing frontier and were "advanced over?" As usual, as *obstacles* to westward-moving Anglo civilization.

Chicano perspectives provide an alternative to the dominant, distorting, and self-deluding east-to-west framework for looking at our nation's past. Rejecting the narrow view that "experience follows the flag"—that the U.S. heritage is only that which occurred *within the national political boundaries of the United States*—I would posit that a more accurate, sensitive, and intellectually valid way of looking at our past is to include the development of *the entire geo-cultural area which ultimately composed the United States.* Such a framework would be based on the *continuous, parallel study* of the various civilizations which developed in the geo-cultural United States. It would continuously include the experiences of the many Native American societies, the northward advance of Hispanic and Mexican civilization concurrent with the westward advance of Anglo-American civilization, and relations between these two expanding societies and Native American civilizations.

Such a frame of reference is not entirely new. The renowned American historian, Herbert Eugene Bolton, championed this approach with his Greater America concept as early as 1927.[3] However, Bolton's theory focused mainly on the comparative expansion and development of elites and institutions—government, church, military, and system of laws. A "Chicano-ized" neo-Boltonian Greater America approach would include such themes, but would also encompass a broader socio-cultural spectrum—the comparative study of the lives, experiences, and cultures of "ordinary" people in these various societies.

Several other ideas should be kept in mind when viewing our Greater American heritage from a Chicano perspective. That heritage should be viewed from multiethnic perspectives—the perspectives of Mexicans, Indians, Spaniards, and Blacks who participated in the northerly expansion of Mexican civilization and in the inter-relationship with other Native Americans and westward-moving Anglo society. That heritage should be viewed from multiclass perspectives—the perspectives not only of the Hispano-Mexican lead-ers (heads of expeditions, government administrators, priests, and large landowners), but also of the many ordinary men, women and children who contributed to the establishment and development of northern Mexican soci-ety. That heritage should be viewed with a recognition of both the unifying historical-cultural patterns of northern Mexican society and the rich internal diversity of the northern Mexican experience. That heritage should be viewed as active, not passive—what the northern Mexican people *did* as well as what was *done to* them (for example, the U.S. conquest of northern Mexico in 1846). Finally, that heritage should not simply be viewed from the out-side as a distant historical phenomenon, but an attempt should be made to *get inside* that experience—to attempt to understand and feel northern Mexican history as an intensely human experience, a meaningful part of the total experience of Greater America and world humankind.

That said, what about the second part of the question—what does this have to do with the American Revolution Bicentennial? Quite simply, a Chicano perspective on the Bicentennial is a south-to-north view of the Revolutionary era. Looking at the *geo-cultural* American experience, it is a westernization of the Bicentennial through the application of the neo-Boltonian Greater America concept.

A Chicano perspective on the American Revolution Bicentennial asks the following—in looking at the Greater American experience of the geo-cultural United States (that area which ultimately would compose the United States and the various cultures and experiences encompassed by that area), what was happening in the west while the east was going through the process of rebellion against England? In functional terms, it issues the challenge—how can the inclusion of the Chicano heritage help make the Bicentennial a true *national* celebration, not just a reinforcement of the traditional east-to-west framework for looking at the American experience?

In the fall of 1970, Dr. Mario Barrera (a young political scientist then at the University of California, Riverside, now at UC San Diego), R. Alex Campbell (a professional filmmaker for the Kaiser Permanente Medical Care Program), and I pondered that question. Our answer was to make a motion picture, a filmic documentary attempt to provide a Chicano perspective west-ernization of the American Revolutionary era.

We selected as our subject the 1775–1776 expedition of Juan Bautista de Anza, which resulted in the founding of a Spanish colony at what ultimately would become the city of San Francisco. This subject was ideal, because the expedition culminated in the west at the same time that the American Revolution was erupting on the east coast. This meant the film would have a natural linkage to the celebration of the Bicentennial.

The result of our efforts was "Northwest from Tumacácori," a 33-minute, black-and-white documentary film. In it we attempted to re-create not only the story of the Anza expedition, but also the feeling of the expedition—to immerse the viewer in it. While realizing the limitations of discussing a film which few of the readers have seen, I will attempt in the next few pages to explain how this film provides *a* Chicano perspective on the American Revolution Bicentennial.

Northwest from Tumacácori traces the story of the 1775–1776 second Anza expedition to California. It picks up the expedition in the village of Tumacácori, one of the many small towns in which Anza garnered recruits for the California colony. From there the film follows the expedition to San Francisco Bay, where the colonists founded the Mission Dolores and dedicated it to their patron saint, Francis of Assisi.

While maintaining the film's basic chronological framework, we also attempted to extend its scope in both time and space. Moving from the 1775–1776 timeline, we employed both flashbacks (such as Anza's 1774 expedition to California and his preparations for the second expedition) and flashforwards (the U.S. conquest of northern Mexico in 1846). To broaden the geographical scope, we discussed the Pacific coast geo-political confrontation among England, Russia, and Spain, and introduced the variety of Native American civilizations in the area. The use of a narrator made such extensions possible without destroying the essential temporal and spatial unity of the film.

The very selection of the subject matter—the Anza expedition and the Mexicanizing of California—was an implementation of the Greater America concept. It focused on an aspect of the total heritage of the geo-cultural area that ultimately became the United States. We attempted to humanize and give visual dramatization to the spread of a civilization north into the area and its interrelationship with existent Native American societies—a process which occurred long before Anglo-Americans penetrated the territory. Through the film we tried to provide material for the development of a truer understanding of our nation's multicultural past. Now let us briefly consider the manner in which the film implements some of the concepts that I proposed as important elements of a Chicano perspective on our national heritage.

An essential element of a Chicano perspective is the recognition of the multiethnic nature of history. No ethnic group holds a monopoly on our nation's past. Yet that past has generally been presented from Anglo perspectives—interpretations from the point of view of the dominant society. Even the Boltonian western counter-attack did not break away from the "dominance" syndrome. It merely replaced Anglo perspectives with Spanish institutional and upper class points of view.

A Chicano perspective goes beyond traditional Boltonianism by subjecting history to multiethnic scrutiny. How did various ethnic groups participate in and view the Greater American heritage? What are the perspectives of members of various ethnic groups on critical historical phenomena?

We determined that three major ethnic perspectives on the Anza expedition needed to be expressed in the film—Mexican, Spanish, and Indian.

The first critical distinction was in our conception of the terms Mexican and Spanish. The territory at that time was claimed by Spain (as well as by many Indian civilizations). The Spanish administrative unit was the Territory of New Spain. In so far as the Anza expedition represented an extension of the King's political control, the establishment of a new Church mission, and the erection of a new governmental unit, the event was a Spanish phenomenon. However, in so far as the expedition represented the movement of American-born (in the Western Hemispheric sense) people, the extension of *their* local experience, and the development of the Greater Mexican geo-cultural heritage, the event was a Mexican phenomenon.

One of the persistent aspects of Spanish Borderlands mythology has been the idea that this northward socio-cultural movement was purely Spanish. In point of fact, while a few Spaniards did make it to northern Mexico and Spanish institutions were established in the borderlands, the essence of this movement was Mexican. It was an extension of the experience of American-born people, who took to the north a society which was not pure Spanish import, but rather culturally (and biologically) mestizo—a continuous, dynamic mixture of Spanish and Indian elements which resulted in a new Mexican civilization. And the people who spread this new civilization north to the borderlands should most accurately be referred to as Mexicans.

The double standard of European longevity has been applied too long. Eastern U.S. history does not begin in 1776 or 1783, but in 1607 with the founding of Jamestown. And U.S. history books have traditionally referred to Americans, American this, and American that, long before the Atlantic coast story reaches the independent United States. According to that rationale—that the socio-cultural history of a nation long precedes its national political birth—the term Mexican should be used for socio-cultural phenomena as they occurred, not put into the historical deep freeze until some political document provides the legal name change.

In these terms, the Anza expedition was almost entirely Mexican. Anza himself was born on the northern Mexican frontier, the scion of two generations of northern frontier people. Most of the rest of the expedition was also of Mexican lineage. A notable exception was Padre Pedro Font, who hailed from Barcelona.

In "Northwest from Tumacácori," Mexican perspectives on the expedition are presented through the voices of two members of the expedition—Anza himself and José Antonio Sánchez, one of the ordinary members of the settlement party. Spanish and Indian aspects of the event are presented either by the narrator or by inference through the commentary of Anza and Sánchez. The Spanish aspect of the expedition includes references to King Carlos III of Spain, the Viceroy of New Spain, and the geo-political importance of the expedition for Spain. A special distinction is made by indicating that Padre Font was a Spaniard from Barcelona in contrast to the Mexican mestizoes, creoles, and Indians who comprised nearly the totality of the expedition.

The introduction of Native American perspectives required more subtlety. As the movie is designed as a multiperspective recreation of a significant event of Greater American history, we avoided "taking sides" in the often polaric Hispanicist–Indianist historical controversy. Resisting the temptation to use "good vs. bad" clichés, which often undermine the study of intergroup relations, we attempted to include Indians as a significant part of the story even though no Indians speak in the film.

The narrator points out that Indians make up a large part of the expedition. Other Native American societies play a collateral role. Apaches provide both a constant threat and a real impact, when at one point they steal all of the expedition's horses, necessitating a lengthy delay. In contrast, such Indians as the Yumas and Cogats provide food for the expedition en route. To sharpen this contrast and to underscore the "not all Indians are alike" theme, Sánchez points out that the Yumas, like the Mexican settlers, also fear the Apaches. Finally, Anza announces that one of his major goals is to convert the San Francisco Bay Indians to Catholicism and make them loyal subjects of the King of Spain.

The issue of Indian–Mexican conflict is dealt with in a number of ways. While Anza tells the Mexican families that they will be settling land belonging to the King of Spain, Sánchez expresses some doubt about land ownership with the statement, "But we knew the Indians thought it was theirs." While Anza rhapsodizes about his preparations for dealing peacefully with Indians through gifts, he also takes ten professional soldiers in case this "peaceful" approach fails. We provided a note of visual irony to Anza's "peace talk" by backing his words with a picture of soldiers and Indians locked in combat.

Finally, there is the Indian revolt at Mission San Diego. Anza, resting at Mission San Gabriel near present-day Los Angeles, interrupts his expedition to quell the revolt. Although Sánchez follows Anza's orders, he introduces an Indian point of view by stating, "I don't know why the Indians revolted. They may have good reason." It would have been ahistorical to transform Sánchez, an illiterate Mexican villager, into an informed social philosopher by having him launch into an in-depth discussion of the Hispanicist–Indianist controversy. However, his injection of uncertainty into the land ownership and San Diego revolt questions creates a multiethnic relativity of viewpoints. This clash of perspectives is further dramatized in the final symbolic image of the San Diego revolt sequence. After Anza suppresses the rebellion and proclaims his success in "pacifying the land," the camera, shooting from within a prison cell from behind an Indian holding onto the window bars, focuses through the bars on a huge cross outside of the prison. To the Indian, civil authority (prison bars) and the Church (cross) may well be mutually supporting elements of oppression.

A second basic component of a Chicano approach to the Greater American heritage is a consideration of multiclass perspectives. In some respects these may be similar to multiethnic perspectives. In other respects class divisions may cut across ethnic lines.

The Anza expedition, although clearly Mexican in its human components, was divided rigidly along class lines. In contrast to the leader-oriented perspective of most previous studies and presentations of the stories of Hispano-Mexican expeditions into northern Mexico, "Northwest from Tumacácori" clearly delineates the divergent experiences and perspectives of the elites and masses in the Anza expedition. The principal vehicles for this dual perspective and divergent experience are Anza and Sánchez.

In the film, Anza represents the expedition's elite, Sánchez, its masses. They view the world differently. Anza organizes the settlement expedition as a mechanism for solidifying Spain's control over California. Sánchez, with little awareness of the complexities of international geo-politics, voices his hope that the move will mean a new and better life for his family. Anza considers all of the land claimed by Spain to therefore belong to Spain. Sánchez expresses an awareness that Indians consider it theirs. Anza views Indians as potential obstacles which must be overcome if they resist and as potential subjects to be made loyal to the Crown and converts to the Church. Lacking Anza's world view and frontier experience, Sánchez has greater fear of Indians, who represent the threatening unknown, but also greater sympathy for Indian reaction against the Church and Crown, as in the San Diego revolt. In furnishing food, clothing, animals, arms, and equipment to the colonists, Anza expresses his general contempt for the masses, remarking that he did not give them money, "which they would have spent foolishly or gambled away." Sánchez, on the other hand, expresses gratitude for the commander's gifts.

In terms of experience, as well as perceptions, the elites and masses of the expedition provide a contrast. Anza and the priests have personal servants during the march; Sánchez and his fellow colonists, of course, have none. Anza and the priests enjoy wine, hams, spices, and fine chocolates; the colonists receive sugar, beans, and tortilla flour. While the colonists struggle across the swift Colorado River, Padre Francisco Garcés is carried across on his back.

The internal variations of experience are also affected by sex difference. Although there are no women speakers in the movie, the special tribulations suffered by women are introduced by a discussion of sick women in danger of miscarriage and, more cogently, by the death of one woman during childbirth. An indication of the particular hardships of women on the journey is the fact that, after giving birth, María Dolores (Sánchez' wife) resumes the trip "three days later, when she was able to ride again," according to Sánchez. Compare this with the experience of U.S. pioneer women in their relatively luxurious wagons!

Possibly most central in our conception of "Northwest from Tumacácori" was the idea of trying to bring the viewer inside of the expedition, to re-create to the degree possible the experience of the expedition. This experiential approach was not used at the expense of providing information *about* the expedition, but in an attempt to extend the film beyond the traditional "outside looking in" style of most historical documentaries.

Historical information was presented in abundance: the historical setting—the geo-political situation, Anza's background, and Anza's first expedition to California; the second expedition, including a lengthy discussion of its size, composition, and logistics; California of that period—the missions, El Camino Real (the coast road), and San Francisco Bay as Anza found it; Mexican culture of the period—supplies of the expedition, life in the missions, and the Catholic Church.

But while providing information, we tried to do more. We tried to create experience. We tried to involve viewers *in* the expedition. We tried to help viewers see the expedition as its members saw it, feel it as they felt it.

Several elements went into our attempt to create viewer experience. We emphasized music and visual imagery to create the mood, with a concomitant restriction of dialogue, which was kept to a minimum. In order to build the feeling of the length and tedium of the expedition, we purposefully established and maintained a slow, measured pace. In our attempt to portray tedium, we consciously accepted the necessary risk of all filmmakers who seek that end—the danger of generating viewer boredom rather than an empathetic sense of tedium. But as our goal was to create understanding through a sense of experience, not to engage in competition with the entertainment industry, we adhered to our intellectualized game plan.

And what were the kinds of viewer experiences we tried to create? Here are a few examples. The climatic challenges faced by the expedition—raging rivers, mountain snowstorms, and seemingly endless deserts with little pasture, little firewood, and no water. The sense of time—nearly a year from José Antonio Sánchez' departure from Tumacácori to the dedication of Mission Dolores at San Francisco Bay. Physical suffering—constant illness, women in danger of miscarriage, damage from snowstorm, even death. Varied colonist feelings about Native Americans—fear, conflict, gratitude for their generosity, and confusion over their claims to land and rebellion against the Church. The all-pervading emotional impact of the Catholic Church— symbolized by the opening and closing sequences of Mass, first in Tumacácori, later at San Francisco Bay.

This, then, was our concept in making "Northwest from Tumacácori." In a general sense, the film represents an attempt to provide a south-to-north perspective on the Greater American heritage. At its most basic, the film says, "Others besides those depicted in the traditional east-to-west approach to U.S. history played a part in our nation's geo-cultural heritage. Here is the experience of some of those others not generally found in stories of our country."

In these terms, the film provides the opportunity for the development of greater intercultural understanding. Mexicans and Native Americans can obtain increased factual knowledge and, even more important, gain greater emotional insight into their heritage. Moreover, descendants of "east-to-west Americans" can expand their knowledge of our country's geo-cultural past and of the experiences of the ancestors of others.

But while we consider this film as a bridge to better intercultural under-standing in a general sense, it has an even more timely significance for the celebration of the American Revolution Bicentennial. The Bicentennial should be a time for the rededication of the United States to the highest principles for which the revolutionaries fought and which our nation has yet to fully achieve. The elimination of social injustice and the development of better understanding of ourselves and others should rank at the top of the list of Bicentennial goals. And to develop this better understanding, historical dis-tortions and omissions must be rectified. By providing an insight into the western, Mexican, and Native American experiences which paralleled in time the outbreak of the independence movement in the east, "Northwest from Tumacácori" contributes to the ethnic, cultural, and geographical democra-tization of the Bicentennial celebration. As such, it is one small step in the ongoing struggle for understanding and justice.

NOTES

1. Throughout this article, the terms Chicano and Mexican American will be used interchangeably.

2. Raymond Starr, "The Great Frontier Thesis as a Framework for the American History Survey in Secondary Schools" *History Teacher,* VI (February, 1973), pp. 227–232.

3. A discussion of the Bolton Theory can be found in Lewis Hanke, ed., *Do the Americas Have a Common History? A Critique of the Bolton Theory* (New York: Knopf, 1964).

The corresponding Chapter for this Selection can be found on pg. 3.

SELECTION 2

TEACHING THE CHICANO EXPERIENCE

THE MEXICAN AMERICAN WAS BORN IN DECEMBER, 1845, WHEN the United States annexed the Lone Star Republic into the union as the state of Texas, thereby transforming 5,000 Mexican Texans (Texans of Mexican descent) into Mexican Americans.[1] The following year, as part of United States war operations against Mexico, United States military forces invaded and occupied the Mexican Northwest (today the U.S. Southwest). Through the ensuing 1848 Treaty of Guadalupe Hidalgo, the United States obtained official sanction for this gigantic land grab (one third of Mexico's territory) and, at the same time, added to the Chicano[2] population by proffering United States citizenship to the 75,000 Mexicans living in the dismembered territory.[3]

Since those mid-nineteenth-century events, the Mexican American population has grown until Chicanos now form the nation's second largest ethnic minority (some six to ten million)[4] and make their homes in every state in the union.[5] Yet despite their long, rich history, their growing population, and their increasing geographical dispersal, not until the Chicano Movement of the 1960's and 1970's did Mexican Americans truly begin to penetrate the American[6] consciousness. And only in the last few years have significant numbers of American educators become interested in incorporating the study of the Chicano experience into our educational system.

Source: James A. Banks (Ed), *Teaching Ethnic Studies: Concepts and Strategies* (Washington, D.C.: National Council for the Social Studies, 1973), pp. 181–199.

Reprinted by permission of the National Council for the Social Studies.

Unfortunately, this long-overdue educational reform has met with uneven success. In part this has resulted from continued lack of knowledge and awareness by many educators, lack of reformist concern by others, and even outright resistance to change by some. Even those interested in making the study of the Chicano experience an intrinsic part of our educational system have encountered difficulty in transforming commitment into effective pedagogy. To a degree this difficulty stems from the short time during which educators have dealt seriously with teaching the Chicano experience. But this difficulty also stems from the very nature of our society and our educational process.

Within the social studies, three basic elements are necessary for the effective teaching of the Chicano experience—awareness of the major obstacles to understanding, development of new exploratory concepts for analyzing the Chicano experience, and use of innovative teaching strategies for exploring the Chicano experience. In the following pages, I will devote myself to these three basic issues.

OBSTACLES TO EFFECTIVE TEACHING

Four major obstacles impede the effective teaching of the Chicano experience. These are: (1) the persistence of societal stereotypes of the Mexican American; (2) the inadequacy of existent social studies textbooks; (3) the general lack of knowledge about the Mexican American past and present; and (4) the rigidity of traditional frames of reference for examining the Chicano experience.

Our educational system does not operate in a vacuum. It reflects the society around it and deals with students produced by that society. Unfortunately, the teaching of the Chicano experience is severely limited by the fact that students come to school pre-conditioned in their perceptions of the Mexican American.

In both historical and contemporary terms, U.S. society has been pervaded subtly and sometimes not too subtly by anti-Mexican prejudice. The roots of this prejudice stretch back over the centuries to the European power struggle for New World domination. Since Spain had arrived first from Europe and had claimed most of the New World, it became the prime target for other European contenders. Through its own vigorous internal debate over the treatment of Indians, Spain unwittingly furnished fuel for its antagonists' propaganda machines. Using Spanish cruelty toward Indians as the base and blending in other anti-Spanish themes, these contending nations propagated a collection of anti-Spanish stereotypes which became known as the Black Legend *(leyenda negra)*. English colonists carried this Hispanophobia to the New World. Here their constant conflict with Spaniards and residents of

Spanish possessions reinforced anti-Spanish attitudes and made anti-Hispanism an intrinsic, if sometimes unrecognized or unadmitted, part of the national psyche.[7]

Paralleling anti-Hispanic prejudice in the Anglo mentality was a feeling of Anglo superiority over non-Whites, including Native Americans.[8] Moreover, Englishmen and Anglo Americans took a particularly scornful view of the genetic and cultural offspring of Hispanic–Indian fusion—the mestizo—whom they considered a "mongrelized" product of two inferior peoples.[9]

As the United States expanded westward during the early nineteenth century, it found this Mexican mestizo in its way. Texas Revolution and Mexican War propaganda emotionally supercharged the already existent anti-Mexican attitudes, as did such other anti-Mexican prose as nineteenth-century travelers' accounts and the popular dime novel, which commonly used the theme of the triumph of the good Anglo-American cowboy over the degenerate Mexican mestizo.[10] The dime novel, with its blatant racism, has disappeared. However, it is clear that its prejudice-producing role has been taken over by more subtle image purveyors.

From the time he is born, an American is bombarded by anti-Mexican impulses, including those spread by the mass media. Let us take a few examples. Frito Bandito and his serape-clad, sombrero-wearing, mañana-saying Mexican brothers in the U.S. advertising menagerie leap to mind as obvious perpetrators of anti-Mexican stereotypes.[11] Comic strips, such as "Gordo," the living Mexican stereotype, help to reinforce these negative Mexican images. Whether intentionally, uncaringly, or unwittingly, the motion picture industry has produced a long series of prejudice-building movies. For example, in the "my-bad-guy-is-better-than-yours" movie genre, such films as *The Magnificent Seven, The Professionals,* and *The Wild Bunch* celebrate the victory of tiny bands of Anglo gunmen over whole armies of Mexicans—the reassertion of Anglo superiority even at the bad-guy-to-bad-guy level.

In short, the classical anti-Spanish Black Legend has given way to a Modern Black Legend: anti-mestizo, anti-Mexican, and anti-Chicano. This Modern Black Legend is a negative attitude toward, stereotype of, or prejudice against the Mexican American created by the steady bombardment of the American mind by anti-Mexican sensory impulses, made more effective by the absence of any significant institutionalized defense or counter-attack against these impulses.

In teaching the Chicano experience, therefore, social studies teachers must confront the Modern Black Legend's pervasive effects on their students. But the problem does not end here. Not only must teachers contend with anti-Chicano prejudice-creating and stereotype-building aspects of society, they must also come to grips in the classroom with text materials which, in relation to the Chicano, are almost always inadequate and often clearly destructive.

INADEQUATE TEXTBOOKS

The Mexican American has always suffered in social studies textbooks.[12] For the past four years I have been deeply involved in analyzing elementary and secondary school social studies textbooks and have found little in them which would specifically contribute to the pride of the young Mexican American, but much that could assault his ego and reinforce a concept of Anglo-American superiority over the Mexican American. Social studies texts usually either ignore or distort the Mexican-American experience (as well as the experiences of other ethnic minorities). Relatively few texts specifically discuss the Mexican American, and those which do devote at most a few inadequate (and often inaccurate) pages to this topic. Therefore, the student's image of the Chicano experience is derived tangentially—from depictions of his Indian, Spanish, and Mexican ancestors—and the image is a defeatist one.

U.S. history texts generally say little about the Mexican American's Indian heritage, except for an occasional line or so on Aztec and Mayan civilization. The long, rich history of the Mexican Indians—including their many scientific, educational, cultural, societal, governmental, and economic accomplishments—remains missing from these books. The major impression of the pre-Columbian Indians is one of defeat at the hands of the Spanish conqueror.

Then what about Spain, the conqueror? Usually these books contain a few more lines about Spain, but these, too, are suffused with negativism. The student gets no sense of Spain's brilliant culture or contributions to world civilization, but merely receives a unidimensional Black Legend image of Spaniards as oppressors of New World Indians. However, when faced with an English rival, the Spaniard, too, turns out to be a loser, usually dramatized by a lengthy, culturally chauvinistic depiction of England's victory over the Spanish Armada in 1588.

Independent Mexico receives somewhat more attention than Spain or pre-Columbian Mexico, but the emphasis on defeat remains. Mexico seldom appears in U.S. history texts except when being defeated or invaded by the United States or by those of Anglo American descent, as in the 1835–1836 war for Texas independence, the 1846–1848 U.S.–Mexican War, and the 1914 U.S. occupation of Vera Cruz. By selecting Anglo victories over Mexico as the principal means of portraying the latter, textbook authors, whether intentionally or unintentionally, reinforce feelings of Anglo superiority and Mexican American inferiority.

So much for traditional U.S. history texts. But what about the modern inquiry method social studies textbooks? Although their framework is often altered from chronological historical narrative to topical treatment of various aspects of life, society, and culture, the traditional cultural biases generally remain when these books deal with matters directly pertinent to or tangentially relevant to the Chicano experience.

Ironically, the Mexican American suffers from tokenism even in exposés of textbook treatment of minorities and in so-called multiethnic syllabi. In Michael B. Kane's 148-page *Minorities in Textbooks: A Study of Their Treatment in Social Studies Texts*, Mexican Americans receive only one page as part of a six-page section on the "Spanish Speaking."[13] And in Warren I. Halliburton and William Loren Katz's *American Majorities and Minorities: A Syllabus of United States History for Secondary Schools*, Chicanos receive limited, sporadic, and inaccurate treatment.[14]

KNOWLEDGE AND FRAMES OF REFERENCE

To societal stereotypes and inadequate textbooks must be added two other basic pedagogical obstacles—limited knowledge about and rigid traditional frames of reference concerning the Chicano experience. Our knowledge is limited not only by the relatively modest amount of research done on the Chicano past, but also because most of that research has been concentrated on a small number of topics. Most major areas of the Chicano experience have been barely touched upon or entirely ignored by researchers. We have only begun to illuminate the totality of the Chicano experience. Our current knowledge, which only hints at that vibrant past, must be used sensitively with this limitation in mind.

Similarly, the teacher must also contend with invalid traditional frames of reference, whose persistence in society and education has hindered the study of the Chicano experience. Let me mention merely five of these frames of reference:

1. the idea that U.S. history is an essentially unidirectional east-to-west phenomenon;
2. the attempt to explain the Chicano experience by labeling it "just like" the experiences of Blacks, Native Americans, or various immigrant groups;
3. the view of the Chicano experience as essentially homogeneous, with most Mexican Americans following a single stereotyped historical pattern;
4. the concept of the "awakening Mexican American," arising from a century-long siesta; and
5. the attempt to explain the Chicano experience by presenting a parade of Mexican heroes and individual Mexican American success stories.

In their place, I would like to suggest and briefly discuss the following five alternative frames of reference, which I call exploratory concepts for analyzing the Chicano experience:

Traditional Frames of Reference	*Suggested Alternative Exploratory Concepts*
1. U.S. history as an east-to-west phenomenon	1. Greater America concept
2. "just like" explanations	2. comparative ethnic experiences
3. Chicano homogeneity	3. Chicano diversity
4. "awakening Mexican American"	4. history of activity
5. heroes and success stories	5. the Chicano people

THE GREATER AMERICA CONCEPT

One of the basic structural concepts of U.S. social studies has been the culturally distorted idea that the United States is strictly an Anglo product which began on the east coast and flowed west. At best, most books on U.S. history and society give only token recognition to the fact that cultures existed in the West prior to the coming of the European, that explorers and settlers came north from Mexico into that area during the sixteenth, seventeenth, eighteenth, and early nineteenth centuries, and that Mexicans were living in the Southwest when the United States invaded the area in 1846. Little substantive attention is paid to the northward flow of culture and society from central Mexico or its impact on the pre-1846 American Southwest.

In order to create true intercultural understanding, the social studies must be reoriented on the basis that the Greater American heritage developed from the dual advance of societies from the Atlantic coast west and from Mexico City north, as well as from the fusions and conflict between these advancing cultures and the already existent Southwestern civilizations.[15] For students to understand the Greater America in all of its cultural and ethnic dimensions, the study of the Mexican heritage of the United States must become an intrinsic part of the social studies process, beginning with the first year of school. The teaching of social studies must include, from grade one on, the continuous, parallel study of Anglo and Mexican cultural and societal patterns, their contributions, their conflict, and the process or failure of fusion or coexistence.

In this manner, the social studies would begin operating on the reality of this dual heritage by examining such bicultural topics as:

1. explorers and settlers of both the Mexican Southwest and the Atlantic colonies,
2. Native American civilizations and their relations with expanding U.S. society from the east and expanding Mexican society from the south,
3. types of economic systems that developed in the western and eastern sections of our country,

4. various concepts of law, land, and water rights which became implanted throughout the country within different cultural settings,
5. Mexican and U.S. political systems,
6. Mexican and U.S. class and caste structures, and
7. ethnic relations in the United States and Mexico.

This continuous Greater America approach can reduce the inherent ethnocentrism which has always plagued U.S. social studies and place in proper perspective the bicultural heritage and multiethnic reality of the United States.

COMPARATIVE ETHNIC EXPERIENCES

The teaching of the Chicano experience has also suffered from misguided attempts to describe Chicanos by explaining them in terms of superficially similar experiences of other U.S. ethnic groups. This means simplistic depictions of the Chicano experience as "just like" those of Blacks, Native Americans, or various immigrant groups.

The Chicano experience does have certain similarities with the experience of each of these groups. However, social studies teachers must avoid the comfort of easy generalizations, for just as there are similarities, there are salient differences which invalidate a simple "just like" approach. For example, like Blacks, Native Americans, and Asian Americans (but unlike European immigrant groups), Chicanos can rightfully attribute part of their sufferings to racial prejudice. Like Native Americans (but unlike Blacks, Asian Americans, or European immigrants), Chicanos were one of the two major ethnic groups which established large-scale societies *prior* to the coming of Anglos and, through military conquest, became aliens in their own land. Like European and Asian immigrants (but unlike Blacks or Native Americans), Chicanos have seen their numbers increased in the nineteenth and twentieth centuries by a major flow of free immigration.

These few examples demonstrate that the Chicano experience has parallel aspects in other ethnic experiences, but that, as a unique composite, it contrasts with any other individual ethnic experience. Moreover, just as these three factors—racial prejudice, conquest and alienation in their own land, and flow of free immigration—are useful analytical tools for comparing ethnic experiences, any number of such categories can be devised for ethnic comparative analysis. This conceptual frame of reference should help students in developing logical analytical thinking, help sensitize them to cultural nuances, and help eradicate the distorting tendency to explain the Chicano (or other ethnic) experience in simplistic "just like" terms.

CHICANO DIVERSITY

In examining the Chicano experience, social studies teachers must avoid not only simplistic "just like" depictions. They must also reject another equally convenient, but equally distorting traditional frame of reference—the view of the Chicano experience as essentially homogeneous, with most Mexican Americans following a single stereotyped historical pattern. Instead, teachers should adopt a third exploratory concept—the great internal diversity of the Chicano experience and the Chicano people.

In applying this concept, an almost unlimited number of questions can be devised. Let me suggest a few which could prove useful in probing Chicano diversity. For example, what aspects of the Chicano experience are essentially Spanish, Mexican Indian, Native American, Black, American (U.S.), or simply variations of universal human experience (for when we go beyond ethnic categories, all people have co-participated in such universal experiences as fear, love, hunger, cold, heat, and hope)? What have been the geographical variations in the Chicano experience—between regions, states, sections of states, cities, or barrios? What have been the comparative experiences of various Mexican immigration waves? What have been the differences in experience of different generations of Chicanos? What have been the varieties of urban and rural experience? What have been the experience differences of various Chicano social classes, economic groups, and political groupings? What have been the experience differences of Mexican American men and women? For that matter, what differences in the Chicano experience have spawned such diverse appellations as *Chicano, Mexican American, Latin American, Spanish American, Hispano, Latino, Tejano, Californio,* or *American of Mexican descent?*

These are only a few of the questions which may help in examining the diversity of the Chicano experience. Not only will this line of exploration lead to an awareness of the variety in the Chicano past and present, but it will also provide an antidote to textbook and societal stereotyping of the Mexican American.

HISTORY OF ACTIVITY

Ironically, some of these stereotypes have developed as byproducts of the Chicano Movement. Scholars and journalists, in jazzing up their treatment of the Movement, have come up with such catchy but pernicious phrases as "the awakening Mexican American" and "the siesta is over." These invalid, ahistorical concepts imply that, prior to the Movement, the Mexican American had been taking a century-long siesta and is now just emerging from more than a century of somnolence and passivity. Nothing could be further from the truth.

There are many sources for this misconception. For one thing, even more than the Black and Native American, the Chicano has lacked national visibility. As America's true "invisible man," he has failed to gain admission into traditional narratives of the U.S. past. Therefore, when the Chicano Movement forced the nation to notice its second largest ethnic minority, many writers treated the Movement as a deviancy in Mexican American history—a sudden shift from passivity to activity.

In part, too, the historical myth of Chicano passivity has been reinforced by the recent flood of scholarly and journalistic accounts of Anglo prejudice against, discrimination against, and exploitation of ethnic minority groups. These are certainly major verities of U.S. history. However, the preponderance of books and articles about Anglo activity toward (usually against) Chicanos as contrasted with the few studies of Chicano activity itself has unfortunately produced the distorted impression of the Chicano experience as an essentially passive one, with the Chicano merely the passive recipient of Anglo discrimination and exploitation.

But the reality of Chicano–Anglo relations belies this. Since the 1846 conquest, Chicanos have established a long activist heritage of resistance against Anglo discrimination and exploitation. Therefore, in examining Chicano–Anglo relations (and they should be examined in social studies classes), teachers must avoid the trap of using a simple active Anglo (exploiter–discriminator) and passive Chicano (exploited–discriminated against) model.

Moreover, although discrimination, exploitation, and resistance are essential aspects of the Chicano experience, they comprise only part of it. These themes should not be permitted to monopolize the study of the Mexican American past. The Chicano experience is a unique composite of a vast variety of human activities. By using the "history of activity" exploratory concept, teachers can help eradicate the distortions produced by the purveyors of "the awakening Mexican American" and "the siesta is over" image.

THE CHICANO PEOPLE

Finally, while applying the "history of activity" concept, social studies teachers must avoid the limitations of still another commonly used but distorting frame of reference—the attempt to explain the Chicano experience simply by presenting a parade of Mexican heroes and individual Mexican American success stories. Certainly heroes and success stories comprise *part* of the Chicano experience. Chicanos can develop greater pride and non-Chicanos can develop greater respect by learning about Chicano lawyers, doctors, educators, athletes, musicians, artists, writers, and businessmen, as well as Mexican and Chicano heroes (heroes either to their own culture or to the nation at large). However, the teaching of the Chicano experience often becomes little more than the display of Emiliano Zapata, Pancho Villa, Benito Juárez, and Miguel Hidalgo posters or an extended exercise in "me too-ism"—the listing of Mexican Americans who have "made it" according to Anglo standards.

In falling into these educational clichés, the very essence of the Chicano experience is overlooked. For this essence is neither heroes nor "me too" success stories, but rather the masses of Mexican American people. The social studies teacher should focus on these Chicanos, their way of life, their activities, their culture, their joys and sufferings, their conflicts, and their adaptation to an often hostile societal environment. Such an examination of the lives of Mexican Americans—not Chicano heroes or "successes"—can provide new dimensions for the understanding of and sensitivity to this important part of our nation's heritage.

TEACHING STRATEGIES

So much for exploratory concepts. But what of specific teaching strategies for implementing these concepts? Many of the strategies already developed in social studies education are applicable or adaptable to the Mexican American. However, in view of the obstacles and exploratory concepts I have discussed, let me suggest three teaching strategies which are particularly useful for studying the Chicano experience:

1. the critical analysis, from a Chicano perspective, of social studies textbooks and other image-creating (often stereotype- or prejudice-creating) elements of our society;
2. the selective use of Mexican American supplementary materials; and
3. the constant use of local community resources, with a strong emphasis on oral investigation.

CRITICAL ANALYSIS

As I discussed earlier, the ethnocentrism of our social studies textbooks is a major obstacle to understanding the Chicano experience. However, the teacher can mitigate the negative impact of these textbooks and even make effective use of their cultural biases and distortions.

Young students cannot be expected to have the knowledge or critical facility to analyze fully or erect effective defenses against the inherent cultural deficiencies and biases in our social studies textbooks. Teachers provide the main and possibly only line of defense between these distortions and students' developing minds. After carefully analyzing books to be used in the classroom, teachers should present them to their students in proper perspective, indicating ethnic biases—including how the book may reaffirm Anglo superiority and neglect or distort the role or image of the Mexican American. Going one step further, teachers should help students learn to identify and analyze cultural distortions in textbooks and encourage them to use this critical thinking with all text materials, including such supposedly objective supplementary works as almanacs, atlases, encyclopedias, and dictionaries.

Moving beyond these standard materials, teachers should have students apply a Chicano perspective (as part of a multiethnic perspective) in analyzing other societal elements which create images (including stereotypes) and ideas (including prejudice). Motion pictures, comic strips, advertisements, speeches, newspaper and magazine articles, official government publications, and all types of books provide fine raw material for students to use in studying anti-Chicano biases which pervade society. In short, the teaching of critical analysis, particularly involving the development of sensitivity to ethnic and cultural nuances, should become an intrinsic part of social studies education.

CHICANO SUPPLEMENTARY MATERIALS

Considering the deficiencies of social studies textbooks in relation to the Mexican American, teachers must also adopt a second teaching strategy— the selective use of Chicano supplementary materials. The current Chicano Renaissance has produced a sudden affluence in Chicano poetry, short stories, essays, novels, art, manifestoes, and plans.[16] Chicano magazines and newspapers—many cooperating through the Chicano Press Association— have increased rapidly in number and geographical distribution.

Chicano scholarly journals now provide a forum for research results and intellectual debate over subjects vital to the Mexican American people. A small number of Movement films and movies treating history from a Chicano perspective are now available. When used effectively by the social studies teacher, these varied materials should prove stimulating and enlightening in the examination of the Chicano experience.

USE OF LOCAL COMMUNITY RESOURCES

But these supplementary materials notwithstanding, effective teaching of the Chicano experience requires expanding the classroom beyond four walls. The use of general Chicano books, magazines, journals, articles, films, art, and ephemera must be complemented by student discovery of Mexican American heritage at the local level. Particularly in the Southwest, but increasingly in other sections of the country, potential materials are all around, including the richest resource of all—the Mexican American people.

Students can explore their local communities to obtain information on the Chicano experience. Newspapers, city council and school board minutes, and records of such organizations as local clubs, churches, Mexican American chambers of commerce, benevolent societies, and community settlement houses are all potential sources. However, since Mexican Americans generally have been neglected in local books, newspapers, and other written sources, only the fringe of their experience can be discovered through reading. This study process must be supplemented by oral investigation if students are to develop a true knowledge and understanding of local Mexican American society, culture, and history.

Every Mexican American is a potentially valuable source of knowledge. There are no class, caste, educational, or linguistic qualifications for being a part of history, having a culture or society, having family or barrio traditions, perceiving the surrounding community, or relating one's experiences. Ideally, all Mexican Americans should have the opportunity to tell and record their own stories and those of their families and friends—their personal contributions to the documenting of the Chicano experience.

The teacher can use various means to involve the student in the process of oral exploration. For example, students may be assigned to write the biography of a local Mexican American individual or family, including their own. The assignment may provide some non-Chicano students with their first personal contact with Mexican American life. By hearing history and obtaining a perspective on society as viewed, recalled, and repeated by Mexican Americans, non-Chicano students should obtain a new outlook on the American past and the community around them. For Mexican American students, the assignment can have a double payoff. First, it can help them discover a personal sense of historicity based on their own families' past, as contrasted to the generalized experience presented in books. Second, it can contribute to family pride. As parents and other relatives relate their stories to students, they should become increasingly aware that they are a meaningful part of our nation's heritage, a part worth being studied and recorded.

Or the teacher may bring local Mexican American residents into the classroom. Here they can share their experiences and views with students, relate their oral traditions, answer questions, give new outlooks on society and history, and open doors of investigation for students.

Using these family biographies and classroom interviews as basic data, students can test hypotheses, reevaluate previous conceptions (or misconceptions), and develop new generalizations of the Chicano experience. Moreover, this process of oral investigation can give students of all ethnic backgrounds a first-hand, localized awareness of and sensitivity to the varieties of cultures in our country. It can open intellectual doors for them, stimulate within them a desire to continue their study of the local community, and, by revealing the community's past and present problems and possibilities, create the commitment to resolve these problems and fulfill the possibilities. Finally, it can "humanize" the study of the Chicano experience by revealing on a personal and affective level what students might never be able to discover in books.

The study of the Chicano experience offers both challenge and opportunity to the social studies teacher. Obstacles may be frustrating, new concepts may be demanding, and innovation may be difficult. But more difficult, yet, have been the lives of Mexican Americans for the past 125 years. America is finally recognizing the Chicano presence, and educators are finally recognizing that the study of the Chicano experience is a vital part of becoming aware of our nation's multiethnic and culturally pluralistic heritage. It is up to the social studies teacher to turn this overdue societal recognition into educational reality and thereby help create an open society of the future.

NOTES

1. Prior to the admission of Texas, the Mexican-American population consisted of a handful of Mexican immigrants into the United States.

2. In this article, I use the words Chicano and Mexican American interchangeably, except when referring to the Chicano Movement.

3. The Treaty of Guadalupe Hidalgo is *must* reading for anyone interested in the Chicano experience.

4. Not until 1970 did the Census Bureau include Mexican Americans as a population category. The Chicano population prior to 1970 can only be "guesstimated" on the basis of such occasionally used census categories as persons of Mexican birth, persons of the Mexican "race," persons of Spanish mother tongue, and White persons of Spanish surname. These categories were further limited in value by not being applied nationally, but only to selected states, particularly in the Southwest. Even the 1970 census has come under severe criticism because the Chicano and Puerto Rican categories were not included on the short form which went to everybody, but only on the long form which went to a 5-percent random sample.

5. Although Chicanos are most numerous in the Southwest, they are rapidly increasing in number throughout the rest of the country.

6. For convenience, I use the term American in referring to the United States. However, it should be remembered that, strictly speaking, this term applies to all nations and inhabitants of the Western hemisphere.

7. For a history of the development of the Black Legend, see Philip Wayne Powell, *Tree of Hate: Propaganda and Prejudices Affecting United States Relations with the Hispanic World* (New York: Basic Books, 1971). In particular, pages 131–144 contain a discussion of the Black Legend's impact on U.S. education.

8. For an analysis of English and Colonial U.S. attitudes toward Native Americans, see Roy Harvey Pearce, *The Savages of America : A Study of the Indian and the Idea of Civilization* (Baltimore: Johns Hopkins Press, 1953). A major study of English–Anglo attitudes toward people of color is Winthrop Jordan, *White Over Black: American Attitudes toward the Negro, 1550–1817* (Chapel Hill: University of North Carolina Press, 1968). Although Jordan focuses on White–Black attitudinal relations, his book has serious implications for the history of Anglo–Chicano relations.

9. Américo Paredes presents a slight variation on this theme. In summarizing one of the elements of the Anglo-Texas anti-Mexican legend, Paredes writes that Anglo-Texans traditionally assumed that "The degeneracy of the Mexican is due to his mixed blood, though the elements in the mixture were inferior to begin with. He is descended from the Spaniard, a second-rate type of European, and from the equally substandard Indian of Mexico, who must not be confused with the noble savages of North America." See Américo Paredes, *"With His Pistol in His Hand": A Border Ballad and its Hero* (Austin: University of Texas Press, 1958), p. 16.

10. Cecil Robinson, *With the Ears of Strangers: The Mexican in American Literature* (Tucson: University of Arizona Press, 1963), pp. 15–30.

11. Thomas M. Martínez, Advertising and Racism: The Case of the Mexican-American, *El Grito*, II (Summer, 1969), pp. 3–13.

12. The most intensive multiethnic analysis of current social studies textbooks is *Report and Recommendations of the Task Force to Reevaluate Social Science Textbooks Grades Five Through Eight* (Sacramento: Bureau of Textbooks, California State Department of Education, 1971).

13. Michael B. Kane, *Minorities in Textbooks: A Study of Their Treatment in Social Studies Texts* (Chicago: Quadrangle Books, 1970).

14. Warren J. Halliburton and William Loren Katz, *American Majorities and Minorities: A Syllabus of United States History for Secondary Schools* (New York: Arno Press, 1970).

15. The classical champion of studying the American past on a two-directional basis was Herbert Eugene Bolton. A discussion of the Bolton theory can be found in Lewis Hanke (ed.), *Do the Americas Have a Common History? A Critique of the Bolton Theory* (New York: Knopf, 1964).

16. In Mexican and Chicano tradition, a plan is a manifesto of goals and grievances, issued by groups or individuals upon initiating a social or political movement.

The corresponding Chapter for this Selection can be found on pg. 8.

CONCEPTS AND STRATEGIES FOR MULTIETHNIC EDUCATION

HOW DO WE PROCEED WITH DEVELOPING MULTIETHNIC EDU-cation in the schools? Involved in the effort are:

1. creating multiethnic teaching concepts;
2. developing multiethnic teaching strategies; and
3. incorporating multiethnic concepts and strategies into all aspects of the K–12 curriculum.

Here I shall deal only with the first two items. I shall describe eight concepts that should be considered in the development of a multiethnic curriculum and suggest ways to implement them in the classroom. Although the concepts and strategies are only indicative of the possibilities for multiethnic curriculum development, it is my hope that these ideas will stimulate systematic thinking and action in regard to multiethnic education.

U.S. HISTORY AS A MULTIDIRECTIONAL, GEOCULTURAL PHENOMENON

A basic structural concept that pervades U.S. education is the ethnocentric view of the country as a strictly unidirectional product of civilization that spread from Western Europe across the Atlantic to the east coast of what is today the United States

Source: Excerpt from his monograph (with Fay Metcalf and Sharryl Hawke), *Understanding You and Them: Tips for Teaching about Ethnicity* (Boulder, CO: ERIC Clearinghouse for Social Studies/Social Science Education Consortium, 1976), pp. 8–14. Also published in *Social Science Education Consortium Newsletter, 24* (November, 1975), 1–4.

Reprinted by permission of the Social Science Education Consortium.

and then west to the Pacific. Within this approach, ethnic groups appear almost always in two forms—as *obstacles* to the advance of westward-moving Anglo civilization or as *problems* which must be corrected or, at least, kept under control.

The underlying rationale for this frame of reference is for the most part *political*—the idea that the development of the United States should be viewed as a process that occurred in an east-to-west direction *within* the national political boundaries of the country. However, in applying this frame of reference, educators have been somewhat inconsistent. Most surveys of and courses on U.S. history discuss the geography of the area that ultimately composed the United States. Yet the fertile lands, valuable minerals, and important rivers that helped make the United States wealthy and powerful were all here before there was a United States. These books also dwell on the 13 British colonies, although they did not become part of an independent nation until 1776. And such historical events as the Texas Revolution of 1835 and the Lone Star Republic are generally included in surveys of United States history, although Texas did not become a part of the United States until annexation in 1845. Thus, even the traditional study of U.S. history does include phenomena outside of the political boundaries of the country as a part of the United States experience.

Yet educators have deviated inconsistently from this rigid political framework. While including land, minerals, rivers, English colonists, and Texas as significant parts of the U.S. experience *even before* they became part of the political unit, educators have not adequately included those Native American, Hispanic, and Mexican civilizations that developed on land that ultimately would become part of the United States. While focusing on the east-to-west flow of civilization from Europe, U.S. schools have devoted little substantive attention to the northwesterly flow of civilization from Africa to America, the northerly flow of Hispanic and Mexican civilization, and the easterly flow of civilizations and cultures from Asia. At best, most books and curricula on U.S. history, society, and culture give only token recognition to the development of cultures in America prior to the coming of the European; the growth of the Native American, Hispanic, and Mexican civilizations *before* the U.S. conquest of their territory; and the flow of civilizations into the United States other than east-to-west from Europe.

Let us reject the distorting, unidirectional approach to the study of the United States. Instead, let us introduce the variety of cultural experiences that have composed the *total* U.S. experience. The rationale for this alternative is *geocultural* instead of political. Rather than look just at the political U.S., our educational system must deal *consistently* with the development of the entire geocultural area which eventually became a part of the United States. Moreover, the flow of cultures into the United States must be viewed multidirectionally, with the rich diversity that resulted for our nation.

For students to obtain an understanding of the United States in all of its cultural and ethnic dimensions, the school curriculum should include, from the first year, the continuous, parallel study of the various civilizations which developed in the geocultural United States. Through this conceptual framework, we can examine such multiethnic topics as:

1. the varieties of Native American civilizations;
2. the European- and African-descent explorers and settlers of both northern Mexico (later the U.S. Southwest) and the Atlantic colonies;
3. the relations of Native American civilizations with the expanding U.S. society from the east and expanding Mexican society from the south;
4. the types of British colonial, United States, Spanish colonial, Mexican, and independent Native American economic systems, political systems, philosophies, cultural patterns, class and caste structures, literary and artistic traditions, and concepts of law, land, and water rights;
5. the social and cultural origins of the varieties of peoples who entered the United States from various directions;
6. the impact of these people on the development of U.S. culture and society and the converse impact of the United States on them; and
7. the process of cultural and ethnic conflict, fusion, and co-existence.

MULTIETHNIC PERSPECTIVES

Schools need to provide more than dominant-society perspectives. Note—I did not say *the* dominant-society perspective. There is no such thing. There is no monolithic dominant-society viewpoint any more than there is a monolithic ethnic-group perspective. In other words, not everybody of any group thinks alike.

However, almost all textbooks and curricular designs for the presentation of U.S. society are based on some perspective from the dominant society. To correct these distortions, we need to introduce multiethnic perspectives throughout the entire study of the U.S. experience.

Described below is an application of the multiethnic perspective to a selected event, the Cherokee Removal—the U.S. government's forced movement of the Cherokees (as well as Choctaws, Chickasaws, Creeks, and other Native Americans) from their homes in the South to the western United States. There are a number of dominant-society perspectives on this event. One perspective holds that Indians were obstructing the westward expansion of U.S. civilization and had to be moved in order to provide room for Anglo-American westward migration and settlement. A second perspective holds that the United States should be ashamed of the injustices committed through this forced removal and should continue making amends through various forms of compensation. A third perspective holds that, although the Cherokee Removal was unjust, it happened long ago, the clock cannot be turned back, and contemporary Anglos should not be forced to shoulder the guilt for events that occurred more than a century ago.

While there are variations in these perspectives on the Cherokee Removal, usually missing from general U.S. history books are perspectives from U.S. ethnic groups. What did the "removed" Indians think? What were the varieties of opinions about the Removal among Cherokees, Choctaws, and others? What did the western Native Americans think when they saw eastern Indians being moved onto *their* land? How did Black people perceive this forced movement of another "colored" population? How did northern Mexicans (soon to be conquered and annexed to the United States) view this massive forced population movement? Were there any differences among white ethnic groups in their attitudes toward the Removal?

By asking such questions multiethnic perspectives can be incorporated into the study of the U.S. experience. Nontraditional sources, excerpts from ethnic writings, provocative questions, and role-playing are kinds of techniques that teachers, curriculum developers, and textbook writers can use to introduce multiethnic perspectives.

COMPARATIVE ETHNIC EXPERIENCES

The teaching of the experiences of U.S. ethnic groups has suffered from reliance on simplistic depictions of the experience of one ethnic group as "just like" that of another group. While there may be certain similarities among the experiences of various ethnic groups, there are also salient differences that invalidate such a "just like" approach. As a unique composite, the experience of each ethnic group differs from all others.

The "just like" approach blurs the special qualities and demeans the uniqueness of each group. Moreover, it leads to the creation and reinforcing of broad, distorting stereotypes of "ethnics." Finally, by creating such misunderstanding, it ultimately impedes valid analysis and decision making.

In contrast to the "just like" approach, we should teach about ethnic groups through the study of comparative ethnic experiences. A series of categories of experience that cut across ethnic lines can be developed and used to guide comparisons of various groups. Let us take two examples.

1. What different forms of prejudice and discrimination has each ethnic group experienced? What have been the differential effects of these different types of prejudice and discrimination? What have been the varying attempts of society to eradicate this prejudice and discrimination in relation to each group? How successful have these efforts been in reducing prejudice and discrimination toward each group?

2. By what means did various ethnic groups become a part of U.S. society—conquest, free immigration, or forced migration? When did these groups become part of U.S. society? What have been the differential effects on these various groups of the time and manner in which they entered life in the United States?

These questions indicate the types of analytical categories that can be developed for comparing ethnic experiences. The goal of this comparative approach is *not* to make value judgments about various ethnic groups but to develop an understanding of the different ethnic group experiences.

SOCIETY AS THE PROBLEM

Most journalistic and scholarly discussions of minority groups are based on the implicit assumption that these groups are *problems.*

Such descriptions take various forms—characterizations of ethnic groups as racially inferior, culturally deprived, underachieving, overly traditional, and/or unassimilated. In each case the thrust of the discussion is unidirectional—the ethnic group is the problem. Change the group, make it conform to U.S. society *as the author conceives of it,* bring it into the mainstream, and the problem will disappear.

The pervasiveness of the ethnic-group-as-problem idea has had a deleterious classroom impact. It leads to asking loaded questions: What about an ethnic culture impedes educational attainment? What about ethnic groups makes them violent or unambitious or undependable? What about the nature of some ethnic groups prevents them from achieving as other Americans? Such lines of inquiry create their own answers—stereotypes. Although the details may vary, the student is directed to operate on one basic assumption—the ethnic group is the problem.

Moreover, the constant classroom reference to and textbook depictions of ethnic groups as problems has disastrous consequences for student self-image and intergroup understanding. How long can ethnic students be expected to experience their group being designated a "problem" before this repetition creates a negative self-image? And what are the long-range effects of this same repetition in convincing Anglo students to view ethnic people as problems?

Teachers should reject the ethnic-group-as-problem frame of reference in favor of an alternative analytical concept—society as the problem. With the society-as-problem exploratory concept in mind, the examination of the social problems faced by ethnic group members assumes an entirely different tack.

Instead of asking what about ethnics is a problem, the question should be, What aspects of our society create problems for members of ethnic groups? What facets of our economic system lead to low income and poor jobs for ethnic group members? How does the political process keep ethnic groups generally in a position of powerlessness? What features of our educational system lead to underachievement by ethnic children? Such lines of inquiry—an outgrowth of the society-as-problem frame of reference—will help eliminate negative stereotyping, reveal the obstacles faced by ethnic group members, and lead to a new understanding of the societal reforms needed to create true equality within our nation.

HISTORY OF ETHNIC ACTIVITY

In applying the society-as-problem concept, teachers must drop still another invalid frame of reference—the concept of ethnic passivity. The recent flood of scholarly and journalistic accounts of prejudice against, discrimination against, and exploitation of ethnic minority groups has helped create a greater awareness of the historical and contemporary inequities of our society. However, the preponderance of books and articles about actions toward (usually against) ethnic groups as contrasted with the relatively few studies of ethnic activity itself has produced the distorted impression that the experience of ethnic groups has been essentially a passive one—as the passive recipients of discrimination and exploitation.

In examining intergroup relations, the teacher must avoid using a simple ethnic passivity (exploited/discriminated against) model. Although discrimination and exploitation are essential aspects of the ethnic experience and should be examined honestly in school, these themes should not be permitted to monopolize the study of ethnic groups.

The experience of each ethnic group is a unique composite of a vast variety of human activities. In studying these experiences, teachers should focus not only on what has been done to ethnic groups, but also what ethnic people have done. By using the history-of-ethnic-activity exploratory concept, educators can help eradicate the distortions produced by the purveyors of the mythology of ethnic passivity.

THE ETHNIC PEOPLE

While applying the history-of-activity concept, the teacher must also avoid the limitation of still another commonly used, distorting frame of reference— the attempt to describe the multiethnic experience through a parade of ethnic heroes and success stories. Certainly heroes and success stories compose *part* of that experience. Children of an ethnic group can develop greater pride and others can develop greater respect for that group by learning about its heroes (heroes either to their own culture or to the nation at large) or its lawyers, doctors, athletes, musicians, artists, writers, and other "successes." However, the teaching of the multiethnic experience often becomes little more than a glorification of ethnic heroes or an extended exercise in "me-too-ism"—the listing of ethnics who have "made it" according to dominant society standards.

The over-reliance on these educational clichés obscures the very essence of the multiethnic experience. This essence is neither heroes nor "me too" success stories, but rather the experiences of ethnic people as a whole. Educators should focus on the diverse aspects of ethnic people of all walks of life—their activities, their culture, their life styles, their joys and sufferings, their conflicts, and their adaptation to an often hostile societal environment. Moreover, in the discussion of heroism and success, attention should be paid to the worth of each individual's life and the values of each ethnic group, not only the standards established by the dominant society. In human terms, should a bank president or athletic hero automatically be considered more of a success than a laborer, a devoted parent, or a good neighbor?

All members of ethnic communities—not just ethnic leaders—make ideal sources for study. Writing family biographies and autobiographies, doing research in the community, and bringing local ethnic people into the classroom to talk with students are all effective strategies for implementing this concept.

ESSENTIALS OF EXPERIENCE

The study of ethnic people must be just that—the study of the *experiences* of ethnic people. Unfortunately, much of current ethnic studies has not progressed beyond the superficial presentation of the symbols of ethnic groups.

Ethnic studies is not simply demonstrating Mexican dances, designating a soul food day in the cafeteria, displaying traditional Asian clothing, playing Native American music, or showing white ethnic art. All of these can be valuable parts of "multiethnicizing" the educational process. But too often this incorporation of the external symbols of ethnic groups comprises the totality of a school's commitment to ethnic studies. This is no more than educational tokenism.

The presentation of these ethnic symbols—rituals, music, art, poetry, clothing—must be augmented by the study of the essentials of each group's experience reflected by these symbols. While developing an appreciation for the aesthetics of ethnic music, poetry, art, dance, clothing, food, and other such cultural elements, students should delve into the experiential significance behind these symbols. What do the varieties of Mexican dances reveal about the Mexican culture and experience? How did soul food develop historically and how does it reflect the Black experience? What brought about the creation of different kinds of Asian clothing? What Native American cultural values are dramatized by the rich diversity of Native American music? What do the creations of white ethnic artists say about their respective cultures and experiences?

Teachers must strive not only to develop among *all* students an appreciation of the external symbols of *all* ethnic groups. Using the essentials-of-experience concept, they must also strive to promote an understanding of what these symbols say about those groups, reveal about their experiences, and express about their values.

In addition, teachers should provide opportunities for students to participate *internally* in the experiences of ethnic groups. The reading and hearing of ethnic poetry, short stories, novels, plays, and essays can create a feeling for the experience of an ethnic group. Ethnic music, art, and dance can reveal the fiber and emotion of the group. Autobiographies of ethnic people provide intimate personal views of what it means to experience life in the U.S. as a member of an ethnic group. Living autobiographies can be presented to students by having them visit ethnic communities and inviting members of ethnic communities to discuss their experiences with the class. And students should be placed in role-playing situations, where they can experience—if only in an artificial and transitory manner—what it means to be a member of various ethnic groups. In short, to paraphrase a traditional Native American expression, ethnic studies should enable all students to "walk a mile in the moccasins of others."

INTERRELATIONSHIP WITH SOCIETY

While applying the essentials-of-experience frame of reference, educators must not restrict their focus to the experience *within* ethnic cultures. Obviously the study of ethnic cultures is a vital aspect of developing a multiethnic curriculum. Ethnic literature, art, music, family structure, religion, values, and traditions deserve sensitive attention.

But multiethnic education must push beyond the study of ethnic cultures to the study of the historical and contemporary interrelationship of each ethnic group with the rest of U.S. society. This will help students develop an understanding of the unique problems each ethnic group has faced and currently contends within U.S. society. Moreover, the application of this concept can reveal the kinds of changes necessary for creating a society of equal opportunity for all regardless of ethnic origin.

CONCLUSION

Finally, multiethnic educational reform necessitates the full incorporation of the study of ethnicity and ethnic groups throughout the entire school curriculum, beginning with preschool and kindergarten, in every subject area from social studies to literature, from mathematics to music, from science to industrial arts, from language arts to physical education. Such an educational process can help students acquire greater understanding of their own heritage and the heritage, culture, and experiences of others. It can help create better intergroup relations based on the solid foundation of serious study. And it can help develop in our young people the commitment to and the tools for building a better society for all.

The corresponding Chapter for this Selection can be found on pg. 13.

THE SOCIETAL CURRICULUM: IMPLICATIONS FOR MULTIETHNIC EDUCATION

S CHOOLS DO NOT MONOPOLIZE MULTIETHNIC EDUCATION NOR will they do so in the future, even if they so wish. Why? Because all students, all people, continuously receive multiethnic education—both positive and negative—outside schools. Aware of it or not, we are all students of the societal curriculum.

What is the societal curriculum? It is that massive, ongoing, informal curriculum of family, peer groups, neighborhoods, churches, organizations, occupations, mass media, and other socializing forces that "educate" all of us throughout our lives. Much of this informal education concerns ethnicity and ethnic groups.[1]

The recognition of the inevitability, omnipresence, and continuous pervasiveness of the multiethnic societal curriculum raises significant questions for both society in general and educators in particular. What does this curriculum "teach" about ethnicity? How does it affect what people "know" about ethnicity and ethnic groups? How does it influence beliefs, perceptions, attitudes, and behavior related to different ethnic groups? How does it increase or limit the effectiveness of school multiethnic education? What are its implications for schools, including school curriculum development? How can educators more effectively use it in school multiethnic education?

Source: James A. Banks (Ed.), *Education in the 80's: Multiethnic Education* (Washington, D.C.: National Education Association, 1981), pp. 24–32.

Reprinted by permission of the National Education Association.

The multiethnic societal curriculum comprises at least four general components: (1) home, peer group, and neighborhood; (2) organizations and institutions; (3) the media; and (4) personal interethnic experiences. For each person, some aspects of that curriculum work positively to increase sensitivity to and understanding about ethnic groups. For each person, other aspects have a negative impact through spreading distortions, building stereotypes, or increasing prejudice. For example, studies have shown that many children develop well-formed attitudes about ethnic people, including prejudices and stereotypes, by the time they reach school.[2] While we have no way of determining the specific content of each person's individual societal curriculum, educators should remain alert to the general processes and diverse content of societal curriculum multiethnic education.

For most people, multiethnic education begins in the home, long before they enter school—through conversations about ethnic people or ethnic groups, through offhand remarks (including ethnic epithets and stereotyping), and through observation of actions of family members and friends. Multiethnic education also comes from the neighborhood peer group through conversations and the spreading of children's "knowledge" about ethnic groups. These statements do not label the home and the neighborhood as multiethnic educational villains; they describe a reality. In fact, the family and the neighborhood may provide *either* or *both* positive or negative multiethnic education, even if not conscious that they are doing so.

Societal institutions and organizations other than school and mass media institutions also serve as multiethnic educators. These include such institutions as churches, social clubs, political organizations, occupational associations, even the workplace itself. Each organization "educates," in such ways as providing religious and moral instruction, informing members of societal developments affecting their livelihoods, or exhorting members to take certain positions on issues. Some of this education may relate clearly to multiethnic concerns; other aspects may have less obvious, but no less significant, ethnic implications.

A few specific examples of the ongoing institutional multiethnic curriculum include labor unions counseling members about undocumented aliens and minority job training programs; religious leaders delivering sermons about desegregation; professional associations discussing affirmative action; private businesses or government agencies providing cultural awareness training for their employees; and social clubs maintaining ethnically oriented membership policies.

The media—television, motion pictures, radio, newspapers, and magazines—rank among the most powerful and pervasive aspects of the societal curriculum. Television, for example, has been receiving increasing scholarly attention. One study reported that young people between the ages of 3 and 16 spend one-sixth of their waking hours with the television set.[3] By the time of graduation, the average high school senior will have spent 12,000 hours in the classroom and 15,000 hours in front of the television set, according to another estimate.

Some examples of the multiethnic educational impact of the so-called entertainment media include the following. In a pioneering study, Ruth C. Peterson and L. L. Thurstone discovered that viewing the classic silent film *The Birth of a Nation* increased student prejudice toward Black Americans.[4] Irwin C. Rosen found that the film *Gentleman's Agreement* improved student attitudes toward Jews, even though most of the students tested stated that the film *had not* changed their attitudes.[5] Another study reported that White children felt that TV comedies like "The Jeffersons" and "Sanford and Son" accurately portrayed Black family life, although these same children admitted that such shows contrasted with personal experiences with their own Black friends, whom they labeled as exceptions.[6] A teacher in one of my multiethnic education courses discovered that her elementary school students had deeply rooted preconceptions about gypsies. In discussing where they had "learned" so much, students responded with answers ranging from "my folks" to "Wolfman" movies! These examples provide evidence of both the actual and potential multiethnic educational impact of the media.

Finally, of course, is the curriculum of personal experience. Increasing national mobility has drastically reduced the possibility of living in total ethnic isolation. Most people have some sort of personal interethnic contact—in school, on the job, through travel, or in their communities. Personal experiences vary, as do the ways in which they are perceived, interpreted, reacted to, and remembered. Yet these experiences comprise an important part of each person's multiethnic societal curriculum and become integrated into the personal storehouse of multiethnic knowledge and attitudes.

TOWARD UNDERSTANDING OR MISUNDERSTANDING

The societal curriculum has both positive and negative multiethnic effects. Good interethnic personal experiences can increase positive perceptions of other ethnic groups; negative experiences can create or reinforce prejudice. Some families make a conscious effort to bring multiethnic understanding into the home, provide positive interethnic experiences, and avoid ethnic slurs and stereotyping; other families take the opposite tack, leaving a terrible legacy for our society in terms of interethnic misunderstanding.

Businesses and government agencies that provide training in intercultural understanding serve as positive multiethnic educational forces; those that ignore this need or implement procedures and practices that discriminate, *however unintentionally,* against persons of certain ethnic backgrounds make multiethnic negativism a part of their day-to-day curriculum. By showing *The*

Autobiography of Miss Jane Pittman, Roots, and *Holocaust,* television probably contributed to multiethnic understanding. Theatrical and television films
ranging from traditional anti-Native American westerns to the recent plague
of ethnic gang movies, however, have helped to heighten interethnic fears,
distrust, and stereotyping.

For better or for worse, the multiethnic societal curriculum has had and
will continue to have a powerful educational influence. Moreover, whether
because of neglect or ineffectiveness of multiethnic education, schools have
not successfully offset the negative aspects of the societal curriculum. In fact,
as analyses of ethnic content of textbooks and children's stories have demonstrated, schools may contribute in some respects toward interethnic negativism.[7] In a late 1970's social studies assessment project of the California
State Department of Education, seventh grade students in 65 California public schools were asked to select one of four answers to "Which of the following is an example of an ethnic group in the United States?" Fourteen percent selected "The United Auto Workers," 24 percent each answered " All
the people who live in the same town" and "The Chinese," and 34 percent
answered "People on welfare"! The societal curriculum had done its job.

INTEGRATING THE SOCIETAL CURRICULUM
INTO THE SCHOOL CURRICULUM

When designing and implementing multiethnic education, educators should
constantly and seriously consider the societal curriculum. To ignore it is to
operate in a land of make-believe, because students will learn about ethnicity and ethnic groups from the societal curriculum and this learning will
affect their school multiethnic education. I would suggest at least two basic
lines of educational reform. First, integrate the multiethnic societal curriculum into the school curriculum. Second, attempt to make the societal curriculum a more positive multiethnic educator.

There are myriad ways to integrate the societal curriculum into the school
curriculum. I will discuss three of these strategies: (1) building from student
"knowledge;" (2) studying the local community; and (3) bringing media into
the classroom.

One of my favorite strategies is to build from preexistent student beliefs.
Prior to teaching about a particular ethnic group in school, have students
keep records of the ways in which they have observed the societal curriculum "teaching" about that group—through personal experiences, neighborhood, media, and other institutions. Such an approach will help raise student
awareness of the existence and content of the societal curriculum as well as
of their own particular beliefs. Moreover, this strategy can "prime" students
for the classroom study of the group by helping educators avoid what philoso-

pher Paul Tillich has labeled one of the basic failings of education—"to throw answers like stones at the heads of those who have not yet asked the questions." Most important, this approach can contribute to preparing students for a lifetime of continuous understanding of the multiethnic societal curriculum.

A second strategy is to use the local community as a source of study. Effective multiethnic education requires expanding the classroom beyond four walls. Every human being is a valuable source of knowledge. There are no class, caste, educational, or linguistic qualifications for being a part of history, for having a culture, for participating in society, for having family or ethnic group traditions, for perceiving the surrounding community, or for relating one's experiences.

Teachers can use various means to involve students in community study. For example, in the early elementary grades, persons of different ethnic backgrounds can be brought into the classroom to talk about their experiences, cultures, traditions, and beliefs. For older students, teachers can use field trips into local ethnic areas, student "cultural mapping" of the area around the school, and individual or team investigation into the historical development of local ethnic communities.

The writing of biographies of local individuals or families, including one's own, combines the development of research and writing skills with the discovery of personal or community roots. This strategy may provide some students with their first in-depth personal contact with persons of different ethnic backgrounds. By hearing history and obtaining perspectives on society as viewed, recalled, and interpreted by persons of diverse ethnic backgrounds, students should obtain new and broader multiethnic perspectives on the U.S. past and the community around them.

Using these classroom interviews, field trips, community investigations, and family biographies as basic sources, teachers can help students test hypotheses, reevaluate previous conceptions (or misconceptions), and develop new generalizations about ethnic groups. Moreover, this process of community investigation can both increase interpersonal communication skills and give students a localized awareness of and sensitivity to the ethnic backgrounds in the community. Finally, community investigation can "humanize" the study of ethnicity for students by providing direct involvement in the workings of society.

A third strategy is to make multiethnic analysis of media an integral part of the K–12 curriculum. Feature films, radio, television, newspapers, magazines, and advertising can be stimulating and significant aspects of the school curriculum. So what's new? Haven't such sources been used for years in the classroom? Certainly, but seldom as sources for multiethnic analysis.

Too often the visual media, in particular, have served simply as surrogate teachers, as substitutes for the written word, or as spoken textbooks from which students are asked to recall factually and memorize uncritically.

Media should not be viewed as transmitters of information, providers of facts, and pipelines of truth. Rather, they should be used as sources to be considered analytically, including an examination of their multiethnic perspectives, interpretations, and implications. How have different media portrayed, treated, or depicted different ethnic groups? What assumptions about ethnic groups and ethnicity do different media reflect? What historical forces and societal conditions have influenced media treatment of ethnicity during different eras?

In the early elementary grades, teachers can use children's stories about different ethnic groups as well as photographs, drawings, and animated films that include ethnic groups to introduce the concept of image formation. Advertisements in magazines and newspapers, on television, and even on billboards and bumper stickers, can be used throughout the elementary grades for the analysis of role depiction of ethnic groups.[8] The secondary school teacher may ask students to analyze the local newspaper or local or national news telecasts for the kinds of stories carried about specific ethnic groups and for the interpretations of and attitudes toward ethnicity-related issues, such as immigration and desegregation. Feature films, television entertainment series, and newscasts make excellent classroom sources—not for what they "tell" about ethnicity, ethnic groups, or intergroup relations, but for the examination of the perspectives and interpretations they present. The goal, of course, is to raise the level of critical thinking and awareness of the process of media multiethnic education.

CHANGING THE SOCIETAL CURRICULUM

While multiethnicizing the school curriculum, educators should also strive to help the societal curriculum become more of an ally and less of an antagonist in our multiethnic quest. While our ability to modify the societal curriculum is limited, there are avenues to effect change. Let me give some examples from my own experience.

Some of my most rewarding multiethnic education workshops have been for school district parents. In these workshops I not only explain and illustrate multiethnic education, but also suggest how parents can contribute multiethnically. Parents can be an extraordinary force for interethnic understanding— or misunderstanding. To maximize multiethnic educational effectiveness, school districts should make parent participation an integral part of their total program.

Societal institutions can be outstanding allies in the effort for multiethnic understanding. At the present time I am working with one religious denomination in developing a multiethnic approach to church school education using the theme, the Bible as a multicultural document. Educators should encourage governmental agencies to expand awareness training to help employees more effectively provide equitable services to persons of all ethnic and cultural backgrounds.

Many private businesses are introducing forms of multiethnic education into their employee development programs, a trend we should support. Why? Because of growing private industry awareness that the traditional "culture-blind" managerial training is merely "blind"—it does not necessarily prepare, and in some cases may actually disprepare, people to deal effectively and sensitively with a multiethnic work force and public.

IMPLICATIONS FOR TEACHER EDUCATION

Effective multiethnic education requires effective multiethnic teachers—teachers with multiethnic knowledge, skills, and attitudes. Such effectiveness ultimately requires the multiethnicizing of teacher education, both pre-service and in-service. This includes education in the multiethnic societal curriculum. Two strategies are the use of societal curriculum journals and training in multiethnic analysis of media.

Whenever I present in-service training courses, I ask each teacher to keep a multiethnic societal curriculum journal—a record of the education on ethnicity each observes outside school. Even those teachers possessing considerable awareness usually express surprise about the degree of multiethnic education occurring in the societal curriculum. "Awareness training," which helps teachers develop a better understanding of the societal influences on their own and their students' beliefs and attitudes about ethnicity and ethnic groups, should become an integral part of teacher education.

A second component of teacher education should be training in multiethnic analysis of media. In the spring of 1979, for example, Dr. Leon Campbell and I presented A Filmic Approach to Race and Ethnicity in the History of the Americas as one of the series of film-and-history courses offered at the University of California, Riverside. In that course we paired two feature films about three ethnic groups—a U.S. film and a Cuban film about Blacks in their respective societies, a U.S. film and a Bolivian film about the Indian experience in the two countries, and a U.S. film and an Argentine film about Italian-descent people in their nations. Students not only analyzed the treatment of ethnic groups and interethnic relations in the films, but they also investigated the historical and societal factors affecting those filmic interpretations. In addition, they wrote papers comparing class films with others viewed in the societal curriculum. The result—a growth in both general critical thinking and specific understanding of the multiethnic educational nature of the media.

CONCLUSION

Schools exist to prepare young people for the future. Throughout that future, students will constantly "go to school" in the multiethnic societal curriculum. How they perceive that curriculum, how it affects their beliefs and attitudes, how it influences their interethnic behavior will to a great extent be a result of school successes or failures in preparing them to be multiethnically literate.[9]

How well are schools preparing students to deal with that curriculum—to be aware of it, to comprehend it, to analyze it, and to resist its more noxious effects? By helping students develop a knowledge base for a multiethnic societal curriculum, teachers will be preparing a citizenry that is more aware, sensitive, and constructive.

NOTES

1. For example, see Randall M. Miller (ed.), *The Kaleidoscopic Lens: Ethnic Images in American Film* (Englewood, NJ: Jerome S. Ozer, 1979); and Cherry A. McGee Banks, A Content Analysis of the Treatment of Black Americans on Television, *Social Education* 41, 4 (April, 1977), pp. 336–339, 344.

2. Mary Ellen Goodman, *Race Awareness in Young Children,* (2d ed. rev.; New York: Macmillan, 1964).

3. Wilbur Schramm, Jack Lyle, and Edwin B. Parker, *Television in the Lives of our Children* (Stanford, CA: Stanford University Press, 1961), p. 30.

4. Ruth C. Peterson and L. L. Thurstone, *Motion Pictures and the Social Attitudes of Children* (New York: Macmillan, 1933), pp. 35–38.

5. Irwin C. Rosen, The Effect of the Motion Picture "Gentleman's Agreement" on Attitudes Toward Jews, *Journal of Psychology,* 26 (1948), pp. 525–536.

6. Bradley S. Greenberg, Children's Reactions to TV Blacks, *Journalism Quarterly,* 49 (Spring, 1972), pp. 5–14.

7. For example, see Michael Kane, *Minorities in Textbooks: A Study of Their Treatment in Social Studies Texts* (Chicago: Quadrangle Books, 1970).

8. James D. Cullery and Rex Bennett, Selling Women, Selling Blacks. *Journal of Communication,* 26 (Autumn, 1976), pp. 160–174.

9. James A. Banks, Teaching for Ethnic Literacy. A Comparative Approach, *Social Education,* 27 (December, 1973), pp. 738–750.

The corresponding Chapter for this Selection can be found on pg. 17.

SELECTION 5

GLOBAL PERSPECTIVES AND MULTICULTURAL EDUCATION

MULTICULTURAL AND GLOBAL EDUCATION ARE NATURAL, IF OFTEN unaware, partners. While they differ in emphasis, these two educational reform movements are linked by common concerns. Both seek:

to improve interpersonal and intergroup relations;

to increase awareness of the impact of global and national forces, trends, and institutions on different groupings of people, including national and ethnic groups;

to reduce stereotyping and increase intergroup understanding;

to help students comprehend the significance of human diversity, while at the same time recognizing underlying, globe-girdling commonalities; and

to improve intercultural communication.

In this quest for culturally sensitive, globally aware adults, multicultural and global educators need to plan and work together to help students become "multicultural global literates"—people with the knowledge, skills, and attitudes to live more effectively, sensitively, and constructively on our multicultural planet earth (Banks, 1973).

Source: Global Perspectives: Education for a World in Change, Feature Section (February, 1980), pp. 3–6.

This article was adapted from his chapter in *Curricular Dimensions of Global Education,* a 1979 joint publication of the Pennsylvania Department of Education and Research for Better Schools, Inc. Reprinted by permission of Research for Better Schools and the American Forum for Global Education.

The challenge, of course, is to break these general aims into a few common goals, each of which expresses a central, teachable concept. This and the further step of identifying some useful guidelines for the design of appropriate teaching strategies and learning experiences are the general parameters of this article.

What are some of the common areas of concern which could serve as the basis for such cooperation? Following are four goals which represent conceptual concerns that are central to both multicultural and global education and that can be integrated into a wide range of subject areas:

1. understanding of the function of groupness in our society and in the world—in other words, the significance of the fact that every person belongs to many groups;
2. understanding of the process by which people form images of ethnic groups and of foreign cultures;
3. understanding of global interrelatedness, including its variable significance for persons of different ethnic groups and different nations;
4. development of skills for living in a world of diversity.

UNDERSTANDING OF GROUPS

No person belongs to *a* single group. Each person belongs simultaneously to *many* groups—sex, age, economic, social, regional, national, religious, cultural, and ethnic groups, to name a few. At various times in a person's life, the fact of belonging to one or more of these groups may have a significant, in some circumstances determining, influence.

Education, then, should help students:

• to develop an awareness that each of us belongs to many groups,
• to understand how this multigroupness affects values, attitudes, beliefs, goals, and behavior; and
• to perceive how world trends and events have a differential impact on persons belonging to different groups.

ETHNIC GROUPS TREATED DIFFERENTLY AROUND THE GLOBE

The study of groups can provide students with a framework for analyzing the complex interplay of human diversity and global commonalities. While examining how the strength of and respect for ethnic traditions is handled in other nations, global education should continuously compare and contrast ethnicity elsewhere with the function of ethnicity in the United States. This should include the study of how Americans of different ethnic groups have maintained, modified, or lost aspects of their foreign heritages, how and why they are similar to or different from those living in their foreign root cultures, and what transnational connections still exist between foreign nations and cultures and U.S. ethnic groups. In this way, the examination of such global concepts as migration, cultural adaptation, and international communications can enhance student understanding of the experiences of American ethnic groups.

One cooperative effort to address this complex topic—the relationship between U.S. ethnic groups and their foreign root cultures—took place under the auspices of the University of Denver's Center for Teaching International Relations. That project compared the transnational linkages of four American ethnic groups: Black Americans, Irish Americans, Mexican Americans, and Arab Americans—with their corresponding root cultures in Africa, Ireland, Mexico, and the Arab world. The four project monographs provide a valuable source for teachers interested in addressing the global concepts of international linkages and intranational groupness (Smith, 1976).

UNDERSTANDING OF IMAGE FORMATION

How are images of groups developed over time, and more particularly, how do people come to form stereotypes, which can poison interethnic relations and impede global cooperation? Beginning in kindergarten, students should be introduced to the ways in which images of groups are formed, the differences between generalizations and stereotypes about groups, and the pernicious effects of stereotyping. As various foreign areas and ethnic groups are studied throughout the K–12 curriculum, the global concept of image formation, including the development of group stereotyping, can be examined with increasing complexity. The educational goals might be conceived as follows:

- to help students to better understand the process of stereotyping,
- to learn to detect stereotyping in operation,
- to monitor one's own stereotypical thinking,
- to use generalizations about groups as flexible clues rather than as mental straitjackets, and thereby
- to become more thoughtful, sensitive citizens.

THE SOCIETAL CURRICULUM

A major force in image formation is the "societal curriculum"—that massive, continuous, informal set of subtle teachings by family, peer groups, neighborhoods, churches, organizations, occupations, mass media, and other socializing forces that "educate" all of us throughout our lives. From the societal curriculum, as well as in school, people learn about culture, ethnicity, race, other nations, foreign areas, and the world as a whole. While some aspects of the societal curriculum increase multicultural and global understanding, other aspects provide misinformation, present distortions, spread stereotypes, and contribute to misunderstanding (Miller, 1979). Studies have shown that many children develop well-formed attitudes about members of ethnic groups and foreign areas, including prejudice and stereotypes, by the time they reach school (Goodman, 1964; Lambert and Klineberg, 1967).

In this respect, the media have a particularly powerful impact, often outweighing school and personal experience. One survey of U.S. fourth, eighth, and twelfth graders found that television had the greatest impact on their attitudes toward foreign nations and peoples. An illustration of the negative educational potential of the media occurred during the fall of 1977 television showing of *The Godfather Saga,* when NBC repeatedly cautioned the audience that:

> *The Godfather* is a fictional account of the activities of a small group of ruthless criminals. The characters do not represent any ethnic group and it would be erroneous and unfair to suggest that they do.

Convincing and effective? No. Merely gratuitous posturing which could have done little to soften the film's impact on perceptions about Italian Americans. Yet that very posturing dramatized an awareness of the power of the multicultural societal curriculum.

LINKING SOCIETAL AND SCHOOL CURRICULA

Educators must learn to deal directly with the societal curriculum. In essence, they should find ways to integrate into the school curriculum an ongoing examination of *what* and *how* the societal curriculum "teaches" about different cultures and different global issues.

The general aim, then, is two-pronged: to help students understand and evaluate the societal curriculum; and to help students monitor and actively counter tendencies to let themselves become reactive to, and therefore subtly manipulated by, events, trends, and interpretations fostered by the societal curriculum.

Children's stories about different nations, cultures, and ethnic groups, as well as photographs, animations, and printed cartoons, can be used to introduce the concept of image formation to early elementary school students.

In the later elementary grades, advertisements in magazines and newspapers, on television, and even on billboards and bumper stickers can be used provocatively for the study of image making.

For older students, feature films are marvelous sources for study. In comparing films on common themes, but produced in different countries, students can isolate and compare specific global and cross-national concepts. Such concepts include the family, the city, sex roles, economic dislocation, migration, stresses of acculturation, the conflict between law and justice, and comparative race and ethnicity in the Americas. By using the medium of film, already a potent force in most students' lives, they can begin to come to grips with both the universality of such global phenomena and the variations in the way they are treated by different national and ethnic groups.

In working with this approach to linking multicultural and global education, the teacher should bear in mind the fact that motion picture themes of ethnicity and foreignness cannot be fully understood in isolation from each other. For example, in the study of such films as *Tarzan* and many World War II feature films, account should be taken of the effect they had on the formation of images of Black Americans and Japanese Americans.

UNDERSTANDING OF GLOBAL INTERRELATIONSHIPS

As we become more globally interconnected, events and trends almost anywhere are increasingly likely to send shock waves throughout the world and affect even the most distant human being . . . even those not conscious of that impact. Moreover, the effects are not felt equally by all persons. For example, the global oil crisis has been particularly onerous for the poor, who have less budgetary flexibility for dealing with rising prices. Or, as the saying goes, when the United States catches a cold, minority groups usually get pneumonia.

Thinking in Terms of Systems

Education should strive to increase student *awareness* of the importance of thinking in terms of "systems," of interrelated parts—of the variable ramifications of events, institutions, and global forces for different nations and persons in different intranational groups. Whether it is the passage of a local zoning ordinance or the complex financial manipulations of a multinational corporation, the impact will be different for persons of different groups. Furthermore, a coordinated K–12 educational process should help students learn to *evaluate* how global factors affect their local communities, including the lives of persons of different backgrounds. Student ability to analyze, synthesize, and apply systems of multiperspective thinking should be developed continuously and with increasing complexity from the beginning of a child's schooling.

In elementary grades, teachers can have students analyze how events at school—for example, the establishment of new classroom procedures or school regulations—affect various groups of students differently. Students can role play and then analyze children's stories in which events or conditions have variable effects on the different characters. In high school, students can evaluate the significance of a court decision for different ethnic groups, the impact of the construction of a freeway on different groups in the community, the importance for different groups of a world shortage of selected products, and the multiple ramifications of changes in national immigration policies.

SKILLS FOR THE FUTURE

Both global and multicultural education are deeply concerned with helping students develop the appropriate thinking and communication skills, as well as the knowledge and the attitudes, for living in a culturally diverse and globally interrelated world. Following are some skills which are important to learn today and will become increasingly essential to exercise tomorrow:

> the skill of weighing evidence of relevant multicultural factors in decisions and situations in the face of changing global conditions;
>
> the skill of assessing future trends and their likely impact on individuals, ethnic groups, and nations;
>
> the skill of dealing effectively with disagreement and conflict and of developing cooperation across ethnic, cultural, and national boundaries;
>
> the skill of communicating interculturally, whether within the United States or around the world.

Intercultural Communication

Take, for example, the skill of intercultural communication. The obvious recommendation would be that everyone should learn at least one other language. In addition, schools need to help students—including monolingual students—to develop the skills of observing, becoming sensitive to, and interpreting the verbal and nonverbal aspects of intercultural communication. This also entails being aware of the variable meanings that the same or similar words (in different languages) have for persons of different cultures. This should include the study of body language, gestures, personal space, conversational distance, and social customs. Examples drawn from sources like the books of Edwart T. Hall, such as *Beyond Culture* (1976), and the recent *Gestures* (1979) by Desmond Morris, *et al,* can help students develop insights into patterns of intercultural communication.

Language arts and literature courses can be given multicultural and global dimensions by teaching about the intercultural variations of words and concepts. For example, teachers can use stories by persons of different ethnic groups and nations dealing with the same theme, such as family, environment, mobility, home, religion, social customs, and cultural mores. The examination of these stories can help students understand that the same or similar words in different cultural, ethnic, or national contexts may have commonalities or strikingly different connotations in meaning. In sum, the development of the skills of communication—whether interethnic, interlingual, or international—is a goal toward which global and multicultural educators should constantly and systematically strive.

These four suggested areas illustrate both the challenge and the opportunities for cooperative multicultural and global education. Such education is a necessity for all students . . . not just students of ethnic minorities, students in ethnically mixed schools, or students contemplating careers in foreign trade or international relations. All students will ultimately have to learn to take their places as citizens of our multiethnic nation and of a multicultural, interdependent world.

The corresponding Chapter for this Selection can be found on pg. 21.

SELECTION 6

THE EDUCATION OF LANGUAGE MINORITY STUDENTS: A CONTEXTUAL INTERACTION MODEL

IT WAS ALMOST INEVITABLE THAT THE RISE IN PUBLIC CONCERN with issues concerning relations between ethnicity and schools would ultimately be reflected in a rise in scholarly attention to that topic. As a result, the last two decades have seen a major expansion in scholarship on facets of this general theme. Such scholarship has provided new insights, but it has also revealed the enormous knowledge gaps that still exist and some of the critical directions that future scholarship should take.

There are many ways to group ethnicity-and-schools scholarship. I will look at this scholarship in terms of three, necessarily overlapping, categories: (1) works that analyze the historical development of various relationships between ethnicity and schools or that document the current situation within education, although the lengthy delays that often exist between research, writing, and publication often transform such "contemporary" analyses into historical slices of life; (2) studies that identify those factors that influence the education of minority students and that need to be addressed in the process of attempting to improve that education; and (3) scholarly literature that provides recommendations for the modification of educational policies and practices. However, it must be recognized that many studies touch upon all three categories. (For

Source: Excerpt (pp. 14–23) from chapter in California State Bilingual Education Office, *Beyond Language: Social and Cultural Factors in Schooling Language Minority Students* (Los Angeles: Evaluation, Dissemination and Assessment Center, California State University, Los Angeles, 1986), pp. 3–33.

Reprinted by permission of the Evaluation, Dissemination and Assessment Center.

example, Weinberg, 1977, provides historical analysis, needs assessment, and recommendations for action.)

HISTORICAL–CONTEMPORARY ANALYTICAL SCHOLARSHIP

Numerous themes have emerged, with the following merely serving as examples. The struggle over desegregation continues to absorb scholars, particularly those with a bent toward reconstructing and analyzing the history of this process (Coleman *et al.,* 1966; Wollenberg, 1976; Weinberg, 1977). The educational experience of ethnic minority students has drawn the attention of other scholars, particularly educational anthropologists, who have documented these experiences through first-hand observation and interviews as well as by school records (Parsons, 1965; Rist, 1978; Kleinfeld, 1979; Philips, 1983). The development and modification of educational conditions affecting students have been examined, sometimes from a perspective of hope (things have improved or are improving), sometimes from one of despair (severe structural restraints in the educational system and society render educational change in favor of minorities relatively meaningless or virtually impossible) (Carnoy, 1974).

FACTORS THAT INFLUENCE THE EDUCATION OF MINORITY STUDENTS

In general, three types of factors have been identified:

1. Overall societal dynamics that influence education through such means as setting the societal agenda for school priorities, contributing to minority self-concept and teacher perceptions of minority students (such as through the mass media), and restraining or galvanizing educational reform (Kirp; 1982; Appleton, 1983).
2. School forces that influence minority education, such as teacher expectations and behavior, counseling practices, school structure, curriculum, and testing (Kane, 1970; Jencks *et al.,* 1972; "Perspectives on Inequality," 1973; Samuda, 1975; Longstreet, 1978). This second category of scholarship also includes those research studies that attempt to analyze and differentiate schools in which minority and poor students tend to achieve from those in which they tend to do poorly (Brookover *et al.,* 1979; Purkey and Smith, 1983; Cuban, 1984).
3. Educationally relevant sociocultural factors within minority communities or identified as part of ethnic minority students such as language, culture, socio-economic situation, and personal and group experiences

both within and outside of the educational system (Dinnerstein *et al.,* 1979; Clark, 1983; Grossman, 1984).

PRESCRIPTIONS FOR REFORM

Curricular and textbook reform aimed at making education more relevant to minority students by emphasizing their histories and cultures and at creating better intergroup understanding has been advocated by scholars dealing with the issues of multicultural, multiethnic, and bilingual education (Banks, 1981a, 1981b). Others have addressed various modifications of teacher behavior, ranging from raising their expectations for minority students to adopting culturally sensitive teaching styles (Ramírez and Castañeda, 1974; García, 1982). Some have moved beyond the classroom into such areas as reform of testing, placement, counseling, and other school practices (Atkinson, Morten, & Sue, 1979). Finally, there is a growing, increasingly sophisticated body of scholarly literature on language aspects of instruction, addressing such topics as bilingual education and English-as-a-second-language (ESL) education (California State Department of Education, 1981; Fishman and Keller, 1982).

CONTEXTUAL INTERACTION MODEL

Yet, while this research has contributed to our understanding of the complex and changing relationships between ethnicity and education, no consensus has emerged concerning two basic questions. First, why do members of some minority groups *tend* to have higher educational achievement than members of other minority groups? Second, why do members of some minority groups *tend* to have lower educational achievement than mainstream American students?

Over the years, analysts have posited a number of explanations for group achievements and underachievements. However, these explanations generally fall short of being convincing, for a number of reasons.

First, some analyses have relied too heavily on single-cause explanations. Group educational differentials have been attributed, at various times, to language difference, to socio-economic status, to racism and other forms of prejudice, to cultural conflict, to discriminatory instruments (such as I.Q. tests), or to the cultural insensitivity of educators. Yet as surely as one of these has been posited as *the,* or at least *the principal,* cause of group achievement differentials, then other situations are discovered in which these factors exist, and yet group achievement differentials do not occur.

Second, a tendency that both distorts on its own and contributes to the misguided dependence on single-cause explanations is the confusion of correlation and cause. Sometimes correlations are found, as between language and educational achievement, between socio-economic status and educational achievement, or between race and educational achievement. Yet, without evidence-based demonstrations that these correlations actually reflect causation—for example, that language difference, socio-economic status, or race have actually *caused* lower educational achievement—such correlations are no stronger than arguing that a cock's crowing "causes" the sun to rise simply because the two phenomena are strongly correlated.

Third, there has been a tendency to decontextualize explanations. That is, explanations about the relationships between sociocultural factors and educational achievement often posit causation without consideration of the context in which these factors operate. For example, while there may be causative connections of such sociocultural factors as language, race, ethnicity, socio-economic status, learning style, and group history to low educational achievement, there are also situations in which limited English proficient students, students of different racial and ethnic backgrounds, and students from poor families succeed dramatically in school. Why do students of similar linguistic, racial, ethnic, and socio-economic backgrounds vary so widely in their academic achievement? More specifically, under what conditions do students with similar sociocultural characteristics succeed educationally and under what conditions do they perform poorly in school? In other words, within what contexts—educational and societal—do students of similar backgrounds succeed and within what contexts do they do less well?

The question of the educational influence of context stretches beyond our national borders. For example, why do Koreans tend to succeed in United States schools and society, but not in Japan? Why do native Maoris do worse in New Zealand schools than do those immigrant Polynesians who have language and culture similar to the Maoris? Why do West Indian students do better in United States schools than they do in the United Kingdom? An analysis of group culture alone does not provide the answers to these questions. It is also necessary to evaluate the societal and school contexts in which those cultures operate.

This article moves beyond the three fallacious analytical tendencies that have been noted and posits a Contextual Interaction Model for evaluating the educational process, in general, and the educational experiences of language minority students, in particular. This model integrates two previous conceptual formulations: my historical concept of the Societal Curriculum (Cortés, 1981) and the Interaction Model for Language Minority Students developed by the Bilingual Education Office. The latter model, presented in the publication, *Basic Principles for the Education of Language-Minority Students: An Overview* (California State Department of Education, 1983), was adapted from James Cummins' article, "Linguistic Interdependence and the Educational Development of Bilingual Children" (Cummins, 1979).

The Contextual Interaction Model illustrates the way in which non-school societal factors affect three aspects of the school's context and process, which are labeled educational input factors, instructional elements, and student qualities (see Figure 6.1). Among these societal factors are:

1. family (including home culture and language use);
2. community (both the general community and subcommunities, such as ethnic communities);
3. non-school institutions (such as religious institutions, voluntary associations, and government agencies);
4. the mass media (including television, motion pictures, radio, newspapers, and magazines);
5. heritage, culture, and ethnicity (including individual backgrounds, ethnic group experiences and life styles, and varying societal elements from the local to the national level);
6. attitudes (ranging from national to local);
7. perceptions (including not only how individuals and groups perceive themselves and others, but also how they interpret how others perceive them);
8. socio-economic status (family and surrounding community); and
9. educational level (self, family, and peers).

These and other factors create the societal context in which educational institutions function. Moreover, operating through the societal curriculum (the massive, on-going educational and socializing process carried on by society at large, as contrasted with the educational and socializing process conducted within schools), these societal factors directly affect the school's context and process. In particular, they influence at least three areas of school education:

1. *Educational input factors,* such as educators themselves (including the knowledge, skills, expectations, and attitudes of teachers, administrators, counselors, school board members, and other educational personnel), fiscal resources, governmental policies, and the educational theories and assumptions that undergird and inform the school educational process.
2. *Student qualities,* such as their proficiency in one or more languages, academic skills and knowledge, self-image, prosocial skills, educational motivation, and goals for the future.
3. *Instructional elements,* including curriculum, subject emphases, textbooks and other educational materials, pedagogical strategies, teaching styles, counseling, student placement, evaluation plan, staff development, and parent involvement.

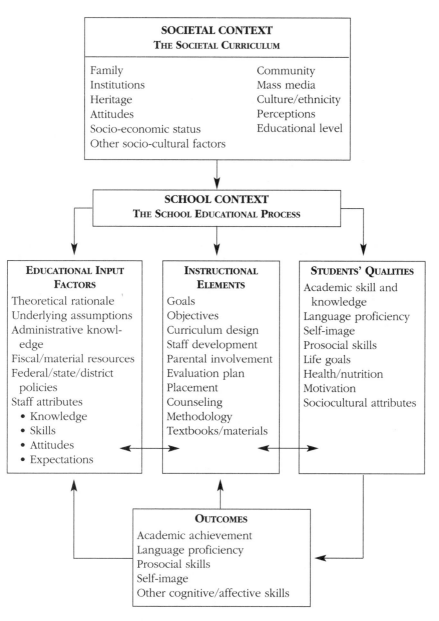

FIGURE 6.1
School and Society: Contextual Interaction Model.

In addition, these three components of the educational process affect each other. Both the general educational input factors and student qualities (including perceived qualities) influence the selection and implementation of instructional elements. Furthermore, these instructional elements affect students, with this impact sometimes observed and evaluated as cognitive and affective outcomes, although many of these outcomes are neither perceived nor assessed by schools. In turn, these student outcomes should be evaluated for purposes of modifying educational input factors and instructional elements.

Finally, the model illustrates the dynamism of these interactions over time. As days, weeks, months, years, and decades pass, the content of the model changes, continuously and sometimes dramatically. Society changes over time. The educational context and process—general educational factors, instructional treatments, students, and student outcomes—change over time. The ways in which society interacts with and influences schools—both via society in general and via specific societal elements, including ethnic groups—change over time. Finally, as the future adult citizens of our society, students who emerge from the schooling process ultimately influence, modify, and reinforce schools, the societal context, and the content of the societal curriculum. In other words, the Contextual Interaction Model is dynamic, interactive, and historically changing (see Figure 6.2).

As conceptualized in this model, the school and societal educational processes are themselves extremely complex and interact in complex ways. For example, take one aspect of the societal curriculum, the visual media (motion pictures and television). Scholars and societal analysts have long recognized the impact of motion pictures on American society. Film historian Lewis Jacobs (1939) noted:

> The content of American motion pictures since their inception has been, in fact, not only an important historical source but a stimulant and educator to American life itself. Besides offering a social occasion and an emotional experience, they supplied audiences with information and ideas. (p. 3)

The rise of television, through both its own programming and its recycling of theatrical feature films, has extended the impact of the visual media. In 1977, social psychologist George Comstock reported that there had been more then 2,300 research papers on television and human behavior. According to him:

> Several writers have argued that television is a powerful reinforcer of the status quo. The ostensible mechanisms are the effects of its portrayals on public expectations and perceptions. Television portrayals and particularly violent drama are said to assign roles of authority, power, success, failure, dependence, and vulnerability in a manner that matches the real-life social hierarchy, thereby strengthening that hierarchy by increasing its acknowledgement among the public and by failing to provide positive images for members of social categories

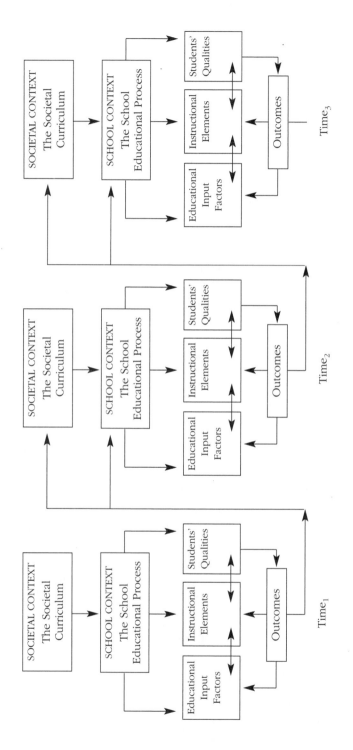

FIGURE 6.2
Contextual Interaction Over Time.

occupying a subservient position. Content analyses of television drama support
the contention that portrayals reflect normative status. (pp. 20–21)

Among those influenced by film and television are persons involved in
the educational process, including teachers, administrators, counselors, curriculum developers, textbook writers, school board members, and students.
It affects their perceptions of themselves and their perceptions and expectations of others, thereby influencing curricular content and pedagogical decisions. To the extent that media teaching conforms to or conflicts with school
teaching, it reinforces or challenges school instruction.

Moreover, both school learning (student outcomes) and societal learning will affect the future societal context. Students of today become the societal decision makers and context providers of the future. In turn, that future
societal curriculum will influence school education of the future.

This example illustrates the complex and dynamic nature of the historical interaction between schools and society, as well as the multiplicity of factors that influence students, including their school achievement. Moreover, it
demonstrates the need to examine both societal and school contexts in analyzing student achievement and in suggesting educational change to increase
that achievement. In short, the Contextual Interaction Model provides a means
of visualizing the total educational process for purposes of analysis.

While the Contextual Interaction Model applies to the school education
of all students, it can be used to examine the education of specific groups
of students, such as language minority students (see Figure 6.3). For example, the societal context influences the students' proficiency in English (L_2)
and their primary language (L_1), their motivation to strengthen their primary
language and acquire proficiency in other languages, their perceptions and
expectations of teachers and schools, and their self-image (including educational motivation, life goals, and hopes for the future). It influences educators, such as their knowledge, perceptions, and expectations of language
minority students, their multiple language facility, and their beliefs and underlying assumptions about education, including language learning. Therefore,
it influences the instructional elements adopted by these educators in addressing language minority students, including approaches to language use and
instruction, the treatment and coordination of other subject areas, their interaction with students, and the use (or non-use) of student or community socio-
cultural factors in developing instruction. The result will be educational outcomes, including English language learning, the further development of the
students' home languages, cognitive achievement in other subject areas,
improvement in prosocial skills, and such elements of the students' affective
domain as self-image, perceptions of others, and orientation toward society.

The examination of a wide variety of societal and school factors, including their interaction both at one point in time and dynamically over time,

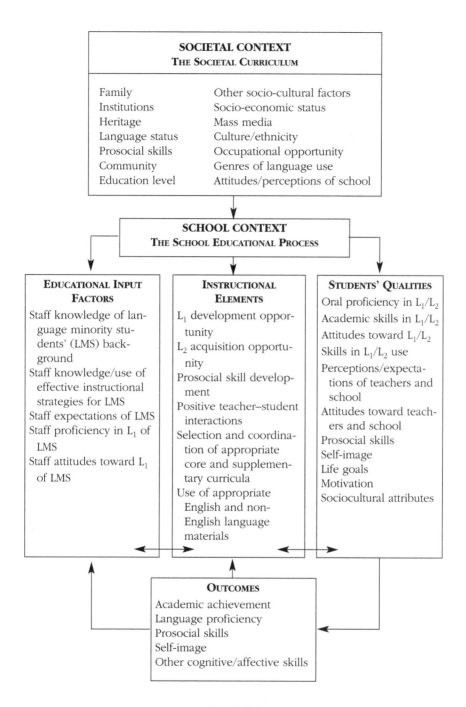

FIGURE 6.3
The Education of Language Minority Students: A Contextual Interaction Model.

provides the essence of the Contextual Interaction Model. This model rejects single-cause explanations and instead seeks to incorporate a multiplicity of factors that may influence educational achievement. It rejects static correlations and instead substitutes the consideration of observable dynamic interactions over time in an attempt to assess causation. It rejects the examination of societal and school factors outside of a specific context and instead examines the dynamic operation of these multiple factors within specific contexts. Finally, it provides a basis for the comparison of contexts in order to identify different ways in which sociocultural factors interact with and influence educational experience, including educational achievement.

Moreover, a careful examination of the contextualized relationship between sociocultural factors and educational achievement can lead to the identification of other school dilemmas. Analysts may determine that certain verifiable realities exist within an educational situation, but that the actors in that situation may perceive things quite differently and, most importantly, act and react on the basis of those assumptions. For example, within the Contextual Interaction Model, the *fact* that a teacher is not prejudiced against a linguistic minority group may be less important than the perception by students or parents that the teacher is prejudiced, with the resulting effect on the educational actions of those students or parents. Likewise, "objective" analysis may determine that certain curricular content exists within the educational system or within society itself, but within the Contextual Interaction Model the meaning and importance that individuals or groups assign to that content becomes additionally significant. The objective "fact" that educational opportunity exists is important, but also important is whether or not a student *believes* that opportunity exists within a specific school situation or that school education enhances future opportunities within society.

In other words, the Contextual Interaction Model incorporates both objective and subjective elements. It integrates a consideration not only of the existence of sociocultural factors, but also of the way in which these factors operate and the perception of their operation by the actors, primarily educators and students. Finally, it provides a framework for viewing the dynamic interaction of multiple factors over time.

ACKNOWLEDGMENTS

I would like to thank Daniel Holt and Dennis Parker for their insightful comments on earlier drafts, and James Banks both for his critique and for allowing me to read a chapter of his forthcoming book, *Multicultural Education in Western Societies,* which he co-authored with James Lynch.

The corresponding Chapter for this Selection can be found on pg. 26.

HOLLYWOOD INTERRACIAL LOVE: SOCIAL TABOO AS SCREEN TITILLATION

"MISCEGENATION (SEX RELATIONSHIP BETWEEN THE WHITE AND black races) is forbidden." So reads Section II, Rule 6 of Hollywood's 1930 Motion Picture Production Code (the Hays Code), which prescribed U.S. movie content from 1934 until the mid-1960s. Resting beneath rules II-4 ("Sex perversion or any inference to it is forbidden") and II-5 ("White slavery shall not be treated") and poised above rule II-7 ("Sex hygiene and venereal diseases are not proper subjects for theatrical motion pictures"), the "miscegenation rule" formally encoded the established informal Hollywood practice—using the interracial love plot convention to preach against this industry-proclaimed social deviation while simultaneously employing it to titillate moviegoers (Stanley and Steinberg, 1976).

Since the beginning of motion pictures, American moviemakers have consciously addressed or casually injected this theme—exploring it, exploiting it, and manipulating it. Interracial love's very status as a societal taboo and, for a period, as Code-forbidden fruit (even though it had long been a social reality) made it a plot convention with special power to titillate, disturb, and antagonize. According to film critic Michael Wood:

Source: From Paul Loukides and Linda K. Fuller (Eds.), *Plot Conventions in American Popular Film* (Vol. II of *Beyond the Stars).* (Bowling Green, Ohio: Bowling Green State University Popular Press, 1991), pp. 21–35.

Reprinted by permission of the Bowling Green State University Popular Press.

> Movies bring out . . . worries without letting them loose and without forcing
> us to look at them too closely. They trot around the park in the half-light. . . .
> It seems to be enough for us if a movie simply dramatizes our semi-secret
> concerns and contradictions in a story, allows them their brief, thinly disguised
> parade. (Wood, 1975, p.16)

Movies have used interracial love to manipulate personal phobias, probe psychological recesses, critique social practices, and sometimes attack legal statutes. In its continuities and changes, consistencies and variations, this plot convention has occasionally suggested or revealed the status and reality of interracial love in the United States. More often, however, it has provided glimpses, often unintended glimpses, into pervasive American angsts, concerns, and tensions.

Hollywood's interracial love stock convention has passed through three main phases. First came the pre-Code period, from the beginning of film until the 1930 completion and 1934 industry-wide adoption of the Hays guidelines. Second came the era of the Hays Code, which ruled Hollywood until the mid-1950s and then slowly, agonizingly declined until its demise in the late 1960s. Third came the post-Hays years, beginning with the 1968 adoption of Hollywood's new multi-lettered movie rating system.

In dealing with and manipulating the theme of miscegenation, Hollywood has extended a centuries-old literary tradition. For example, Shakespeare addressed it in *Othello*. The love between Othello, the heroic Moor, and Desdemona provides a weapon for the villainous Iago, who wounds Desdemona's father by goading him that "an old black ram is now tupping your white ewe."

Throughout the pre-movie era, American writers regularly dealt with miscegenation (as threat and reality) in geographical genres that might be categorized as Easterns, Westerns, and Southerns. Easterns embraced so-called "Indian captivity narratives," which often contained sensationalistic revelations by real or fictitious abducted White women concerning their lives (including their sex lives) among the Indians. Westerns, too, abounded with tales of Indian captivity, but they also expanded the ethnic dimensions of the miscegenation theme by adding the sexual threat of Mexican men, usually the *mestizo* (mixed blood) offspring of Indian–White relations. Finally, in Southerns, Black men served as the interracial sexual threat. (Surveys conducted for Gunnar Myrdal's 1944 classic, *An American Dilemma: The Negro Problem and Modern Democracy*, asked southern Whites what discriminatory lines were most important to maintain. Their most common answer— "the bar against intermarriage and sexual intercourse involving White women.") (Myrdal, 1944, p. 60). The perceived sexual threat to White women by colored men ("colored" defined by mainstream American racial perceptions, not by genetics or categorical "objectivity"), then, served as a plot convention in nineteenth-century American literature.[1]

However, the reversing of genders brought a fundamental change in this popular plot convention. In contrast to their non-White brethren, colored women in U.S. literature often served as interracial sexual conveniences, particularly for young White men going through their sexual rites of passage (after all, boys, at least White ones, will be boys). Yet, while White men had access to colored (black, brown, red, or yellow) women, such fictional liaisons almost always proved transitory, usually ending sadly.

Therefore, when movies came into existence, they could draw upon a long popular literary tradition. Colored men had become consistent sexual threats, often resorting to force in their lustful pursuits. Colored women had become readily available sexual conveniences, who seldom achieved permanent interracial bliss. As early movies mindlessly adopted and casually adapted this literary legacy, colored sexual threats and sexual conveniences leaped from the printed page to movie screens.[2]

SILENT SCREEN INTERRACIAL LOVE: THE CONVENTION DEVELOPS

Screen visualization of interracial love involved additional complications. In particular, it raised three thorny questions. First, for movie purposes, who was White and who was colored? Second, what should be the basic parameters of the miscegenation plot convention? Third, what variations could filmmakers employ and what limits could they test within the convention?

In practical movie terms, whiteness and coloredness did not always emerge clearly. With the popular beliefs of mainstream White Americans as the guiding principle, the movie categorization of coloreds evolved in the following general pattern. African Americans were colored, along with Black Africans and mixed-blood mulattoes. Asian Americans were colored (also Asians, Eurasians, and Pacific Islanders). Native Americans (American Indians) were colored, along with "half-breeds" (although those with lesser amounts of Indian ancestry sometimes played White on screen). Movie Arabs, too, fell into this racial twilight zone.

Latinos presented an even more complex challenge. Most Mexicans, the preponderant U.S. Latino population during the early movie era, enjoyed mixed racial ancestry, principally White and Indian. But some Latinos came from pure or heavily European descent. So to what racial agglomeration did Latinos belong, White or colored? Hollywood soon answered—"both." Indianized or Africanized Latinos were colored; Europeanized ones were White (usually inaccurately labeled as "Spanish" to differentiate them from colored "Mexicans"). For screen Latinos, physical appearance and stated (or implied) ancestry became the racial dividing line. Within the interracial love plot convention, "Spanish" Latinos played White, while "Mexicans" usually functioned as colored, thereby permitting the screen co-existence of the Latin lover (White) and the lecherous Latino greaser (colored).

Rapidity of racial categorization proved particularly critical during the early days of moviemaking. In ten-minute one-reelers, filmmakers had little opportunity to develop plot or character subtleties. Established stereotypes, reified by popular literature, provided convenient shortcuts to reach movie audiences—colored men lusting after White women and White men sowing their wild oats with colored women.

Film titles also helped condition audience reactions. Titles told viewers when to expect Latinos to provide interracial sexual threats (*The Girl and the Greaser,* 1913) or sexual conveniences (*How Porto Rican Girls Entertain Uncle Sam's Soldiers,* 1899). As for Indian–White love relations, a stream of movies—*Comata, the Sioux* (1909), *A Romance of the Western Hills* (1910), *The Chief's Daughter* (1911), and *The Squaw Man* (1914)—combined audience titillation with moral lecturing on the inappropriateness and tragic consequences of interracial liaisons. By the mid-1910s, Hollywood had solidified the two basic miscegenation conventions.

Two 1915 films both epitomized these themes and helped to invest them with iconic significance. In that year, D. W. Griffith's classic Southern, *The Birth of a Nation* (based on *The Clansman,* Thomas Dixon's novel/play about the Civil War and Reconstruction South) exploded onto movie screens, featuring the inflammatory manipulation of the miscegenation threat. In one climactic moment, a White southern belle leaps to her death from a cliff rather than suffer the advances of a Black man. In the face of pressure from the National Association for the Advanced of Colored People, Griffith reportedly cut several other scenes of Blacks pursuing and sometimes catching White women (Kirby, 1978). But never fear! A stock element of the plot convention involved the timely arrival of the White male hero to rescue the racially/sexually threatened damsel. In *The Birth of a Nation,* the Ku Klux Klan becomes the hero, saving the city (by implication, the South and even the entire nation) from the Black menace, symbolized as a sexual threat.

That same year, *The Cheat* dramatized the colored sexual threat of Asians, in the person of wealthy, lascivious Japanese immigrant businessman Hishuru Tori, played by the popular Japanese American actor, Sessue Hayakawa. Spurned by a White woman, Tori *brands* her! But, like Blacks in *The Birth of a Nation,* like Indians and Mexican "greasers" in myriad westerns, the Asian upstart ultimately receives his comeuppance, being beaten and nearly lynched by an enraged White courtroom mob.

Upset with being asked to play so many stereotypically lustful, villainous Asians, Hayakawa formed his own film company. Usually set in Japan, his movies gently explored interracial love, almost always involving a White man and a Japanese woman, such as in two 1920 features, *Locked Lips* and *Breath of the Gods.* Hayakawa's films typified the gender-reversal flip-side of the screen miscegenation theme—that colored women felt a magnetic attraction to and sometimes preference for White men.

Basic guidelines were developing within American filmdom's interracial love stock convention. "Spanish" Latinos functioned as White. Colored men sexually threatened White women, who spurned their advances and waited for White men to save them. White men could cross the color line with Indian, Asian, and Latin women, although usually for transitory satisfaction and with generally unhappy results. In the case of African Americans, the screen color line became nearly impermeable (although White plantation owners had historically permeated it with regularity).

In only rare instances did silent movies bend the convention. For example, in the acclaimed 1926 film, *The Vanishing American,* love develops between a Navajo man and a White reservation teacher. However, as regularly occurred in interracial love films, death comes to the rescue. The Navajo dies fighting for his people against an unscrupulous Indian agent, thereby providing filmmakers with a convenient resolution for the love affair.

Sometimes movies appeared to break the convention, only to later expose the illusion. In *The Sheik* (1921), Rudolph Valentino's Ahmed Ben Hassan abducts a White woman, but the movie finally reveals that he is really a European, not an Arab. According to a *New York Times* reviewer, "You won't be offended by having a white girl marry an Arab either, for the Sheik really isn't a native of the desert at all" (Michalek, 1989, p. 4).

Running until the late 1920s, the Silent era developed three major parameters for screen interracial love. It created a movie working definition of White and non-White. It established a screen gender gap—love between White men and colored women became transitorily permissible, while colored men provided sexual threats to White women. And it erected a screen pecking order for interracial love, with Latinos requiring the most careful internal differentiation, Asians, Indians, and Arabs enjoying some flexibility, and African Americans becoming the least likely to cross interracial barriers.

THE CODIFICATION OF INTERRACIAL LOVE

Then came the Hays Code. In 1922, former Republican Postmaster General Will Hays became president of the Motion Picture Producers and Distributors of America. Selected by Hollywood to provide a buffer against governmental and public criticism, Hays sought to create a system of industry self-regulation. However, he encountered opposition from studio moguls as he tried to impose his rural Protestant moral standards on film content.

In 1930, Hays commissioned the writing of a Motion Picture Production Code—content guidelines for what Hollywood movies should teach and not teach viewers. At first filmmakers only selectively followed the Code. But increasing threats of federal censorship and growing public pressure, including the 1934 establishment by Catholic bishops of the Legion of Decency to evaluate movies, impelled Hollywood to choose self-censorship via the Code as a lesser evil. So in 1934 the studios reluctantly agreed to submit scripts to the industry's Production Code Administration, whose suggestions had to be followed for a film to earn a Code Seal of Approval, increasingly de rigueur for exhibition.

The Hays Code listed acceptable and unacceptable plot conventions, including the miscegenation prohibition. The fact that interracial love and marriage occurred in the United States took a back seat to the Hays bunch's conviction that Hollywood should teach their inappropriateness. In general, they should not occur; if they occur, they should be punished.

Moreover, both Hollywood's informal traditions and Code formal guidelines reflected other socio-economic factors. Racial bigotry was alive and well in the United States, including a widespread (although not universal) White taboo against interracial love (Hernton, 1965). Some states outlawed miscegenation (the U.S. Supreme Court did not invalidate such laws until 1967). Finally, not wanting to offend White southern moviegoers, whom Hollywood feared would not patronize films about Blacks, studios operated on a self-imposed "southern veto" of movie content.[3]

Although the Code's miscegenation rule specified Black and White, Hollywood applied the rule with variations to other colored groups, while using Hollywood's traditional gender double standard as a further informal guideline. After all, Code or no Code, taboos make titillating screen material. So filmmakers skirted the borders of the Code-hardened convention, teasing audiences with touches or hints of interracial love.

The Bitter Tea of General Yen (1933) employed sexual fantasizing. A White American woman becomes simultaneously repelled by and attracted to the magnetic Chinese warlord, General Yen. Then one night he breaks into her bedroom. However, another Yen, masked and in western clothes, intercedes and saves her, for which she kisses him. Before anything more can happen, she awakens, realizing she has had a "nightmare."

Bordertown (1935), too, reached the sexual edge before stopping. Chicano casino owner Johnny Ramírez proves dangerously attractive to two Anglo women. Not to worry; of course it won't last. One woman goes crazy, the other dies in an automobile accident . . . proper punishment for defying interracial frontiers.

But when filmmakers reversed the genders, the Code became more porous. White men occasionally crossed the interracial line, at least transitorily. Moreover, this usually occurred at a safe geographical distance from the United States, such as in the South Pacific.

In *Bird of Paradise* (1932), for example, an American sailor (Johnny) and a Polynesian princess (Luana) fall in love, although Luana is betrothed to a native prince. However, Johnny's American determination and ingenuity prevail, as he abducts the willing princess during their wedding ceremony and they (implicitly) consummate their love. Yet 1930s' screen interracial affairs do not end happily. Johnny ultimately leaves on an American ship while Luana sadly returns to her people, sacrificing love to lift the curse of an erupting volcano!

With the arrival of World War II, Hollywood transformed the miscegenation plot convention into a patriotic appeal to galvanize public support for the war effort. Historically, to strengthen public wartime resolve, nations have used propaganda to degrade the enemy and suggest the calamitous results of an enemy victory (Keen, 1986). During World War II, film industries worldwide played a critical role in this process. For Hollywood, the interracial sex convention provided an ideal vehicle. In the Pacific, the United States confronted Japan, its only racially different enemy. Movies portrayed Japanese soldiers as being dedicated to rape as well as to military victory, with American nurses in the Philippines facing this threat in films like *So Proudly We Hail!* (1942) and *Cry Havoc* (1943). In fact, Hollywood's version of World War II sometimes made it seem as if the United States were fighting a Pacific war mainly to protect military nurses.

The post-World War II era ushered in a new dimension in American filmmaking. Having focused for four years on evils abroad, filmmakers turned their crusading zeal to evils at home, including the blight of anti-ethnic bigotry. Once again that increasingly chameleon-like plot convention, interracial love, became a message-carrying vehicle. However, screen tradition survived even as movies used the theme to explore racism.

The traditional themes of sexual threat and convenience remained. Indians continued to lust for White women, for example, provoking John Wayne to devote years looking for his Comanche-abducted niece in *The Searchers* (1956). According to Indian-hater Ethan (Wayne), "Living with Comanches ain't being alive."

The minority sexual threat even moved from the old west into modern urban America. In *Trial* (1955), a White teenage girl drops dead from a heart attack while she and a young Chicano are kissing and fondling. With the town superheated over this interracial incident—he *must* have been forcing himself on her—the sheriff barely prevents a lynching. Placed on trial for murder, the boy is saved through the efforts of a dedicated Anglo lawyer and the sensitive decision of an African American judge.

Less fortunate is Black Tom Robinson, wrongfully accused of attempting to rape a White woman in the 1962 film adaptation of Harper Lee's novel, *To Kill a Mockingbird*. Despite an impassioned defense by a White lawyer, the all-White southern jury convicts Tom. Panic-stricken and rightfully fearing a lynching, Tom tries to escape and is killed.

Tradition also survived alongside social critique when genders were reversed. The "love-em-and-leave-em" convention continued, although colored females gained improved stature. In the 1952 western masterpiece, *High Noon,* a series of Anglos cohabit with (but do not marry) small-town Mexican entrepreneur Helen Ramírez. Admired for her business acumen but scorned for her ethnicity, Ramírez embodies strength and intelligence. . . but also tragedy. Appropriately, according to convention, the Anglo town marshal dumps her and marries a White blonde.

Sometimes filmmakers made interracial marriage the central issue. That most formidable screen taboo, Black–White love, began to receive attention, most notably in the 1949 *Pinky.* A southern mulatta, Pinky goes north to study nursing. So light-skinned that she passes there for White, Pinky falls in love with a White doctor. When she goes home to visit her mother, the doctor follows, discovers her secret, but still begs Pinky to marry him and move north. However, instead she decides to dedicate her life to running a clinic and nursing school for young Black women.

Pinky uses interracial love to critique racism, yet it ultimately conforms to Hollywood tradition and the Code convention against interracial love by having Pinky choose to stick to her own race. Even director Elia Kazan expressed some concern:

> I'm worried because people might think we're saying Negroes and whites shouldn't marry. We solve this story in personal terms. This particular boy and girl shouldn't get married. . . . But we don't mean the story to be true of all people with colored and white skins ("Zanuck," 1949, p. 25).

In still another way the movie pulled punches. The filmmakers cast a popular White movie star, Jeanne Crain, as Pinky, thereby adding another fantasy layer for White viewers, their main audience, and making it easier for those moviegoers to identify with Pinky's humiliating experiences (Jones, 1981). (Hollywood has consistently cast White performers as non-White characters, but rarely the reverse.) Despite Hollywood's apprehensions, *Pinky* became one the year's top-grossing movies . . . even drawing sizable southern audiences, casting further doubt on the rationality of the industry's informal southern veto (Campbell, 1978).

At times screen interracial marriages occurred, although seldom without complications. Screen Black–White marriage remained virtually non-existent, but Whites occasionally married other coloreds—almost always involving White men and colored women. Yet interracial marriage still usually spelled "trouble."

In *Giant* (1956), plucky Chicana nurse Juana Villalobos marries the son of powerful Texas rancher Jordan (Bick) Benedict. Yet despite the Benedict name, Juana is denied service at a high-class hotel beauty salon. However, the film ends with a hopeful metaphor, as Bick's two grandsons, one blonde, one mestizo brown, lie together in a crib on top of a black-and-white sheet.

The complications of love between White Americans and Japanese dominate the 1957 *Sayonara,* with marriage leading to tragedy. When the Air Force reassigns an American airman but denies permission for his Japanese wife to accompany him, they commit dual suicide rather than be separated. But *Sayonara,* too, ends on a note of hope as another American airman, a decorated war hero, decides to marry a Japanese actress.

White man–Indian woman relations, generally enveloped by interracial conflict, achieved the broadest spectrum of post-war screen exposure. The 1950 *Broken Arrow* simultaneously celebrates interracial love and suggests its probable tragic consequences, as a White man marries an Apache princess, who is killed soon thereafter (by White racists, of course). Along with death, the sufferings of racially mixed offspring provided the most common unhappy results. The 1954 *Broken Lance* featured a White–Indian marriage, this time involving a Comanche princess (few screen White men marry Indians who are not princesses). Yet their mixed-blood son faces racism both from the young man's all-White half-brothers of his father's first marriage and from local townspeople, including the father of the White woman he loves. Other films, such as the 1952 *The Big Sky* and the 1955 *The Indian Fighter,* use White man–Indian princess marriages as Sayonara-style hopeful conclusions, thereby avoiding the issue of whether or not they and their offspring encounter later interracial problems.

Most post-war interracial marriage films involved two elements that made them more acceptable to the Hays bunch and, presumably, to American audiences. First, love generally occurred either in distant lands or in the distant past, providing an avenue of escapism rather than a role model for contemporary behavior. Second, they injected the element of social class—if a White man marries an Indian, for example, she should be a princess.

Even adaptations of Broadway hit musicals generally followed the basic post-war plot convention—racism critiqued, but interracial love leading to unhappiness. The 1951 film version of Jerome Kern's *Show Boat* used the tragic marriage convention. When anti-miscegenation laws wreck light-skinned mulatta Julie's marriage to a White man, she ultimately plunges into alcoholism.

The 1958 movie adaptation of *South Pacific* features dual World War II interracial dilemmas. Should sweet, bubbly "cockeyed optimist" Navy Ensign Nellie Forbush marry French planter Emile De Becque, even after she discovers that he had been married to a Polynesian and has two mixed-blood children, or should she wash him right out of her hair? Should handsome U.S. Navy Lieutenant Cable marry a beautiful Polynesian girl? Forbush and Cable ponder their dilemmas together in song:

You've got to be taught to be afraid
Of people whose eyes are oddly made
And people whose skins are a different shade.
You've got to be carefully taught.

The musical resolved Cable's moral quandary with the standard screen solution—he is killed by the Japanese. But Cable's death also shocks Nellie into accepting marriage to De Becque. After all, he isn't Polynesian; he merely married one.

The dilemma of interracial love even moved musically into urban America with the 1961 screen version of *West Side Story.* Polish American Tony and Puerto Rican María try to make a go of it in the midst of interethnic turf warfare. María even disregards the musical warning of her friend Juanita to "Stick to your own kind, one of your own kind." This leads, of course, to tragedy—a Puerto Rican shoots Tony, whose death magically brings the gangs together as they join to carry his body away.

By the 1960s, filmmakers increasingly challenged the Hays Code, including the miscegenation rule. That ultimate taboo, Black–White love, received special examination. In the 1965 *A Patch of Blue,* a kind African American man befriends a blind White girl, who falls in love with him. One day she surprises him by passionately kissing him and asking him to make love to her, but he knows better and refuses. Viewing the kiss one studio executive reportedly opined, "There goes Alabama," referring to the movie's assumed southern unsuitability.

In 1964, the sensitive low-budget *One Potato, Two Potato* ventured into new ground by portraying a successful, loving marriage between a Black man and a White woman. Of course, she pays a penalty. Her White ex-husband contests her for custody of their children and wins.

Finally, in 1967, with the Hays code in tatters, Stanley Kramer struck the final blow against the miscegenation rule with his *Guess Who's Coming to Dinner?.* The dilemma—an African American man and a White woman want the blessing of both sets of parents before they marry. At first the parents oppose them, but finally they all come around to accepting the couples' decision, after a long afternoon and evening of haggling. The film suggests that all six (four parents and two children) will live happily ever after, even to the point of enjoying an interracial dinner.

THE POST-HAYS CODE ERA

In 1968, Hollywood laid to rest the moribund Hays Code, replacing it with a multiple lettering system (currently G, PG, PG-13, R, NC-17, and X). This included the burial of the anti-miscegenation rule. Onscreen interracial love and sex, which had gained an increased and more diversified presence in post-war American movies, now lost their codified illegitimacy.

Moreover, the collapse of the Code occurred simultaneously with other changes, both societally and within the film industry, The Civil Rights movement had shaken the nation, challenging bigotry, discriminatory laws, and inequitable institutions while myriad ethnic pride movements arose. Colored Americans were becoming a growing proportion of the population, spurred both by higher minority (as contrasted to non-minority) birthrates and by large-scale immigration from Latin America and Asia. Moreover, white flight to the suburbs was eroding much of the traditional downtown movie house audience, with Blacks and Latinos taking up the slack. Finally, interracial intermarriage was on the rise.

Eager for new themes to take advantage of the civil rights-spawned interest in race relations, the growth in ethnic pride, and the increase of minority moviegoers, Hollywood experienced a short-lived ethnic flip-flop. No longer did White heroes ride to the rescue of threatened White women; now colored heroes (usually African Americans) whipped White villains. Although the ethnic flip-flop lasted only briefly and colored villains soon returned to the screen (take, for example, the rash of Latino drug dealers), colored heroes have continued to prosper.

The ethnic flip-flop shook the interracial love plot convention, as new adaptations provided enlightening glimpses into both new American realities and the changing American psyche. Particularly suggestive have been three variations of screen interracial love and sex: as a symbol of progress toward social equity; as an expression of colored power; and as an embodiment of pluralism within evolving American sexual mores, particularly concerning sexual orientation.

Interracial love became a theme for proclaiming the need for racial equality. Black–White love now led the way. White men develop loving relationships with Black women in films ranging from the 1970 *The Landlord* to the 1987 *Fatal Beauty,* while in the 1972 *Fat City* a Black man loves and cares for an unfaithful, alcoholic White woman. Mixed offspring also fare better. In *Carbon Copy* (1981), a White father, who years before had engaged in a love affair with a Black woman, suddenly discovers that he has a half-Black teenage son when the young man appears at his home. After a period of shock and conflict, they grow to accept and even "bond" with each other.

White men fall in love with Indian women in the old west (the 1972 *Jeremiah Johnson* and the 1980 *The Mountain Men),* with Eskimo women in the far north (the 1974 *The White Dawn),* and with native Hawaiian women (the 1987 *North Shore),* while in modern America White women fall in love with Indian men without being abducted (the 1966 *Johnny Tiger* and the 1972 *When the Legends Die).* Anglo men regularly fall in love with and sometimes marry Latinas in screen modern America (the 1980 *Gloria,* the 1986 *Touch and Go,* and the 1987 *Extreme Prejudice*). Reverse genders—in the 1979 *Walk Proud* a White girl helps a young Chicano outgrow his misdirected youth gang loyalty, while in the 1987 *La Bamba* another White girl provides Chicano rock-and-roller Ritchie Valens with the inspiration for one of his biggest hits, "Donna." Anglo–Asian love predictably flourishes in distant places (the 1987 *Captive Hearts*) and in distant times (the 1988 *Young Guns*), but it also occurs in the contemporary United States. In the 1985 *Year of the Dragon,* a Chinese American female television reporter helps to redeem a violence-prone Polish American police officer.

In the post-Hays decades, interracial love has pervaded American movies. But although the screen gender gap has narrowed, it still remains. The vast majority of love relations—whether they occur in the past or in the present, in the United States or in other nations—still involve White men and colored women.

While many recent movies have used interracial love to suggest progress toward interracial understanding, in other cases they have been used to proclaim colored power through interracial sex. This occurred particularly during the brief ethnic flip-flop era. Some of the so-called "blaxploitation films" of the early 1970s featured Black studs, like the street-smart, drug-dealing *Superfly* (1972), who dominated White men and women alike. Screen Latinos, too, sometimes used sex to demonstrate ethnic power. In *Scarface* (1983), Cuban American drug lord Antonio Montana tries to gain social acceptability by acquiring a blonde Anglo wife. Male Black slaves remained sexual titans, but in a new function—on the sixtieth anniversary of *The Birth of a Nation,* the horrendous, exploitative 1975 *Mandingo* transformed them from sexual threats into unwilling sexual conveniences for White women.

Occasionally, the traditional theme of colored sexual threat reappears. In *Bad Boys* (1983), Chicago Latino Paco Moreno rapes an Anglo girl, but he receives his punishment—a brutal prison-ward beating by her boyfriend. In the ludicrous 1981 *Tarzan, the Ape Man,* a huge Black African prepares to sexually assault terror-stricken Bo Derek, but Tarzan swings to the rescue. Indian men lust for White women in *Ulzana's Raid* (1972), Chinese men abduct them in *Big Trouble in Little China* (1986), and Arabs chase them in *Paradise* (1982)—but Whites continue to emerge victorious.

Moreover, as movies increasingly presented diversity of sexual orientation, interracial love gained admission into non-traditional gender combinations. It spread into movies about homosexuality, whether involving gays (*The Boys in the Band*—1970 or *Norman . . . Is That You?*—1976) or lesbians (*Working Girls*—1987). It spread into pornography, such as the 1983 soft-porn cult classic *Eating Raoul,* in which the Chicano title role burglar takes up with an Anglo woman, although she does help her husband kill Raoul in the end. Name the genre, interracial love has probably left its mark.

A final variation of interracial love (although seldom interracial sex) has emerged in the form of male-bonding movies, where interracial pals often emit stronger screen vibes together than they do with their women. (In his review of the 1989 *Lethal Weapon 2*, which features Black policeman Danny Glover and his White partner, Mel Gibson, *Newsweek*'s David Ansen wrote, "The real love story here is between the cops—the subsidiary romance between Gibson and Patsy Kensit, playing a wan 'good' South African, feels half-hearted.") (Ansen, 1989, p. 53). Black–White buddies (*Skin Game, Nighthawks, White Knights,* and *48 HRS.*), Latino–white buddies (*Freebie and the Bean* and *Cobra*), Indian–White buddies (*Young Guns* and *The Legend of the Lone Ranger*), and Asian–White buddies (*The Karate Kid* and *The Goonies*) now grace the screen.

The Dirty Harry movies became almost role models of cross-categorical bonding. Harry Callahan, the reluctant affirmative action cop, finds himself unwillingly paired with a Chicano (*Dirty Harry*—1971), a woman (*The Enforcer*—1976), and a Chinese American (*The Dead Pool*—1988). Each movie follows the same pattern—first Harry scorns his assigned partners, then he grows to admire them in spite of himself, and finally becomes saddened when they get either killed or mangled by the villain, leaving Harry to finish the job alone.

CONCLUSION

As the 1990s began, interracial love not only had become common in American movies, but it had even entered daytime television soaps. No longer do filmmakers have to tiptoe around the theme or handle it with delicacy. Unfortunately, exploitation of interracial love has become prominent within the old plot convention. In particular, movies now use colored men as monuments to interracial virility, both in melodramas (such as *Mandingo*) or in comedies like the tasteless 1984 *Sixteen Candles,* in which a White girl has an affair with an oversexed Chinese exchange student with the oh-so-clever name of Long Duk Dong (she calls him The Donger).

Moreover, tragedy continues to stalk interracial love relationships. Symptomatic is the 1987 *China Girl,* an updated *West Side Story* (or *Romeo and Juliet*) about a Chinese immigrant girl and an Italian American boy. Their love is buffeted by neighborhood warfare as an expanding Chinatown encroaches on a traditional Italian American neighborhood. Almost predictably, as it has since the beginning of movies, death resolves the film—a Chinese hood shoots and kills both of the young lovers.

Even as variations appear, plot conventions persist. But so do social taboos and societal realities. In August, 1989, in the Bensonhurst section of Brooklyn, a 16-year-old African American named Yusuf Hawkins was killed by Whites. According to some reports, they were angry because they thought Hawkins and his Black companions were friends of a local White girl who had said she was going to date Blacks and Latinos.

FILMOGRAPHY

1915	*The Birth of a Nation*	Dir. D. W. Griffith
1915	*The Cheat*	Dir. Cecil B. DeMille
1920	*Breath of the Gods*	Dir. Sessue Hayakawa
1920	*Locked Lips*	Dir. Sessue Hayakawa
1921	*The Sheik*	Dir. George Melford
1925	*The Vanishing American*	Dir. George Seitz
1932	*Bird of Paradise*	Dir. King Vidor
1933	*The Bitter Tea of General Yen*	Dir. Frank Capra
1935	*Bordertown*	Dir. Archie Mayo
1943	*Cry Havoc*	Dir. Richard Thorpe
1943	*So Proudly We Hail!*	Dir. Mark Sandrich
1949	*Pinky*	Dir. Elia Kazan
1950	*Broken Arrow*	Dir. Delmer Daves
1951	*Show Boat*	Dir. George Sidney
1952	*The Big Sky*	Dir. Howard Hawks
1952	*High Noon*	Dir. Fred Zinnemann
1954	*Broken Lance*	Dir. Edward Dmytryk
1955	*The Indian Fighter*	Dir. Andre de Toth
1955	*Trial*	Dir. Mark Robson
1956	*Giant*	Dir. George Stevens
1956	*The Searchers*	Dir. John Ford
1957	*Sayonara*	Dir. John Ford
1958	*South Pacific*	Dir. Joshua Logan
1961	*West Side Story*	Dir. Robert Wise
1962	*To Kill a Mockingbird*	Dir. Robert Mulligan
1964	*One Potato, Two Potato*	Dir. Larry Peerce
1965	*A Patch of Blue*	Dir. Guy Green
1966	*Johnny Tiger*	Dir. Paul Wendkos
1967	*Guess Who's Coming to Dinner?*	Dir. Stanley Kramer
1970	*The Boys in the Band*	Dir. William Friedkin
1970	*The Landlord*	Dir. Hal Ashby
1972	*Fat City*	Dir. John Huston
1972	*Jeremiah Johnson*	Dir. Sydney Pollack
1972	*Superfly*	Dir. Gordon Parks Jr.

1972	*When the Legends Die*	Dir. Stuart Millar
1974	*The White Dawn*	Dir. Philip Kaufman
1975	*Mandingo*	Dir. Richard Fleischer
1976	*Norman. . . Is That You?*	Dir. George Schlatter
1979	*Walk Proud*	Dir. Robert Collins
1980	*Gloria*	Dir. John Cassavetes
1980	*The Mountain Men*	Dir. Richard Lang
1981	*Carbon Copy*	Dir. Michael Schultz
1981	*Tarzan, the Ape Man*	Dir. John Derek
1982	*Eating Raoul*	Dir. Paul Bartel
1982	*Paradise*	Dir. Stuart Gillard
1983	*Bad Boys*	Dir. Rick Rosenthal
1983	*Scarface*	Dir. Brian De Palma
1984	*Sixteen Candles*	Dir. John Hughes
1985	*Year of the Dragon*	Dir. Michael Cimino
1986	*Touch and Go*	Dir. Robert Mandel
1986	*Working Girls*	Dir. Lizzie Borden
1987	*Captive Hearts*	Dir. Paul Almond
1987	*China Girl*	Dir. Abel Ferrara
1987	*Extreme Prejudice*	Dir. Walter Hill
1987	*Fatal Beauty*	Dir. Tom Holland
1987	*La Bamba*	Dir. Luis Valdez
1987	*North Shore*	Dir. William Phelps
1988	*Young Guns*	Dir. Christopher Cain

NOTES

1. "Colored" in this essay refers to individuals or groups that have been categorized as non-White in American history or culture (primarily by mainstream White American perceptions or official government labeling).

2. For my book-in-progress on the history of the U.S. film treatment of interracial love, I have so far examined more than 500 films incorporating the theme.

3. Thomas Cripps, The Myth of the Southern Box Office: A Factor in Racial Stereotyping in American Movies, 1920–1940, in James C. Curtis and Louis L. Gould (eds.), *The Black Experience in America: Selected Essays* (Austin: University of Texas Press, 1970), pp. 116–144, challenges the validity of Hollywood's vision of this so-called southern market.

The corresponding Chapter for this Selection can be found on pg. 31.

SELECTION 8

LIMITS TO *PLURIBUS,* LIMITS TO *UNUM:* UNITY, DIVERSITY, AND THE GREAT AMERICAN BALANCING ACT

SINCE ITS INCEPTION, THE UNITED STATES HAS ENGAGED IN A continuous, delicate balancing act involving varying and sometimes conflicting principles. One of those balancing acts has involved the alternatives posed by *pluribus* (pluralistic and individualistic) and *unum* (unifying and cohering) imperatives, both deeply embedded in our nation's history and its Constitution. Such *pluribus* values as freedom, individualism, and diversity live in constant and inevitable tension with such *unum* values as authority, conformity, and commonality.

However, this historical balancing act has involved more than values. Intersecting the *pluribus-unum* value tension has been the *pluribus-unum* tension of societal composition, because the United States began and has evolved not just as a nation of individuals, but also as a nation of groups—racial, ethnic, religious, and cultural groups, to name just a few.

Americans vary in their relative emphasis on *pluribus* and *unum.* Some emphasize *pluribus,* giving primacy to the defense of individual freedom and societal diversity. Others emphasize *unum,* arguing that the maintenance of societal unity reigns as the more essential value, often superseding the protection of *pluribus* rights, privileges, predispositions, and desires. While those who emphasize *pluribus* seek a capacious society that permits the maximum amount of socially benign diversity, those who emphasize *unum* focus their attention on upholding the societal core, not on preserving freedom for diversity.

Source: National Forum, LXXIV, 1 (Winter, 1994), pp. 6–8.

Reprinted by permission of the National Forum.

PLURIBUS AND UNUM EXTREMISM

Both *pluribus* and *unum* zealots sometimes become extremists—in support of their own particular versions of *pluribus* and *unum,* of course. Yet both *pluribus* and *unum* must have limits. *Pluribus* extremism can result in societal disintegration, particularly in light of our growing racial, ethnic, and cultural diversity. However, *unum* extremism can lead to the societal oppression of individual rights and group options.

Pluribus extremism sometimes takes the form of the defense of all diversity, whatever the societal costs or threat to *unum.* Knee-jerk supporters of such *pluribus* extremism love diversity so much that they constantly preach "tolerance" of all differences, continuously "celebrate" all diversity, and proclaim non-judgmental "acceptance" of every group, regardless.

I believe deeply in diversity, but I also recognize my *pluribus* limits. I am not "tolerant" of bigotry, even if its roots are cultural—fortunately Black and White abolitionists were not "tolerant" of the culture of slaveholding. I do not "accept" the restriction of opportunities for women simply because that restriction might be traditional within a particular culture. I do not "celebrate" the use of violence to resolve differences of opinion, although such problem-solving techniques might be endemic to some cultures. In other words, I do not subscribe to absolute *pluribus* because that necessitates a rejection of personal values, except tolerance, and an abdication of the right—better yet, the obligation—to make judgments. Such *pluribus* extremism, in short, becomes amorality.

At the opposite end of the ideological spectrum stand the *unum* extremists. Not only do they give primacy to *unum,* but many of them also fear diversity—particularly racial and ethnic diversity—viewing it as a threat to the future of American society. So fearful are they that some even seek to punish others for their diversity.

TWO BALANCING-ACT ISSUES

Since both *pluribus* and *unum* extremists are societally destructive, all Americans consciously or unconsciously grapple with two balancing-act questions. Whose *pluribus* should be limited? Whose versions of *unum* should triumph? To address these questions, I will briefly examine two balancing-act issues: language and ethnicity-based religion.

Language

The First Amendment to the Constitution guarantees freedom of speech and press without restriction on the language to be used.

Today, numerous American organizations are trying to eradicate or radically restrict the use of languages other than English within the United States. While such groups and their supporters sometimes issue pious statements about the right of individuals to speak other languages in their homes, they seek to banish it from schools, governmental services, and sometimes even private industry.

Moreover, they champion the establishment of English as our nation's "official" language, calling this a necessity for protecting *unum* and hyperbolically proclaiming that English is being threatened in our country.

Unquestionably, people in the United States should learn English, both because the nation functions better with a common language of public discourse and because individuals enjoy greater opportunities if they possess a solid facility in English. Immigrants realize this, which is why they flood into adult English-language classes, where they are turned away by the tens of thousands. But while the societal *unum* goal of a common language is laudable, many "official English" zealots appear to ignore the fact that this can be achieved without "boiling out" or punishing linguistic *pluribus*.

Making English the official language and establishing English-only rules in government or private business do not increase English fluency, but rather punish those who are in the process of learning English. Paradoxically, such mandates actually retard the achievement of *unum*—after all, you can study U.S. history, learn about American culture, and become a contributing part of American society using any language *while you are learning English*.

Moreover, English-only rules actually weaken some organizations and institutions by reducing effective communication among limited-English-speaking work crews and employees. In contrast, other institutions continuously draw upon the strengths of their multilingual employees by permitting or even encouraging workers to use their most effective languages when communicating with each other and when serving limited-English-speaking customers, as well as by posting vital information in various languages.

Religion

If language raises certain *pluribus-unum* tensions, religion raises others. This seems to be even more problematic where religions also reflect ethnic diversity.

The First and Fourteenth Amendments to the Constitution purportedly guarantee the *pluribus* right that governments "shall make no law respecting the establishment of religion." Yet two recent U.S. Supreme Court decisions, each involving an ethnicity-based religion, suggest the *pluribus-unum* complexities of the application of these amendments.

In April 1990, in the case of *Employment Division of Oregon v. Smith*, the Supreme Court, by a 5–4 vote, upheld the state's punitive action against a man named Al Smith for his sacramental use of peyote, even though it was a ritual of the Native American Church, of which he was a member. (I should mention that although the Eighteenth Amendment to the Constitution banned the consumption of alcoholic beverages from 1919 until its repeal in 1933, the government nonetheless permitted an exception for the sacramental use of wine as part of religious services. Historical consistency, anyone?)

In the *Smith* decision, the Court ruled that religious groups were not exempt from "neutral laws." That decision dramatically altered the *pluribus-unum* constitutional balance by reversing more than a half century of *pluribus*-oriented First Amendment jurisprudence, which had maintained that the state had to demonstrate a "compelling state interest" in order to restrict religious practices. Under the *Smith* precedent, government need only demonstrate that laws are "neutral," even when those supposedly "neutral" *unum* laws encroach upon religious practices. As Mark Twain once asked when informed that someone was neutral on a critical social issue, "Then whom are you neutral against?"

Let's consider some possible ramifications of that decision. Could Amish children be forced to attend high school because "neutral" state laws require it? What about Jews who always wear yarmulkes, even in situations where "neutral" laws require other or no headgear? Or Laotian Hmongs who object to autopsies? Or Seventh Day Adventists whose religious convictions prevent them from working on Saturdays? Or Jehovah's Witnesses whose religious beliefs forbid them from saluting the American flag? (Responding to the *Smith* decision, congress passed the Religious Freedom Restoration Act in November re-establishing the compelling government-interest test.)

In June 1993, the U.S. Supreme Court again acted, this time protecting an ethnically based religion against a "non-neutral" law in the case of the *Church of Lukumi Babalu Ay v. Hialeah*. Faced with the growing practice of Santería, an Afro-Caribbean religion that blends Yoruba and Catholic traditions and sometimes includes animal sacrifice in its services, the city of Hialeah, Florida, prohibited animal sacrifice as part of religious ritual.

However, by a 9–0 vote, the Supreme Court voided this attempt to restrict *pluribus*. The Court did not approve animal sacrifice in religion, although some media pundits ravingly misinterpreted its actions. Rather, the Court ruled that Hialeah could not single out religion for such restrictions. The city would have to apply this prohibition neutrally if it so wished—meaning a total ban on the killing of animals within city limits, an action that Hialeah does not appear eager to take.

CHALLENGE OF THE FUTURE

The issues of language and ethnicity-based religion merely illustrate the continuing saga of America's historical balancing act. With continuously increasing demographic diversity and inevitably increasing multicultural complexity, the American future will demand thoughtful, nuanced, and constructive ways both to protect and to set limits on *pluribus* and *unum*.

Alfred North Whitehead once argued, "The art of progress is to preserve order amid change and to preserve change amid order." One of America's great twenty-first-century challenges will be to preserve *pluribus* amid *unum* and to preserve *unum* amid *pluribus*.

The corresponding Chapter for this Selection can be found on pg. 35.

BUILDING COMMUNITY FROM COMMUNITIES: DIVERSITY AND THE FUTURE OF HIGHER EDUCATION

D IVERSITY IS AN ISSUE THAT JUST WILL NOT GO AWAY. THAT applies to society—make that the world—at large. And for that reason, as we enter the twenty-first century, diversity will remain one of the greatest challenges, while also providing some of the richest opportunities, for U.S. colleges and universities.

THE CONTEXT OF DIVERSITY

The United States is undergoing the most dramatic demographic restructuring in its history. This involves an enormous increase in the number of those referred to as "people of color." In translation, this means that persons of African American, Hispanic American, Asian American, American Indian, and Pacific Island American ancestry are rapidly expanding their presence in the American mosaic.

Only 10 percent of the U.S. population in 1960, by 1990 people of color had become 25 percent of the nation. Moreover, demographic analysts foresee an acceleration of this trend. According to most projections, somewhere in the middle of the twenty-first century, Americans of those "non-Anglo" ancestries will become half of the U.S. population. (I say "ancestry" because I have no idea how future Americans will construct racial and ethnic categories and identities, particularly in light of the growing number of offspring of interracial marriages.)

Source: Metropolitan Universities: An International Forum, IX, 4 (Spring, 1999), pp. 11–18.

These domestic changes have been paralleled globally. Currently 93 out of every 100 of the world's children are being born in Asia, Africa, and Latin America. Europe, which made up one-third of the global population in 1900, has declined to only one-tenth. As of 1997, White people comprised only 17% of the world, a figure that may drop below 10% by 2010.

IMPLICATIONS FOR HIGHER EDUCATION

This national and global demographic drama inevitably influences the trajectories of American colleges and universities. Institutions of higher education need to prepare students for effective participation in this rapidly changing world. Moreover, according to a 1998 Daniel Yankelovich poll, funded by the Ford Foundation, more than nine out of ten registered American voters (more than half of whom labeled themselves as politically conservative) indicated that growing national and global diversity "makes it more important than ever for all of us to understand people who are different than ourselves."

In addition, these demographic changes are drastically altering the long-range national and global pool from which colleges and universities will draw students. As such diverse students converge on higher education institutions, they increase the variety of campus communities, and in doing so they raise serious questions about the significance of communities as well as the very concept of community.

The word *community* has become one of the most overused and abused terms in the English language. With disregard for the sense of common attachment traditionally inherent in the idea, the word is currently applied with little restraint to just about any geographic locale that happens to be embraced by political boundaries. This leads to such oxymorons as the labeling of suburban commuter polities as "bedroom communities."

However, colleges and universities may be no better when it comes to the jargonistic use of community. Can an individual really find community as a solitary member of an 18,000-student institution? This is a dubious proposition. Rather, most students who discover a sense of college community do so primarily by participating in smaller communities, which, in turn, may serve as launching pads to fuller participation in campus life.

This brings us to the issue of diversity. In relation to higher education, the concept usually elicits images and arguments, often contributing more heat than light, regarding diversity's usual suspects, particularly such polarizing topics as affirmative action and speech codes. Certainly these subjects are important. However, rather than revisit and rehash these oft-discussed topics, I have chosen to focus on four other diversity-related themes that I find of increasing importance and concern as I work with higher education institutions across the country. I believe that these four topics will become

increasingly critical elements of twenty-first-century higher education dialogue and decision making, particularly as they illuminate the complex intersection of diversity, communities, and community.

* the proliferation of campus affinity groups;
* the challenge of facilitating constructive intergroup relations;
* the emergence and modification of identities; and
* the reconstructing of knowledge and restructuring of curricula.

AFFINITY GROUPS

Throughout human history, people have tended to want to be around people with whom they have something in common and have aggregated around
commonalities to form affinity groups. There is no evidence that twenty-first-
century Americans will defy such a timeless, universal human propensity.
Certainly this is true on multiracial, multiethnic university campuses. In fact,
as the United States grows in size and cultural complexity, individuals of all
backgrounds increasingly seek to discover and develop smaller group affinities to go along with their larger American identity. Race, ethnicity, gender,
religion, culture, language, sexual orientation—all of these galvanize affinity groupings, providing sources of identity, foci for community, and even
bases for alternative institutions.

This phenomenon also pervades institutions of higher education.
Contemporary multiculturalism has dramatized the presence of diverse communities. Yet, in fact, affinity groups have long existed on college campuses.
How about Hillels, Newman Clubs, and other religion-based organizations?
How about fraternities and sororities, segregated by race and religion
throughout most of their history? Long before the post-civil rights movement
boom of Black, Latino, Asian American, Native American, and other organizations, college campuses teemed with communities of various social and
cultural affinity groups. Yet I can't recall anybody accusing them of "tribal-
ism." The formation of self-selected campus communities based on perceived
commonalities reflects the inevitable process of group aggregation.

But are communities of affinity groups inevitably good for the building
of campus community? No, just inevitable. Because many students feel the
need to aggregate around affinities in order to find a sense of belonging that
cannot be satisfied merely by being on a megacampus, universities—particularly large universities—need to support such smaller communities of affinity. At the same time, however, campus affinity groups can have their down-
side. This occurs when students latch onto them in order to isolate
themselves, to inhibit the access of others to full and equal participation in
campus life, or to disparage or vilify others on the basis of *their* group affini-

ties. The inevitable process of group aggregation can thereby regress into the avoidable process of self-segregation if students—of whatever background or affinity—become prisoners of single-hyphenation identities. Such thinking and action hinder the development of a sense of campus community by impeding the building of connections with others who do not share those hyphens. Sometimes such self-segregated affinity groups also take actions that demean other campus communities, thereby undermining the idea of community.

Universities face the challenge of facilitating healthy, supportive, and affirming group aggregation while simultaneously trying to inhibit the calcification into self-segregation. To do so, higher education institutions need to work to build bridges among communities. This challenge, then, gives rise to an opportunity—the fostering of intergroup relations through serious, civil intergroup conversation and collaboration.

INTERGROUP RELATIONS

Let's return briefly to the social context. While restructuring rapidly in demographic makeup, the United States is also growing in numbers. Unoccupied (or sparsely occupied) space, America's historical safety valve, is dwindling, even as racial, ethnic, religious, and linguistic diversity grows. As space declines—whether globally, societally, or on campus—it becomes increasingly difficult for affinity group communities to avoid bumping up against each other. During the twenty-first century, Americans of all backgrounds must increasingly share space as they live, work, and study closer and closer together. Such contact can result in more healthy intergroup relations, the discovery of better ways to co-exist and, even more optimistically, the development of the ability to thrive through interaction and cooperation across differences. But, as world history has repeatedly shown, increased sharing of space, to put it mildly, does not always go smoothly or necessarily lead to better understanding. Wars, legal systems that oppress or marginalize selected groups, informal processes of group-based stigmatization and exclusion, and individual clashes arising from group-generated bigotry are often the result.

University campuses are certainly not immune to intergroup difficulties. Increasingly crowded campuses find themselves becoming arenas of proliferating varieties of individuals, communities, and affinity group organizations, who often embody contrasting and sometimes clashing values and behavior. As in society at large, such sharing of space does not always go well. Residence halls, classrooms, offices, dining areas, and public events become sites of informal, sometimes inevitable, interactions among those who come from varying racial, ethnic, cultural, religious, and other backgrounds.

Statements by members of one group may offend the sensibilities or grate on the sensitivities of others, even on campuses that take pride in their communitarian atmosphere. Diverse cultural or religious behavioral patterns sometimes lead to misunderstandings, incompatibilities, and personal clashes, even on campuses that espouse the celebration of diversity. An environment of multiple languages—spoken by faculty and staff as well as by students—sometimes irritates those accustomed to a monolingually English atmosphere.

As one who lectures, gives diversity workshops, and troubleshoots on several dozen campuses every year, I find that the problem of space-sharing amidst growing diversity is virtually a universal higher education challenge that cannot be resolved by glowing mission statements or cheer-leading platitudes about celebrating diversity or treating everyone as part of the human race. The creation of a sense of community that goes beyond the superficial requires a serious engagement with the process of building bridges among groups. Many of the intersections among those from diverse communities will occur naturally at the micro level through informal one-on-one or small group interactions. Yet the creation of a greater sense of campus community among communities also requires pro-active efforts by campus leaders. Based on my observations and interventions, it appears that much, maybe most, of the effort to make diversity work comes from student affairs professionals and staff. For example, some of my most fascinating and enlightening campus visits have involved working with student advisors in residence halls. While faculty have the luxury of extended, often theoretical, discussions of diversity and can always refer their disagreements to omnipresent subcommittees, residence hall advisors operate on the multicultural front lines, dealing with everything from seeming incompatibilities among roommate values and behavior to clustering of group-based communities in the dining hall.

Colleges and universities need to continue to seek innovative ways to promote positive cross-cultural and intergroup relations, particularly among students. These efforts should include at least two dimensions: the development of better understanding of differences; and the recognition, sometimes the discovery, of underlying commonalities. By simultaneously addressing both pluribus and unum, universities can avoid the obfuscation that occurs when people retreat into polar positions, whether "all people are basically alike" platitudes or such a fixation on differences that commonalities get lost in the shuffle.

The building of a more constructive sense of diversity and unity among commuting students creates special challenges, particularly for student affairs professionals. Yet avenues exist for promoting better intergroup understanding. Sometimes coordinated with courses, dialogue groups that focus on critical diversity-related issues can provide the framework and mechanism for facilitating interpersonal and intergroup insight, even friendships. In addition, campus initiatives focused on local communities have the potential for building bonds of understanding among participating students of diverse backgrounds.

Fostering healthy intergroup relations is not simply a matter of keeping the campus running more smoothly by avoiding or resolving problems. It is also part of the fulfillment of the university's responsibility to help students become more effective participants in a diverse democracy. Universities should strive to help students develop the commitment and ability to move and communicate successfully across lines of diversity, thereby contributing to a greater sense of campus community. After all, it is these very students who, in turn, will be the builders—or polluters—of both community and communities as they become more active members of the post-college world.

EMERGING IDENTITIES

Now let's add an additional complication. The multicultural mosaic will not remain fixed. Diversity is dynamic, not static. New campus groups come into existence and flourish, while others diminish and sometimes disappear. New affinities or assertions of identity are constantly emerging, ultimately creating new communities. The following two examples—gay and mixed-race students—suggest the campus-level emergence of affinity groups and identities, either newly formed or socially liberated.

Centers and organizations based on sexual orientation have become increasingly common on college campuses. Moreover, from school to school they have taken different forms and have modified their inclusiveness, often reflected by their titles. Some organizations or centers began as gay (encompassing both men and women), but later evolved into explicitly gay and lesbian. In other cases such organizations specifically recognized other identities, such as bisexual and the transgendered. This has had its analogue in the curriculum, with the burgeoning of courses and majors, including those labeled as Queer Studies.

Parallel to the organizational and curricular rise of gays and lesbians has been the emergence of organizations of mixed-race students. One of the most dramatic demographic changes of the past quarter century has been the growth of interracial marriage, particularly since the Supreme Court's 1967 *Loving v. Virginia* decision eliminating state anti-miscegenation laws. An inevitable result of this process has been the expanding number of students who embody not one but two or more racial heritages (along with students of multiple ethnic, religious, or cultural heritages). This has led to informal aggregations and sometimes campus organizations of students of mixed-race backgrounds. Many such students also encounter special challenges, sometimes resulting from the misperceptions of faculty, staff, and fellow students still mired psychologically in the dominant American monoracial categorical system.

The twenty-first century will find new affinity groups making their presence known and felt on college and university campuses. This process may include the emergence of relatively new identities, such as those of mixed-race faculty, staff, and particularly students. It may include the strengthening of long-standing identities—such as gay, lesbian, bisexual, or transgender—that become more public because of an increasingly receptive environment or, conversely, the desire to form or find smaller communities because of the repressive climate of the larger campus community. Colleges and universities need to be flexible in recognizing and responding to these new and emerging identities, which may involve supporting new kinds of identity-based student or staff organizations. It may involve addressing the special needs of those who encounter difficult situations resulting from these identities. It may include holding forums dealing with these topics, particularly if the very presence of or reaction to some affinity groups creates campus controversy or opposition. It may also involve curricular changes that build from the presence of new groupings, address questions raised by their existence, and explore the significance of their experiences. Perhaps most challenging, it will call upon campuses to continue searching for ways to foster new senses and visions of campus community that are inclusive, not repressive or marginalizing, of these newly voiced identities.

KNOWLEDGE AND CURRICULUM

To this point I have focused mainly on issues of campus climate and student affairs, with occasional references to curriculum. Let us now focus on the latter. Preparation of students for a multicultural future should not be left to the serendipity of student contact or the efforts of student affairs staff. Particularly through curriculum, faculty should also play a critical role in helping students become more constructive participants in a multicultural society and shrinking globe.

Like affinity groups, diversity in the curriculum is not a new higher education issue. It has been integral to higher education dialogues particularly since the 1960s, when the civil rights movement led to student demands for greater course attention to such themes as race, ethnicity, gender, and sexual orientation. Faculty and administrators have responded in a variety of ways. Most dramatic has been the establishment of new majors, sometimes even departments, of women's studies and different varieties of ethnic studies. Such initiatives have had mixed results, ranging from sites of exceptional teaching and research richness to weak, diffuse, and marginalized programs of questionable value. Yet, aside from such lightning-rod, often fractious topics as new departments and majors, dramatic changes have also been taking place within traditional departments and disciplines. Over the past three decades the theme of diversity has become fundamental to many academic disciplines, particularly in the arts, humanities, and social sciences. This has included an extraordinary explosion of diversity-related research and rein-terpretation that has fundamentally altered entire fields of study. Inevitably such knowledge reconstruction has influenced course work and even major requirements.

This has also led to controversy. Particularly in the past decade, oppo-nents of such reforms have launched vigorous attacks on diversity-related scholarship and pedagogy. Some ethnic and women's studies programs have been eliminated, often on the grounds that they were too exclusionary in their focus. (Ironically, religious studies programs with a comparably tight focus have escaped the wrath of the anti-diversity critics. Could it be that the latter have their own brand of political correctness?) Yet, in the curriculum at large, diversity seems to have become firmly entrenched.

As a scholarly and pedagogical issue, the rationale for diversity-related education goes well beyond politics, ideology, student demands, and the media-overblown campus culture wars. According to the 1998 Yankelovich poll, more than ninety per cent of registered voters felt that colleges and uni-versities should prepare "people to function in a more diverse society" and "in a more diverse work force," while two-thirds thought that college grad-uation requirements should include at least one cultural and ethnic diversity course and at least one course presented from the point of view of non-Western societies. At the same time, however, nearly one-third of those inter-viewed expressed concern that such courses *might* be nothing more than political correctness.

That poll suggests that, beyond the issue of student demands, diversity cheerleading, or anti-diversity hyperbole lies a deeper, more widely recog-nized, maybe even consensual public challenge. Including through the cur-riculum, universities need to dedicate themselves more thoroughly to the serious and sobering task of preparing students for citizenship in a diverse democratic society and a shrinking globe. After all, these students will be voting on diversity-related issues. They may enter public service, which means working with diverse communities. They may become part of the pri-vate sector, where they will provide goods and services to diverse consumers, while working in and managing organizations with diverse work forces. They may become involved in global activities, where dealing with diversity is basic to their endeavors.

In short, university curricula should help students obtain a more nuanced grasp of the complexities of diversity, develop a deeper understanding of myriad groups, and become more constructive contributors and bridge-builders in striving for a twenty-first-century sense of inclusive community, as people of different backgrounds increasingly share space in their daily lives. To do so, the curriculum should include a more thorough exploration of such topics as the roles diversity has played in the past, principles and problems of interpersonal and intergroup relations, group-based power and privilege, progress and regress in the areas of justice and equality, and diversity-related challenges and opportunities of the future. A university curriculum that fails to help students grapple with such issues is failing in its obligation to contribute to a better future for both affinity-based communities and diversity-based inclusive community.

CONCLUSION

Nehru of India once said, "Life is like a game of cards. The hand that is dealt you is determinism; the way you play it is free will." Demographic changes and the shrinking globe guarantee that diversity and resulting affinity-based communities will be increasingly critical cards in that hand. Will colleges and universities meet the challenges and avail themselves of the opportunities to help prepare students to play that hand well, thereby contributing to a more just, equitable community of true interpersonal and intergroup understanding? Those are the diversity-related stakes for higher education as we enter the twenty-first century.

The corresponding Chapter for this Selection can be found on pg. 40.

MIXED-RACE CHILDREN: BUILDING BRIDGES TO NEW IDENTITIES

IN APRIL, 1997, A CHARISMATIC YOUNG GOLFER NAMED TIGER Woods stunned the sports world when he outplayed a star-studded field to win the prestigious Masters Golf Tournament. That victory also set off a scramble to ascertain and communicate Woods' ethnic identity. Sports commentators have variously referred to him as Black, as having a Thai mother, or as being multiracial. Nike has marketed him as an African American in the United States and as an Asian American in Asia. Woods has kept the pot boiling by occasionally, with tongue in cheek, identifying himself as a Cablinasian (Causasian, American Indian, African American, and Asian American).

While this label helps clarify Woods' family tree, which includes all of these ancestries, it does little to illuminate his *personal racial identity*. With all due respect, I doubt that his identity is really Cablinasian, but rather surmise that it reflects his having been raised by a father with a deep sense of African American tradition and a mother with a strong attachment to Thai culture. I suspect that Woods has a firm *combination* of racial and ethnic identities. In using the term "race," I am not arguing for its scientific validity, which is under widespread scholarly assault (Omi & Winant, 1994; Webster, 1992). Rather, I am using it as it has become part of the U.S. English vernacular as the result of America's long historical love–hate relationship with diversity.

Source: *Reaching Today's Youth,* III, 2 (Winter, 1999), pp. 28–31.

While unique as a sports figure, Woods is not unique racially. Rather he is part of, perhaps the epitome of, a dramatic national phenomenon—the rapidly growing number of Americans with racially diverse parentage (Root, 1992).

MISCEGENATION IN AMERICA

This phenomenon is no historical accident. Mingling of racial bloodlines has been a part of American tradition ever since Europeans first cohabited with Native Americans and plantation owners had sexual relations with slaves. However, the offspring of those unions were almost always arbitrarily assigned to a single racial category. Put another way, to "qualify" as White in the United States generally required possessing—or being viewed as possessing—a sufficiently high percentage of "White blood" that was often defined by state laws with excruciating attempts to achieve mathematical precision.

In an effort to preserve racial "purity," 36 states (at one point) adopted some form of anti-miscegenation law prohibiting interracial marriage. Most such laws banned Black–White marriages, but others barred various combinations—and often bizarrely, as in laws banning White–Chinese but not White–Asian marriages (Spickard, 1989).

If this sounds un-American (as in "all men are created equal"), it certainly sounded that way to the 1967 U.S. Supreme Court, which overturned those laws in the case of *Loving v. Virginia* (regarding the marriage between a Caucasian man and an African American woman). That decision made it possible, for the first time, for Americans in every state to marry across racial lines. Finally given the opportunity to marry persons whom they loved, regardless of racial designation, growing numbers of Americans have done exactly that.

As of the late 1990s, nearly one third of U.S.-born Latinos are out-marrying (that is, marrying someone who is not Latino). More than one out of every ten African Americans now out-marries. There is a huge variation among Asian Americans. According to some estimates, more than 80% of Japanese Americans now out-marry, compared with about 10% of Chinese Americans and less than 5% of Korean Americans. As the result of such unions, the United States now has a growing number of Tiger Woods-style Americans.

THE MULTICULTURALIZING OF SCHOOLS

This strong trend is increasingly evident in schools, as each year more students of racially mixed marriages enroll. During back-to-school nights or parent–teacher conferences the teacher may be surprised when a parent does not conform to the educator's perceptions of a student's "race." Because such students do not fall into neat single-race categories, they also complicate district efforts to compile racial records necessary to comply with funding requirements and help determine school district programs.

In my multicultural education workshops, no topic has elicited a greater response than when I raise the theme of interracial marriage and its ramifications. Many teachers and administrators seem eager to talk about, or are at least relieved that they can discuss, their own personal situations—ancestors, spouse, or offspring. Others who view themselves as monoracial are looking for suggestions about how to address the special needs, desires, and circumstances of students who come from mixed backgrounds.

Likewise, educators must also grapple with negative student interpersonal perceptions, as mixed-race students are sometimes rejected by student groups or cliques because of their lack of racial or ethnic "purity." Mixed-race students also can be pressured by other students to ally themselves with a single racial or ethnic identity (and therefore reject other strands of their backgrounds).

There are numerous youth-related dimensions to the growing mixed-race reality. I will briefly discuss four of them: differentiating heritage from identity; supporting the self-determination of individual identity; facilitating student organizations; and developing valid curricula.

HERITAGE VS. IDENTITY

All students have an ethnic heritage. With diligence and luck, most can trace their family trees back far enough to discover at least some of their roots, even though there may be complications due to such factors as adoption, single-parent families, and remarriage.

In the process of studying their own *heritages,* students may also gain greater insight into their personal *identities.* However, the recognition and construction of individual heritage does not automatically translate into a sense of personal ethnic identity. Educators should avoid making the unwarranted leap from heritage to identity, as these are distinct though related concepts. While heritage influences identity, the latter also involves a deeper, more visceral sense of connection and psychic belonging, often with ramifications for values and behavior (Zack, 1993).

The relationship between heritage and identity becomes even more complex when a student's heritage is not just ethnically but also racially diverse. Most European American students do not come from a single European background. (In one of my recent multicultural in-service workshops, only three of the 24 European American teachers had both parents who were of the same Euro-ethnic background.) In fact, some students have so many European national branches in their family trees that they do not have, and may never develop, any sense of specific ethnic identity. They are simply non-ethnic Americans (or as some refer to themselves, "Heinz 57 Americans").

While educators have long recognized European American blending, even after three decades of the post-*Loving v. Virginia* era, many are still unprepared or unwilling to grapple with the personal and societal significance of mixed racial—not just ethnic—heritages. For students and others who come from racially mixed homes, the study of heritage and the issue of identity may be far more complex than for monoracial students, including monoracial students with multiple ethnic heritages (O'Hearn, 1998). This leads to the second dimension of addressing this new reality—supporting the right of students to determine their own racial identities.

IDENTITY SELF-DETERMINATION

If educators truly believe in freedom, individuality, and human dignity in the area of personal identity, they need to drop two questions often included in educational materials and used in the classroom: To what ethnic group (singular) do you belong? What race (singular) are you? These questions may work for some students, but for others they amount to demanding the rejection of either Mom or Dad and of more distant relatives.

Today many students simply do not belong to an ethnic group. And in the post-Loving era, many do not even belong to a racial group (once again, as used in U.S. parlance). Educators need to recognize and respond to this new reality. They should at least support such students as they assert or contemplate their individual identities. At the same time, teachers must avoid the knee-jerk tendency of trying to cram mixed-race students into inappropriate single-race categories. Based on my work and reading in this area, I have developed the following tentative typology for examining and categorizing the variety of identity routes taken by students and others who enjoy multiple racial heritages.

Single Racial Identity. Some gravitate toward one of their racial heritages, developing strong monoracial identities even while recognizing their multiple (two or more) racial heritages.

Multiple Racial Identity. Some students develop multiple racial identities, honoring the role that each plays in shaping their personal sense of being, rather than choosing one as their predominant identity. (This has even become a part of popular culture. For example, the powerful TV series "Homicide: Life on the Streets" features an American policeman who is part Black and part Italian, played by the intense Giancarlo Esposito, who himself has an Italian-born father and an African American mother.)

Multiple Racial/Multiracial Identity. In addition to feeling a strong sense of identity involving each of their racial heritages taken individually (multiple racial), some students additionally feel the special identity of being racially mixed (multiracial), irrespective of the combination.

Multiracial Identity. For some students, this latter multiracial status becomes their racial identity, superseding any sense of individual racial connection. They may not have a name for it, like Tiger Woods' "Cablinasian," but their sense of mixed-race specialness provides them with a unique identity shared with other mixed-race students.

Non-Racial Identity. Finally, I have encountered some students, as well as adults, who assert that they have no sense of racial identity (somewhat analogous to non-ethnic European Americans with multiple national ancestries). I find this non-racial identity most common among immigrants from cultures that view race quite differently than U.S. Americans. (While some sports pundits have labeled Sammy Sosa as Black, I have yet to hear the Dominican home-run-hitting sensation actually state his racial identity, if he has one. He may simply have a Dominican identity.)

Even as I investigate the identity and experiences of racially mixed students, I feel the burden of language's poverty. The very labeling of the previous categories has a cumbersome, somewhat artificial quality. Yet, even without a common, satisfying terminology, educators cannot avoid this growing reality. In particular, they cannot retreat into such clichéd posturing as simply stating "we ought to stop categorizing and labeling people."

Categories provide the very basis for developing generalizations, while labels enable us to communicate about categories of items, including people. Try teaching U.S. history without categories and labels—Puritans, Confederates, Cherokees, African Americans, and Mormons. Without using such categories and labels, the stories of Massachusetts Bay Colony, the Civil War, the Trail of Tears, slavery, and the state of Utah would not make much sense.

One complication of the post-Loving era is that old monoracial labels do not apply to all students with racially mixed backgrounds. While we do not yet have an agreed-upon set of terms for talking about this new reality, teachers should refrain from imposing monoracial categories on students who come from racially mixed heritages. Instead, they should support, respect, and, if necessary, defend students' rights to assert their own racial identities.

STUDENT ORGANIZATIONS

This new assertiveness has sometimes been expressed through the formation of organizations of mixed-race students. These students find associational common ground based on the shared fact that they all have complex racial backgrounds and, as a result, have some commonality of experience.

One of the most pervasive experiential commonalities is the sense of being misrepresented and misunderstood by other students and even by educators. Many mixed-race students face the organically American peer pressure to choose a race: "Either you are one of us—and only us—or you are one of them (meaning the 'not-us'). You can't be both." Multiracial student organizations provide an alternative—a "nest" in which to discover connections, a forum in which to share experiences, and a "think tank" in which to develop more constructive responses to such external pressures.

These organizations deserve the support and encouragement of educators. Unfortunately, problems sometimes are caused by the very individuals who should be providing assistance when educators try to foist their rigid racial categorization ideologies on their students. An example of this occurred during one of my multicultural education workshops at a high school with a thriving organization of mixed-race students. Commenting on that organization, one administrator lamented that so many of its members seemed to have confused personal identities. As evidence, he pointed out that some students belonged not only to that organization, but also to single-group organizations of African Americans, Asian Americans, Latinos, and the like. I responded that possibly the real problem was his confused perceptions. Those students might have had very healthy multiple identities, both racial and multiracial. Unfortunately I have heard such comments from many teachers who, possibly with good intentions, have tried to help mixed-race students clarify their identities by inappropriately encouraging them to choose one race.

CURRICULUM

One principal purpose of the study of history is to address two basic questions: who am I, and what about the past has contributed to my becoming who I am? In a collective sense, that is one of the reasons that schools require U.S. history, so that we as Americans will develop a better understanding of who we are as a nation and what about our country's heritage has made our nation what it is. Likewise, this is one role of single-group ethnic studies courses—fostering an understanding of the unique heritages, experiences, and cultures of different groups of Americans.

Beginning at the elementary level, school curricula should provide opportunities for students to investigate their individual heritages and to develop an understanding of the relationship of their unique pasts to U.S. and global history. This pedagogical process may include creating family trees, conducting oral history interviews with relatives, collecting family artifacts, perusing family records, writing family histories, and studying local communities. It should also include learning about the experiences of various racial, ethnic, and religious groups to which members of their families belong. These are not soft, "feel good" activities designed to foster better self-concepts, although that may well be a result. These should be addressed as good academic activities: good history, good research, good skill development, and good writing.

Yet the contemporary K–12 curriculum provides almost no illumination of the historical process that brought about racially mixed people in the United States. The solution is not simply to include a discussion of *Loving v. Virginia* as part of U.S. history courses. The curriculum should also involve the history of interracial contact and exclusion, the development and use of U.S. racial categories, the ways in which people have been assigned to those categories, the rise and fall of anti-miscegenation laws, and the ramifications of all of this for American life.

Literature should include stories (including biographies and autobiographies) of racially mixed Americans (Williams, 1995), because their lives are a critical and revealing part of the American story. Schools that examine racial and ethnic diversity, yet avoid the theme of racial mixture, distort the American experience. Moreover, such schools do serious if unintended injustice to students of all backgrounds who need to be weaned from their rigid reliance on old categories when grappling with changing realities.

CONCLUSION

Race American-style has been a long-standing part of our nation's history, has pervaded American cultural consciousness (Cortés, 1991), and continues into the present, even as scholars debunk its scientific validity. Schools need to address it both in its traditional single-race and inchoate mixed-raced dimensions.

The issues of identity and self-identification are becoming an increasingly contentious part of our nation's multicultural landscape. Consider the extended battle over whether or not to include a multiracial category in the year 2000 Census. While that category was rejected, respondents were given the option of marking more than one racial category (based on the federal Office of Management and Budget's October, 1997, guidelines for collecting racial and ethnic data).

Certainly the need to address the mixed-race issue raises complications. The topic may be unsettling for educators uncomfortable moving beyond America's traditional racial categories and labels. Moreover, we lack a common language and agreed-upon set of concepts for addressing this complex area. Even current, widely used scholarly paradigms of ethnic identity formation fail to deal adequately with this issue.

Yet schools cannot wait for the languid process of scholarly debate and clarification. They must grapple now with the growing race-mixed reality, spurred by *Loving v. Virginia*. The time for recognizing, honoring, and responding to racial mixture has arrived.

The corresponding Chapter for this Selection can be found on pg. 44.

PRIDE, PREJUDICE AND POWER: THE MASS MEDIA AS SOCIETAL EDUCATOR ON DIVERSITY

18 SEPTEMBER 1986. RELAXING IN MY RIVERSIDE, CALIFORNIA, home, enjoying my customary third cup of morning coffee and scanning the daily newspapers, I chanced to turn on the popular American daytime television game show, 'The $25,000 Pyramid."

"Pyramid" provides the ideal combination of background distraction and distracting challenge for a committed media double-dipper who enjoys basking in a TV ambience while reading. Competition in "Pyramid" involves two pairs of contestants. For each team, a series of words appears on a screen in front of one player, who then gives clues to guide the partner into correctly identifying the maximum number of words within the time limit. The team that gets the most correct words wins.

Then it happened. As I watched, the word "gangs" popped onto one cluer's screen. Without hesitation, he shouted. "They have lots of these in East L.A." (a heavily Mexican American section of Los Angeles). Responding immediately, the guest celebrity partner answered, "Gangs." Under competitive pressure two strangers had instantly achieved mental communion through their coinciding visions of a Chicano community as being synonymous with gangs. Moreover, they had transmitted this ethnic stereotype to a national television audience.

Source: In James Lynch, Celia Modgil, and Sohan Modgil (Eds.), *Prejudice, Polemic or Progress?* (Vol. 2 of *Cultural Diversity and the Schools*). (London: Falmer Press, 1992), pp. 367–381.

Reprinted by permission of ITPS Ltd., Cheriton House.

Unfortunately, East Los Angeles does have Chicano gangs. But it also has a multitude of far more prevalent elements, like families, schools, business, churches and socially contributing organizations. Yet gangs, not such other aspects of East L.A. life, had rapidly and reflexively linked these total strangers. Why?

The answer lies with the media, whose continuous fascination with Latino gangs—from new reports and documentaries to TV series and feature films—has elevated and reinforced them as *the* quintessential popular vision of East L.A. (and many other Latino communities). "Pyramid" both dramatized this media impact and added to the media bombardment. The media, in short, have created a gang-featuring public curriculum on Latinos.

Moreover, the "Pyramid" episode illustrates an even broader phenomenon: the power of the media to influence public perceptions, not just of Latinos, but of any ethnic or racial group—and not just racial and ethnic groups, but also foreign nations and world cultures. Conceived as an educational metaphor, the media provide a public curriculum on myriad topics, including race, ethnicity, culture, and nationality.

The degree to which the media actually *create* intercultural visions and stereotypes, pride and prejudice, can be debated. Beyond debate, however, is the fact that they *contribute* to intercultural, interracial and interethnic beliefs, perceptions and attitudes, including prejudice, as well as to group self-image, including pride (or lack of it). This power to influence rests not only with those involved in the so-called news or factual media, but also with those who create so-called entertainment.

No matter how vociferously mediamakers may disclaim their educational power and no matter how obstinately entertainment mediamakers, in particular, may claim that they merely provide diversion, evidence clearly demonstrates that the media, including the entertainment media, teach. Identifying what different individuals learn from the media, however, poses a considerable challenge.

Numerous complexities arise concerning the media's role in contributing to ethnic pride and intergroup prejudice. This essay deals briefly with five of these questions. How do the media fit within the larger process of educating the public about race, ethnicity, culture and foreignness? What dilemmas must be faced in attempting to assess media impact in these areas? What is the nature of that media influence? What forms of evidence provide insight into that influence? What effective actions can be adopted to address that influence?

THE MEDIA CURRICULUM

The mass media as a social force should be examined within the broader context of societal education. Discussions of education often, and erroneously, use schools and education as synonymous concepts. Certainly schools comprise a powerful component of the educational process. However, they do not monopolize education, nor could they even if they wished.

People learn through schools. But they also learn outside schools through what I have termed the "societal curriculum"—that massive, ongoing, informal curriculum of families, peer groups, neighborhoods, churches, organizations, institutions, mass media, and other socializing forces that educate all of us throughout our lives.[1] Through the societal curriculum, as well as through the school curriculum, people learn language and culture, acquire beliefs and attitudes, and develop patterns of behavior. They learn about themselves and others. They learn about the groups to which they and others belong. They learn about their nation and other nations and cultures of the world. In short, they learn about diversity, including racial, ethnic, cultural, gender, religious, regional, and national diversity.

As a major element of societal education, the media curriculum—through such avenues as newspapers, magazines, motion pictures, television and radio—disseminates information, images, and ideas concerning race, ethnicity, culture, and foreignness. Educating both for better *and* for worse, this media curriculum about diversity functions whether or not individual mediamakers actually view themselves as educators, whether or not they are aware that they are spreading ideas about diversity, and whether or not they operate in the realms of fact or fiction.

This media curriculum can contribute to ethnic pride, but it can also erode self-esteem through the repetition of negative themes or demeaning images. It can contribute to intergroup understanding through sensitive examinations of ethnic experiences and problems, but it can also contribute to intergroup misunderstanding through the repeated presentation of derogatory stereotypes and an over-emphasis on negative themes about selected groups or nations. It spreads fact and fiction, at times striving for truth, accuracy, sensitivity and balance, while at other times consciously distorting for purposes of sensationalism and commercialism. By operating in this dual manner, the media curriculum both challenges and hypertrophies intergroup prejudice.

Moreover, an analysis of the media curriculum must involve both the news and entertainment media. Audiences learn not only from programs and publications intended to provide information, but also from media presumably made only to entertain (as well as to make money). Moreover, it has become increasingly evident that audiences have great difficulty distinguishing media fact from fiction. For example, a 1989 survey revealed that 50 per cent of U.S. television viewers considered "America's Most Wanted" to be a news program, while 28 per cent thought it entertainment.[2] My own research on feature films reveals that cross-cultural learning from fictional media has become an international phenomenon.

While some members of the so-called entertainment media proclaim that they merely offer diversion, in fact they simultaneously teach, whether intentionally or incidentally. Let us reverse the equation. Whatever the stated or unstated goals of the media, audiences learn from both fictional and non-fictional media, although in the case of fictional media they usually do not realize that such media-based learning is occurring.[3]

As entertainment-packaged, often-unintended multicultural textbooks, feature films and television have been a major part of the century-long teaching–learning environment in which people develop intercultural beliefs and attitudes. Plato recognized the power of fictional narrative when he asserted. "Those who tell the stories also rule the society." In more recent times George Gerbner of the University of Pennsylvania's Annenberg School of Communications proclaimed hyperbolically, but with a core of truth, "If you can control the storytelling of a nation, you don't have to worry about who makes the laws."

Television, including cable, has dominated recent media analysis. Experts concur that television viewing has been growing around the world. In the United States, for example, average household TV viewing time has been climbing steadily—from five hours per day in 1956 to six hours per day in 1971 and to seven hours per day in 1983. As early as 1961 scholars concluded that young Americans between the ages of 3 and 16 were devoting one-sixth of their waking hours to television.[4] According to another estimate, by the time of high school graduation the average U.S. student will have spent 11,000 hours in the classroom and 22,000 hours in front of the television set.[5] Sometimes movie viewing and television watching become synonymous, particularly with TV, cable, and videocassettes now serving as prime recyclers of feature films.

Likening television to schools and television programs to school courses, sociologist Herbert J. Gans argued:

> almost all TV programs and magazine fiction teach something about American society. For example, "Batman" is, from this vantage point, a course in criminology that describes how a superhuman aristocrat does a better job eradicating crime than do public officials. Similarly, "The Beverly Hillbillies" offers a course in social stratification and applied economics, teaching that with money, uneducated and uncultured people can do pretty well in American society, and can easily outwit more sophisticated and more powerful middle-class types. . . . And even the innocuous family situation comedies such as "Ozzie and Harriet" deal occasionally with ethical problems encountered on a neighborhood level. . . . Although the schools argue that they are the major transmitter of society's moral values, the mass media offer a great deal more content on this topic.[6]

I have come to similar conclusions through my own research on the history of the US motion picture treatment of race, ethnicity, and foreignness.

Because of my special interest in the attitude-shaping role of the entertainment media—the power of entertainment media to influence ethnic pride and prejudice—I will emphasize that theme in this article.[7]

THE DILEMMA OF ASSESSING MEDIA IMPACT

Despite the extensiveness of the media curriculum on race, ethnicity, culture, and nationality, caution must temper assertions concerning the *precise* content of audience learning. In particular, we must avoid falling into the common trap of media determinism, assuming the "hypodermic needle" effect so popular (and so fallacious) in many early media studies and still rampant in protest group proclamations.

As all educators know, teaching and learning are not synonymous. We teach and then, through examinations, often to our chagrin, we discover great variations in the extent, content, and quality of student learning. With that in mind, while recognizing the teaching power of the media, we must also respect the conscious and unconscious filtering power of the learner. To assume and make definitive assertions concerning media impact based only on an examination of content, as some scholars and many public pundits have done, is a fallacy equivalent to assessing student learning on the basis of analyzing reading assignments and professorial lectures (in the words of Samuel Butler, "drawing sufficient conclusions from insufficient premises"). Identifying the exact content of learning—from whatever source—can be frustratingly elusive.

Scholarly and popular analyses of the societal impact of the media, particularly the entertainment media, have tended to become polarized on the issue of the media influence on public perceptions and attitudes. Many analysts, including some scholars, have taken a nearly deterministic position, drawing direct causal (sometimes unicausal) links between media and the development of individual, group, and national attitudes and behavior. At the opposite extreme stand most feature filmmakers and creators of entertainment television, who generally claim that they make fictional media merely to entertain, reject responsibility for what their films might incidentally or unintentionally teach, and at times even deny their teaching potential. In the middle stand those scholars who agree that media, including movies and fictional television, do teach, but argue that research to date has generally failed to reveal the precise nature of audience learning. For example, in *The Media Monopoly* Ben Bagdikian argues, "It is a truism among political scientists that while it is not possible for the media to tell the population what to think, they do tell the public what to think about."[8]

Assessing media impact, therefore, poses a major challenge, but research to date does provide some insights. Scholarship on the impact of movies and television on intergroup perceptions has been sporadic and temporally limited, focusing almost entirely on short-range effects of specific films or television shows, often in empirically controlled settings. While research results vary, they do coalesce around two basic conclusions. First, these studies make it clear that feature films and fictional television do influence interethnic perceptions; viewers do learn about race and ethnicity from the entertainment media. Second, the nature of that influence varies with the individual viewer, who provides a key variable concerning the extent, content, and tenacity of that conscious or unconscious learning. In short, scholarship confirms that old social science axiom, *"Some* people are influenced by *some* media, at *some* time."

Research has identified the influence of selected films and television shows on intergroup attitudes and perceptions, sometimes reinforcing prejudices, other times modifying them.[9] One pioneering study of the 1930s involved the classic 1915 silent film, *The Birth of a Nation,* which included a degrading portrayal of Black Americans during the post-Civil War reconstruction period of U.S. history. That research revealed that, when students viewed *Birth* as part of their study of U.S. history, an increase in student prejudice toward African Americans resulted.[10]

But entertainment media can also reduce prejudice. Another study found that the anti–anti-Semitism film, *Gentleman's Agreement,* had such an effect. Students who saw it reported improved attitudes toward Jews, even though most of the surveyed students stated that the film *had not* influenced their attitudes![11]

Other analysts have taken a broader view of the media's impact on intercultural perceptions. Sam Keen's *Faces of the Enemy: Reflections of the Hostile Imagination* and Vamik Volkan's *The Need to Have Enemies and Allies: From Clinical Practice to International Relationships* argue that people *need* to hate and that "the other"—the racial other, the ethnic other, the cultural other, the national other—serves as a convenient outlet for that hate.[12] In his article, "The Convenient Villain: The Early Cinema Views the Mexican American," Blaine Lamb asserts that Mexican characters served that "other" role for early U.S. movie audiences, who needed an easily identified, easily despised foil.[13]

Other scholars have examined media impact on pride and prejudice within the context of larger intergroup and international themes, For example, in his *War without Mercy: Race and Power in the Pacific War,* historian John Dower identifies the nature of racial pride and cross-cultural stereotypes of the enemy that developed in both Japan and the Allied nations prior to and during World War II. He does so by exploring multiple Japanese and Allied sources—from scholarly studies to propaganda tracts, from government reports to military training materials, from popular periodicals to motion pictures. But Dower takes an additional step, pointing to political and military decisions made by both sides that reveal how these stereotypes became operationalized, even when operating on those stereotypes led to military and diplomatic excesses and blunders.[14]

While research has demonstrated conclusively that people learn about race, ethnicity, culture, and foreignness from the media, including the entertainment media, it has also demonstrated that learner responses vary, even to the same media stimulus. Analyses of two highly acclaimed U.S. television comedy series—Norman Lear's "All in the Family" and "The Cosby Show"—have teased out this content-impact gap.

In 1971 "All in the Family" burst onto the American television scene. This popular weekly series portrayed anti-hero Archie Bunker as a classic bigot—racist, sexist and just about every other kind of anti-"ist" imaginable. The show sought to critique racial and ethnic prejudice by making Bunker's expressions of bigotry appear to be comically absurd. Viewers would laugh at Archie, bigotry would appear to be imbecilic, and prejudice would be reduced. The ploy succeeded . . . but only for *some* viewers. Unfortunately, other viewers identified with the cuddly, ingratiating, laugh-provoking Archie, the lovable racist, and found his expression of bigoted beliefs to be a confirmation of the validity of their own prejudices.[15] One study of "All in the Family" confirmed the operation of the "selective perception hypothesis"—that is, already "high prejudiced viewers" tended to admire Bunker and condone his racial and ethnic slurs.[16]

The far less controversial "The Cosby Show" has even drawn mixed responses. At first glance "Cosby" would appear to be the ideal pride-producing, positive role model minority show, featuring a well-educated, sophisticated, financially successful African American family. Yet it has drawn its share of concerned reactions. In particular, some analysts have expressed reservations on the grounds that the show's concentration on well-heeled African Americans might unintentionally encourage viewers to ignore the fact that the majority of American Blacks still face tremendous social and economic problems. As media scholar Paula Matabane wrote:

> "The Cosby Show," for example, epitomizes the Afro-American dream of full acceptance and assimilation into U.S. society. Both the series and Bill Cosby as an individual represent successful competitors in network television and in attaining a high status. Although this achievement is certainly not inherently negative, we should consider the role television plays in the cultivation of an overall picture of growing racial equality that conceals unequal social relationships and overestimates of how well blacks are integrating into white society (if at all). The illusion of well-being among the oppressed may lead to reduced political activity and less demand for social justice and equality.[17]

While some scholars have addressed media impact by examining individual shows, others have examined the process of media learning by posing and applying different theories of audience reception. Some use schema theory, according to which each learner (viewer) develops an internal mental and emotional schema based on his or her own personal experiences, including school and societal learning. This personal schema then becomes the reception framework by which learners process, interpret, and organize new information, ideas, and images, including those disseminated by the media. Psychologist Leon Festinger proposed his "theory of cognitive dissonance," according to which once an individual's cognitive structure takes firm shape, it tends to repel those ideas that seem too dissonant.[18] The application of this theory suggests that media or school frontal assaults on firmly rooted prejudices, when those attacks lack subtlety, may well be rejected by some because they create too much dissonance.

Moreover, learners are not usually aware of either their reception schema or many of their prejudices, including those learned, reinforced, or shaped by the media. Psychologist Albert Bandura, for example, has described the "sleeper effect," which may provide a key to understanding how media teaching/learning works.[19] In relation to the media, the "sleeper effect" suggests that ideas, clothed as entertainment, can subconsciously enter and become part of a viewer's cognitive or affective storehouse, then lie dormant until provoked by some external stimulus, like an event, a personal contact, or even another media presentation. For example, people may not realize that they have prejudices, including media-fostered prejudices, about a certain group until they encounter individuals from that group, at which point these "sleeping" beliefs and attitudes awaken and move into action.

THE NATURE OF MEDIA INFLUENCE

Given these dilemmas of assessing media impact, what can be said with some degree of certainty (or at least reasonably hypothesized) about media impact, including the impact of feature films and fictional television? How do media contribute to pride, prejudice and other aspects of self-concept or intergroup perceptions, particularly to the reinforcement or modification of racial or ethnic bigotry? My own research suggests at least five basic types of media influences on the creation, strengthening, and reduction of ethnic pride and intercultural prejudice.

1. Media Provide Information about Race, Ethnicity, Culture, and Foreignness. People cannot be at all places at all times, so they must rely on the media to bring the world to them. Because they cannot develop in-depth knowledge about each and every racial or ethnic group or nation on the basis of personal experience, they necessarily acquire much of what they know about race, ethnicity, culture, and foreignness through what historian Daniel Boorstin has termed the "pseudoenvironment," principally the mass media.[20]

Certainly newspapers, magazines, television news, and documentary films provide information (selected, organized, edited, filtered, and often decontextualized information of varying accuracy and quality), but so do the entertainment media. Some years ago an elementary school teacher, with whom I had been working, came to me with consternation. Preparing to teach about Gypsies to her fourth-grade class, she began by asking students if they knew anything about them, only to be overwhelmed by the flood of Gypsy "information" that students "knew." When she asked where they had obtained that information, they cited old Wolfman and Frankenstein movies among their main sources.

Moreover, the issue of media as an information source about race, ethnicity, culture, and foreignness goes well beyond the question of accuracy. In news, the constant reiteration of certain themes, even when each story is accurate in and of itself, may pound home an image of an ethnic group, with the relentless drumming of negative themes likely to contribute both to prejudice against the group and to the decline of group pride. Similarly, the repetition of ethnic images by the entertainment media adds to viewers' pools of "knowledge," particularly if news and entertainment treatment coincide in theme, approach, and frequency.

2. Media Help Organize Information and Ideas about Racial, Ethnic, Cultural, and National Groups. More than providing information, media help shape viewer and reader structures for perceiving, receiving, and thinking—the way people organize information. Movies and television, for example, perform the same roles that folk stories and fairy tales have done for years.[21] They provide a type of "ritualized glue" that helps audiences make sense of the pseudoenvironment's increasing information overload, which assaults and often overwhelms readers, viewers and listeners. In his book, *Information Anxiety,* Richard Saul Wurman opines that the amount of information now doubles every half decade, while a single weekday issue of *The New York Times* contains more information than the average resident of seventeenth-century England was likely to encounter in a lifetime.[22]

Reporting that there had been more than 2,300 research papers on television and human behavior, social psychologist George Comstock addressed the relationship of media to the reification of social structures:

> Several writers have argued that television is a powerful reinforcer of the status quo. The ostensible mechanisms are the effects of its portrayals on public expectations and perceptions. Television portrayals and particularly violent drama are said to assign roles of authority, power, success, failure, dependence, and vulnerability in a manner that matches the real-life social hierarchy, thereby strengthening that hierarchy by increasing its acknowledgement among the public and by failing to provide positive images for members of social categories occupying a subservient position. Content analyses of television drama support the contention that portrayals reflect normative status.[23]

To the degree that media express and reiterate the normality of racial, ethnic, and social hierarchies, the more they legitimize taboos and reinforce the validity and even the naturalness of these relationships. When news media present a pattern of thinking about race and ethnicity, they contribute to reader and viewer frameworks for organizing future information and ideas about these groups. When the entertainment media repeatedly depict ethnic or racial dominance or subservience, present ethnic slurs as an acceptable form of expression (for example, when uttered by movie heroes), or portray members of specific ethnic groups in limited spheres of action, they contribute to the formation of viewer schema for absorbing future images into a meaningful, consistent, if distorted, mental framework.

3. Media Help Create Values and Attitudes. Critics of the media have been asserting this for decades. The Payne Fund studies of the 1930s, for example, included Henry James Forman's provocatively titled *Our Movie Made Children.*[24] In 1975 media historian Robert Sklar chose *Movie-Made America* as the title for his widely read cultural history of U.S. motion pictures, although in his book he avoids the "hypodermic" leanings that pervade the Payne Fund studies.[25]

Hollywood's 1930 Motion Picture Production Code (the Hays Code) provides a primer on Hollywood's recognition both that movies teach and that filmmakers should take cognizance of the values they are disseminating. One of the Code's value positions, its opposition to interracial love, appeared in its Section II, Rule 6, which read, "Miscegenation (sex relationship between the white and black races) is forbidden." Until the 1950s Hollywood drummed home the repeated message that miscegenation should be avoided. In those rare screen instances where it occurred or seemed about to occur, punishment and retribution predictably arrived. To an extent this element of Hollywood movie textbook values reflected widespread American social mores. After all, when surveys conducted for Gunnar Myrdal's 1944 classic, *An American Dilemma: The Negro Problem and Modern Democracy,* asked southern Whites what discriminatory lines must be maintained, their most common answer was "the bar against intermarriage and sexual intercourse involving white women."[26]

On the other hand, interracial marriage had long occurred in the United States. However, Hollywood chose value lessons over the presentation of reality. In adopting this pattern of portrayals, moviemakers functioned simultaneously as learners (reacting to the presence of such social mores among many Americans and fearing that movies with interracial love might not "sell" in the South) and as teachers of values (creating and operating within these miscegenation "curriculum guidelines").

4. Media Help Shape Expectations. Ruling Hollywood since 1934, before beginning its slow decline in the mid-1950s and being extinguished in 1968, the Hays Code ordained that crime could not pay in American films. All screen criminals must ultimately receive their just desserts. So it came as a shock to audiences who "expected" screen crime to lead to inevitable punishment when Steve McQueen flew away to Europe to enjoy the fruits of his masterfully engineered bank robbery as the 1968 film, *The Thomas Crown Affair,* came to an end.

With the burying of the Hays Code, Hollywood moved from a crime-cannot-pay to a crime-may-or-may-not-pay position of expectation shaping. Ironically and unfortunately, this more permissive instructional position concerning the expected results of criminality occurred simultaneously with the rise in ethnic theme films spurred by the civil rights movements of the 1960s. The result has been a flood of movies with ethnics as the principal perpetrators of crime. In recent years, for example, Italian Americans and Hispanic Americans have become nearly synonymous with screen crime—ergo, "The $25,000 Pyramid" caper that began this essay.

5. Media Provide Models for Action. Anecdotal evidence provides myriad examples of movies and television popularizing clothing styles, verbal expressions ("Make my day") and other forms of behavior. Aware of this penchant for imitation, protesters have railed against the release of such youth gang films as *A Clockwork Orange* (1971), *The Warriors* (1979), and *Colors* (1988) for fear that young people would imitate the screen gang violence. Although a few fights did break out near theatres, massive waves of imitative gang violence did not occur, which came as a shock to those who proclaimed such media deterministic positions.

But more critical and also more difficult to handle is the issue of "disinhibiting" effects. The question is not do the entertainment media provoke people into action? More important and more subtly, do they remove inhibitions to previously repressed actions? Some African American comedians, for example, who had repeatedly used the word "nigger" in their routines, have dropped it because of their concern that they may have unwittingly and unintentionally helped lower public inhibitions against employing this brutalizing word.

RESPONDERS AS EVIDENCE OF MEDIA IMPACT

While precise empirical data on media impact—as contributors to pride and to prejudice—have inevitably been elusive, responses to the media by scholars, governments, groups, and even the media themselves reveal both a recognition and an expression of that teaching power. Three examples—one racial, one ethnic, and one international—provide glimpses into the stereotype and prejudice-producing potential of the media. Moreover, they illustrate the five types of media influence that I have proposed: providing information; helping to organize information and ideas; contributing to values and attitude formation; helping to shape expectations; and providing models for action.

1. Racial. Media-honed audience preconceptions about "other" groups can lead to viewer expectations about their screen behavior. When moviemakers do not fulfill these audience predispositions and expectations, viewers may respond with disappointment, cynicism, or even outrage. Such occurred in 1989 with *Do the Right Thing,* the perceptive examination of interracial conflict, intraracial diversity, and urban pressures in the primarily Black Bedford-Stuyvesant section of Brooklyn.

Written and directed by the brilliant young African American filmmaker, Spike Lee, *Do the Right Thing* received lavish praise from some White critics. However, others challenged its authenticity on the grounds that Lee did not address the issue of drugs—and what's a movie about an African American community without drugs in the forefront? These White critics brought their media-massaged ghetto preconceptions to the theatre, and when Lee failed to deliver, *he* was at fault. (That same criticism descended on the 1990 African American teen comedy film, *House Party,* which also did not deal with drugs.) Certainly, Black communities have a drug problem, but so do middle- and upper-class White communities, not only in the United States but in many other nations. Yet when was the last time that a White filmmaker received a critical roasting for making a drug-free movie about a White community?

2. Ethnic. Sometimes media themselves provide begrudging recognition of their power to contribute to intergroup stereotyping. For example, prior to the 1977 U.S. national network television showing of Francis Ford Coppola's *The Godfather Saga* (a revised and expanded version of the two theatrical motion pictures, *The Godfather* and *The Godfather: Part II*), the following words appeared on screen, simultaneously intoned by a solemn voice: *"The Godfather* is a fictional account of the activities of a small group of ruthless criminals. It would be erroneous and unfair to suggest that they are representative of any ethnic group."

Forewarned that the characters were not "representative of any ethnic group," a nationwide audience watched the violent, multigenerational saga of the Corleone family. The film began in Sicily, large segments were spoken in Italian with English subtitles, and most of the characters bore such names as Clemenza, Barzini, Tattaglia, and Fanucci. Of course, the film and the television showing could not possibly contribute to Italian American stereotyping, because the disclaimer had inoculated viewers against thinking of the characters as members of any specific ethnic group!

Moreover, those worthless words became the model for future media disclaimers. Subsequent controversial films that exploited criminal violence in presenting other ethnic groups, such as the 1983 *Scarface* (Cuban Americans) and the 1985 *Year of the Dragon* (Chinese Americans), copied and only slightly modified the "Godfather disclaimer." While these words could not mitigate the image-influencing impact of these films (in fact, howls of laughter from audiences when I watched the disclaimers suggest that the warnings may have done more harm than good), the disclaimers did serve as a media admission that feature films do, in fact, teach. They can create, reinforce, and modify public images about ethnic groups. In other words, the "Godfather disclaimer" and its clones provide additional evidence that media have the power to demean group images.

3. International. In the popular 1980 movie satire. *Airplane!,* an airline pilot continually tries to seduce a little boy passenger, using subtle and not-so-subtle laugh-provoking advances. At one point he asks the boy, "Have you ever stayed in a Turkish prison?," inciting uproarious audience laughter. Would that line have been as funny if it went, "Have you ever stayed in a prison?" No. How about a "Swedish prison?" Nothing funny there. An "Argentine prison?" No again. But Turkish prison worked as humor. Why? It drew laughter not only because of the movie's content, but also because of the information, ideas, mental schema, and expectations that movie audiences brought into the theatre. It worked because the filmmakers had identified audience "sleeping" predispositions and cleverly played upon them. The filmmakers presumed—and they were proven correct—that audiences would respond to "Turkish prison" as a humorous metaphor for homosexuality.

But how could the filmmakers have predicted that response? Did they assume that most viewers had learned in school about Turkish prisons as centers of homosexuality? Of course not. Few schools (at least American schools) teach *anything* about Turkey. Or that most viewers had read scholarly books about Turkey containing discussions of Turkish prisons? Dubious. Or that they had read articles about Turkish prisons? A few viewers, maybe.

But the makers of *Airplane!* did know that millions of moviegoers had recently been exposed to the powerful imagery of Turkish prisons in the 1978 film hit, *Midnight Express,* adapted from American Billy Hayes' best-selling account of his imprisonment in and escape from Turkey. Simultaneously skilful in execution and sensationalistic in conception, the movie took Hayes' grueling narrative and reshaped it further to dehumanize Turks (in contrast, while the book excoriated Turkish prison conditions, it also presented Turks in a far more human and diverse manner). Moreover, the movie accentuated the themes of prison homosexuality and Turkish brutality.

With *Midnight Express* priming audiences on Turkish prisons, *Airplane!* merely had to present the "Turkish prison" line. Media-prepared audiences did the rest. In other words, rapidly and reactively drawing upon their own pre-existent internal images, audiences functioned as co-creators in the production of the film's meaning. (According to one Chinese proverb, "We see what is behind our eyes.")

Lest this essay be misinterpreted as media bashing, let me assure you that it is not. As I said earlier, media have sometimes been in the forefront of the struggle against prejudice while at other times functioning as purveyors of bigotry. Media have simultaneously contributed to improved interethnic understanding and to hypertrophied intercultural misunderstanding. They have both built and battered group pride, and have even played a role in fostering positive intercultural action.

Media coverage of Ethiopia provides a cogent example of the positive intercultural role of the media. Famine had ravaged Ethiopia for years. Yet, despite many stories written by print journalists, most people paid little attention to the Ethiopian tragedy until the moving-image media succeeded in capturing the horror and pathos of the famine. The resulting television dissemination of the famine story awakened the world to this catastrophe. Suddenly everyone wanted to help Ethiopia: "We are the world, we are the children;" "Hands across America." The visual media had begun the process; music further spread the message. The war against the Ethiopian famine was "in." But what the media place on the agenda, the media can remove by disuse. Famine in Ethiopia continues, but it has receded in media attention and, as a result, the public agenda has moved on, with other media-designated human dramas taking Ethiopia's place.

Or take Richard Attenborough's 1987 film, *Cry Freedom,* an anti-apartheid celebration of the friendship between South African Black Consciousness Movement leader Steve Biko and liberal White South African newspaper editor Donald Woods. Opening on July 29, 1988, in thirty packed South African theatres, *Cry Freedom* was confiscated later that day by the police, fearful of its teaching power—what both Black and White South Africans might learn from it about national racial conditions. In February, 1990, in the wake of the release of Nelson Mandela, the government permitted the film's renewed showing, deeming it now appropriate for South African audiences to be exposed to the film's potential impact as a media textbook on the nation's history.

THE MEDIA CHALLENGE

In short, the mass media teach, although we can never be certain what any one individual may learn from the media. In dealing with race, ethnicity, culture, and foreignness, the media have the power to contribute to pride and to prejudice, to intergroup understanding and to intergroup stereotyping. Both fact and fictional media provide information, help viewers, readers, and listeners to organize that information, contribute to values and attitudes, help shape expectations, and provide models for behavior. But action can be taken to deal with the intercultural teaching power of the media. Action can and should occur in various sectors of society, but three areas stand out as particularly important.

First, the media need to become more responsible in dealing with race, ethnicity, culture, and foreignness. News media should become more self-critical concerning their news selection, balance, and manner of presentation of different groups. Entertainment media should continuously examine their own tendencies in order to identify patterns of ethnic and foreign images that they disseminate, patterns of intergroup relationships that they portray, and patterns of group behavior that they repeatedly present. Simultaneously, they should strive to create character diversity and human complexity in their portrayal of members of all ethnic groups and nations.

The public at large should become more activist. Public awareness of the teaching power of the media appears to be growing, as reflected in a variety of forms. Protest groups have monitored the media and have challenged what they perceive to be "negative images" or distortions of various ethnic themes. Conversely, ethnic groups have presented awards to mediamakers who have contributed "positive images" to the media curriculum on ethnicity. Other groups have worked closely with the media in an attempt to improve images or mitigate negative treatment, while magazines such as the American quarterly, *Media and Values,* for which I wrote a column on minorities and the media, provide discussions of media issues as well as suggestions for teachers, counselors, religious leaders, and others active in working with youth in particular.

Finally, school educators need to dedicate themselves to integrating media analysis into their teaching. Long after school education has ended, each individual will experience life-long learning through the media. To prepare students for this eventuality, schools need to help develop their media analytical literacy, including multicultural media literacy. "To read without reflecting is like eating without digesting," Edmund Burke once opined . . . but so are mindless viewing and listening.

The struggle against prejudice, bigotry, and discrimination may be eternal. Those engaged in this crusade need to dedicate themselves not to spurious quick-fix efforts to eradicate prejudice, but rather to the unending battle for understanding and equity. As English historian E. P. Woodward once wrote, "Everything good has to be done over again, forever."

NOTES

1. Carlos E. Cortés, The Societal Curriculum: Implications for Multiethnic Education, in James A. Banks (ed.), *Education in the 80s: Multiethnic Education*

(Washington, DC: National Education Association, 1981), pp. 24–32.

2. Thomas B. Rosenstiel, Viewers Found to Confuse TV Entertainment with News; *Los Angeles Times,* August 17, 1989, I, p. 1.

3. Garth Jowett, *Film: The Democratic Art* (Boston, MA: Little, Brown and Company, 1976); Robert Sklar, *Movie-made America: A Cultural History of American Movies,* (New York: Random House, 1975); and Robert Singer and Robert Kazdon (eds.), Television and Social Behavior, *Journal of Social Issues,* Fall, 1976.

4. Wilbur Schramm, Jack Lyle, and Edwin B. Parker, *Television in the Lives of Our Children* (Stanford, CA: Stanford University Press, 1961).

5. Jack G. Shaheen, *The TV Arab* (Bowling Green, OH: Bowling Green State University Popular Press, 1984).

6. Herbert J. Gans, The Mass Media as an Educational Institution, *Television Quarterly,* 6 (1967), pp. 21–22.

7. I would like to thank Charles Wetherell, Director of the University of California, Riverside's Laboratory for Historical Research, for his comments on this essay and his valuable recommendations on my long-term film research.

8. Ben Bagdikian, *The Media Monopoly* (Boston, MA: Beacon Press, 1983), p. xvi.

9. Louis E. Raths and Frank N. Trager, Public Opinion and "Crossfire," *Journal of Educational Sociology,* 21, 6 (1948), pp. 345–368.

10. Ruth C. Peterson and L. L. Thurstone, *Motion Pictures and the Social Attitudes of Children* (New York: Macmillan, 1933).

11. Irwin C. Rosen, The Effect of the Motion Picture "Gentleman's Agreement" on Attitudes toward Jews, *Journal of Psychology,* 26 (1948), pp. 525–536.

12. Sam Keen, *Faces of the Enemy: Reflections of the Hostile Imagination* (New York: Harper and Row, 1986); and Vamik Volkan, *The Need to Have Enemies and Allies: From Clinical Practice to International Relationships* (Northvale, NJ: J. Aronson, 1988).

13. Blaine S. Lamb, The Convenient Villain: The Early Cinema Views the Mexican-American, *Journal of the West,* 14, 4 (1975), pp. 75–81.

14. John Dower, *War Without Mercy: Race and Power in the Pacific War* (New York: Pantheon, 1986).

15. John D. Leckenby and Stuart H. Surlin, Incidental Social Learning and Viewer Race: "All in the Family" and "Sanford and Son," *Journal of Broadcasting,* 20, 4 (1976), pp. 481–494.

16. Neil Vidmar and Milton Rokeach, Archie Bunker's Bigotry: A Study in Selective Perception and Exposure, *Journal of Communication,* 24, 1 (1974), pp. 36–47.

17. Paula W. Matabane, Television and the Black Audience: Cultivating Moderate Perspectives on Racial Integration, *Journal of Communication,* 38, 4 (1988), pp. 21–31.

18. Leon Festinger, *A Theory of Cognitive Dissonance,* (Evanston, IL: Row, Peterson, 1957).

19. Albert Bandura, *Social Learning Theory,* (Englewood Cliffs, NJ: Prentice-Hall, 1977).

20. Daniel J. Boorstin, *The Image or Whatever Happened to the American Dream?* (New York: Atheneum, 1961).

21. Bruno Bettelheim, *The Uses of Enchantment: The Meaning and Importance of Fairy Tales* (New York: Knopf, 1976).

22. Richard Saul Wurman, *Information Anxiety* (New York: Doubleday, 1989).

23. George Comstock, *The Impact of Television on American Institutions and the American Public* (Honolulu: East–West Communications Institute, East–West Center, 1977), pp. 20–21.

24. Henry James Forman, *Our Movie Made Children* (New York: Macmillan, 1933).

25. Robert Sklar, *Movie-made America: A Cultural History of American Movies* (New York: Random House, 1975).

26. Gunnar Myrdal, *An American Dilemma: The Negro Problem and Modern Democracy* (New York: Harper and Brothers, 1944), p. 60.

The corresponding Chapter for this Selection can be found on pg. 48.

SELECTION 12

HOLLY AND MELISSA'S MULTICULTURAL CURRICULUM

G ROWING UP, HOLLY AND MELISSA GOT MULTICULTURAL EDU-cation almost every day. Some days they got lessons on intergroup relations. Other days they were exposed to ideas on gender roles. Occasionally they immersed themselves in world cultures or cultural geography. Then, in fall, 1997, Holly entered kindergarten, and education "officially" began.

Holly and little sister Melissa (11 months younger), my two oldest grandchildren, spend lots of time with "grampushe" (their name for my wife, Laurel) and "granddy." Active, ener-getic, and creative, they spend most of their time with us play-ing with toys, enjoying books, doing jigsaw puzzles, painting, drawing, writing, talking, gallivanting in the backyard, visiting their friends, or going to the nearby park. But they do have their down times, when they relax in front of the television set.

When Holly and Melissa stay with us, we restrict their TV time. Sometimes we choose the programs or videos. On other occasions they pick their own entertainment, their own media curriculum ... with our ultimate veto.

Actually, during their preschool years, their curricular requests went something like this. "We want to see *Pocahontas* (or Shirley Temple or *Aladdin* or *The Lion King* or *The Puzzle Place* or *Scooby Doo*)." They made these requests not because they wanted multicultural education or even knew that they were involved in multicultural learning. They just felt like watching one of their shows.

Source: Chapter One of *The Children Are Watching: How the Media Teach about Diversity* (New York: Teachers College Press, 2000), pp. 7–16.

But wait a minute! That's not education. That's entertainment.

Half right. It is entertainment. But it is also education, because when they watch a video—or *Mr. Rogers* or *Sesame Street* or *Barney and Friends* or the *Teletubbies* or Saturday morning cartoons—Holly and Melissa are also learning about many things, including diversity. This happens whether or not the makers of these programs have any pedagogical goals. It also happens whether or not the little girls are actually aware that they are learning.

They learn about good and evil, right and wrong, life and death, villainy and heroism. They learn about family values from *The Lion King* and physical disabilities (later special abilities) from *Dumbo*. They learn about interpersonal, intergroup, and intercultural relations from *Pocahontas* and *The Puzzle Place*. They learn about gender relations from . . . well, from just about every show they see.

How do I know? Because I listen attentively and talk to them about their reactions to that "entertainment." Oh, yes, they learn, including things that I don't expect.

My "research design" has been simple. I often sit in the den while they watch their shows or videos. Because I want to discover what they *autonomously* extract from the videos, I restrain my natural teacher's inclination to ask questions in order to guide them. I do this because the very process of questioning and thereby provoking responses, while good pedagogically, would be obtrusive. It would pollute the relative purity of the direct interaction between these two developing minds and the media, as well as interfering with the spontaneity of their media-generated multicultural dialogue. My intervention would channel them in directions that I wanted, rather than allowing them to pursue directions that they themselves charted.

From an instructional perspective, it is important for parents and teachers to pose questions about the media, clarify and provide context, and try to mitigate deleterious messages that they think young people may be receiving. Although at times I did this, particularly in response to their questions and expressed reactions, my main goal was not pedagogical, but investigatory. I wanted to try to find out what these two little girls were extracting *on their own,* what they were constructing *between themselves,* and how they were reacting *without* my interference . . . unless, of course, they asked questions or initiated the discussion.

In other words, I wanted to discover what *they* were drawing autonomously from TV (including movies on videotape) and what actions might result from such viewing. This was my one chance to observe consciously, over an extended period of time, how two young children independently responded to the media without adult interference or guidance. It was as close as I could come to "unobtrusive measurement"—or at least as unobtrusive as a huge (to them) adult can be, even if silent. And I did find that my mere silent presence did influence their viewing habits. For example, during scenes of male–female affection, they would sometimes crawl under the den table so that I couldn't see their self-conscious reactions.

Watching Holly and Melissa, particularly during their preschool days, has been a revelation to me. Not that these two little girls are universal media children. But at least they are two, which is two more than most media scholars seem to have continuously observed, recorded, and analyzed over an extended period of time. Noting their reactions has increased my skepticism of most pundit and scholarly claims of what young people are learning from the media, especially assertions emanating from those who tend to project *their* hypercritical adult perceptions of the media onto young people. That tendency for people to overestimate the impact of media messages on others is sometimes referred to as the "third-person effect" (Davison, 1983). Relatively rare are studies based on actual observation of the response of young children to the media (Davies, 1997).

The following snapshots of Holly's and Melissa's media-derived multicultural learning hardly qualify as "thick description" (Geertz, 1973). However, they will give you an idea of what Laurel and I have observed as our two girls work their way through their own personal, idiosyncratic, semi–self-selected media multicultural curriculum.

SHIRLEY TEMPLE

Let's start with lessons in gender behavior. One day Laurel and I heard Holly sobbing in the bathroom. We rushed in, only to be met with a face full of joyous dimples reflecting back from the full-length wall mirror.

"What's wrong, sweetheart?," asked Laurel.

"Nothing. I'm just practicing my crying, like Shirley Temple. She cries when she's in trouble, and then people help her. I can do that, too."

Simply from watching Shirley Temple movies, Holly had already drawn a lesson on gender roles and behavior (Kohlberg & Ullian, 1974). Oh, well. After all, movies are just entertainment.

THE LION KING

Throughout their preschool years, *The Lion King* became their most oft-selected video. It even crept into their language.

The Lion King provides an important example of a media product as textbook. Worldwide it has enjoyed the greatest sales of any movie video (at least until *Titanic*) and has become one of the world's all-time highest grossing movies. It has also caught its lumps from critics concerned with its multicultural dimensions (Giroux, 1996).

Some criticized it as sexist. After all, a male is the head of the pride of lions, with his wife serving a minor supportive role. Pride leadership ultimately devolves upon their son, Simba, as it had previously upon his father, Mufassa. However, before Simba can assume that role after Mufassa's death, his evil Uncle Scar drives him into exile. After years of wandering in the wilderness, Simba encounters Nala, his long-lost girlfriend and wife-to-be. Failing at first to recognize each other, they engage in a battle royal, during which Nala gives as good as she gets. In fact, by the time that they finally recognize each other, she is on top of Simba. When we took Holly and Melissa to the store, the girls chose Nala, not Simba, t-shirts . . . with no sign of Simba envy.

Some criticized *The Lion King* as racist. The main targets were the secondary villains, the three hyenas, because they spoke in a kind of street patois (one of the voices was Whoopi Goldberg, another was Cheech Marin), which some critics concluded was Black speech (although not quite Ebonics). In other words, Black equals bad. Lost in this criticism was the fact that Mufassa, the elder Lion King, spoke perfect grammar with the resonant tones of the great James Earl Jones. Need I point out that Jones is Black?

And the Gay & Lesbian Alliance Against Defamation criticized the movie as homophobic. According to this argument, if the secondary villains, the hyenas, were surrogate Blacks, then the primary villain, Mufassa's nefarious, scheming, and murderous brother, Scar, was played as implicitly gay. He had no wife or kids. Also, I might inconveniently add, he had no male domestic partner. Just three hyena pals, whose relationship to Scar did not strike me as the least bit homoerotic. Moreover, as this line of criticism goes, Scar spoke in a decidedly effeminate (codedly homosexual) fashion. Maybe I'm betraying my unconscious heterosexual bias—or maybe I just lack sufficient multicultural sensitivity—but Scar did not seem effeminate to me. Supercilious, yes, with the type of weary, slothful speech sometimes used in the media to suggest British upper class decadence. That his voice belonged to Jeremy Irons, who has made a career playing such self-absorbed elites, further buttressed this impression.

I certainly don't want to make light of these criticisms. The fact that *The Lion King* struck different viewers in these various ways cannot be summarily dismissed. However, apparently this is not what Holly and Melissa saw . . . or at least they said nothing that indicated this is what they saw. But the movie did have an impact . . . in some respects a troubling one.

One day, while watching the movie, Holly asked me, "Why did the wildebeests want to kill Mufassa?" In the movie, the jealous Scar hatches a plot to kill his brother, Mufassa, by having his allies, the hyenas, provoke a stampede of wildebeests into a narrow gorge where Scar has abandoned Simba. Informed that his son is in danger, Mufassa races into the gorge to save him. While Mufassa succeeds, he is then trampled to death after Scar pushes him off a cliff as he is trying to climb out of the gorge.

Holly's primary concern was not Mufassa's death, but the issue of volition. "*Why* did the wildebeests *want* to kill Mufassa?" I explained that they didn't *want* to kill Mufassa, but that he just happened to be in the way when the hyenas frightened them into stampeding. "Then why did the *hyenas* want to kill Mufassa?" Even as I gave my answer—the hyenas had stampeded the wildebeests because Scar had told them to do so—I realized that, like Oedipus, Holly would relentlessly continue asking questions in an effort to resolve her personal mystery. "But why did *Scar* want to kill Mufassa, his own brother? I don't want to kill Melissa?"

It was only then that I recognized the extent of the moral questions that *The Lion King* had generated in that little seeking mind. What other lessons and dilemmas had this dark and fascinating movie generated for the girls?

Quite abruptly, Holly and Melissa decided that they were no longer interested in *The Lion King*. Their growing dislike of Scar had turned into fear. The movie had suddenly become too scary. But just as abruptly, a few months later, they returned to their old favorite. And this time, as Simba sadly looked down at his dead, trampled father, the little girls were smiling. I restrained myself from asking them why, but my perplexed look revealed my wordless question. "That's okay, Granddad. He's not really dead. He's coming back later. It's the Circle of Life."

In truth, Mufassa does reappear later as a vision in Simba's quest to deal with his own personal dilemmas of growing into adulthood, assuming his responsibilities as head of the pride, and coming to grips with his role in his father's death. "The Circle of Life," the movie's theme song, had provided the girls with a metaphor and the language to grapple with both the events of the movie and maybe even with the concept of death itself.

On a lighter note, one day Melissa began whimpering because I had chastised her about something. Her consoling older sister turned to her and said, comfortingly, "That's O.K. Hakuna matata." A tune sung by Simba and his two pals to cheer themselves up, "Hakuna Matata" means "no worries." It worked for Melissa as well as for Simba, because she grinned broadly and stopped whimpering. The girls' superficial imitative behavior may not be as dramatic as purported media-generated copycat killings. Nonetheless, it suggests the way that media surreptitiously become a part of language and action.

But, after all, *The Lion King* is just entertainment.

POCAHONTAS

Pocahontas proved even more problematic than *The Lion King* for Holly and Melissa. That movie, too, has been on the receiving end of multicultural criticism (for example, see Leslie, 1996; Sardar, 1996–1997). It does not accurately depict American Indian life. (Since when did cartoons accurately depict anything?) It does not tell the *true* story of Pocahontas and John Smith. (Did anyone really expect it would?) It ultimately represents Native Americans in a demeaning manner. Now that criticism deserves closer scrutiny, particularly if it turns out that, indeed, some young people who view it develop a negative—or more negative—view of Indians (Tilton, 1994).

Let me return to my observable research universe of Holly and Melissa. Unlike adult critics, they have not expressed any particular concern about the movie's anthropological or historical fidelity. But *Pocahontas* has, in fact, turned out to be a multicultural textbook. Even at their young age, their textual interpretation has gone through phases.

When the girls began their *Pocahontas*-watching cycle, it tested the mettle of even this committed scholarly observer. One assault of the song, "Color of the Wind," was more than enough for my ears. Unfortunately, many more were to come.

Given the amount of (mainly negative) multicultural analysis that *Pocahontas* has received (Kilpatrick, 1995; Lepore, 1996), I was prepared—I thought—for the little girls' probable initial responses. What questions would come first? Racial identity, ethnic conflict, intergroup love affairs? Wrong.

Holly, then three, opened the dialogue with an interrogatory thunderbolt: "Granddad, can I ask you something? Why are Pocahontas' b – – bs" (deletion mine—a prominent part of the young Indian lass' anatomy) "so much bigger than ———'s?" (referring comparatively to a female member of our family). "Yeah," chimed in Melissa, then two, "They're even bigger than Barbie's." It was a pop-cultural gender one–two punch.

Don't ask me where the girls acquired that language. I have no idea. Maybe they picked it up incidentally from the media or maybe from some of their neighborhood or preschool peers. There is only so much informal learning that parents or grandparents can control (Harris, 1998). This goes even for fiercely protective parents, like film critic Michael Medved and psychologist Diane Medved (1998), who have severely restricted their children's media watching and carefully screened their children's friends. Yet they were aghast when one of their daughters informed them of the names of the Spice Girls . . . which she had learned at a Girl Scout meeting!

Gender difference (as well as intragender physical variation) was the first multicultural dimension of *Pocahontas* that attracted their attention . . . or at least the first dimension that they communicated to me. The issue of skin color—particularly the difference between Pocahontas and John Smith—did not arise until several months later.

The girls have always lived in racially mixed surroundings. They have noticed—sometimes even talked about—the fact that kids they know have different skin colors. So much for color blindness. However, our family made a conscious decision not to mention *racial categories* or engage in *racial labeling* around them. Aware that sooner or later they would pick these up—in school, from their friends, or maybe from the media—we would deal with them at that point, hopefully at a serendipitous developmental moment (Trubowitz, 1969). So when the girls met *Pocahontas*, they had given no evidence that racial categories had become part of their linguistic and perceptual structure. In other words, although not *color blind*, they were *race unaware* ... or at least to the degree that we could infer from their verbal comments.

This coincides with Robyn Holmes' (1995) conclusions in *How Young Children Perceive Race*. After extensive observations of five racially and ethnically mixed kindergarten classes, Holmes concluded that even young children classified people by physical characteristics, including gender and skin color (white, brown, and black), as well as other ethnic dimensions (Japanese and Spanish). However, not all used American *racial* categories or the adult language of *racial* labeling. She pointed out that the children in her project "placed people into different categories primarily on the basis of skin color and the native language an individual spoke" (p. 41). Yet the mere noticing of these differences did not seem to result in prejudice or interracial conflict among the young people in her study. (For other interpretations of race awareness among preschool and kindergarten children see, for example: Aboud, 1988; Goodman, 1952; Hatcher & Troyna, 1993; Hirschfeld, 1996; Katz, 1976; Ramsey, 1987).

Pocahontas ultimately had a more deleterious multicultural effect on Holly and Melissa. At first they merely remarked about differences between the "Indians" (sometimes "savages") and the "sailors," including but not limited to the obvious, movie-emphasized distinctions in skin color. But somewhere along the line these seemingly neutral observations (and I emphasize, "seemingly," as I was not privy to what was going on in their minds) turned into value judgments. Indians (Pocahontas and a few others excepted) began to scare them because of what they wanted to do to John Smith. Indians were becoming part of their cognitive and attitudinal structure, at which point I could not hold back from intervening.

But, of course, *Pocahontas* is just entertainment.

O.J.

One day, shortly after she had turned three, Holly wandered into the kitchen and asked me in naive, puzzled, and chilling fashion, "Granddad, what's the N word?" When I interrogated her about the source of that question, she responded that she had just heard it on television.

A quick trip to the den clarified what had happened. The local TV news was on, they were discussing the O.J. Simpson trial, and one (or more) of the newspeople must have used that irritating pseudoeuphemism, "the N word." They had not said the N word, but they had said "the N word."

This puzzled Holly. We have several alphabet books, with a page of words and pictures devoted to each letter. In learning to read and write the alphabet, Holly had absorbed many words that started with each letter, including N. But if that were so, then how could there be *the* (meaning one) N word?

I had to make a quick developmental decision. Was she ready for a full explanation? Was it the right time for cutting open the apple to get to the core of the topic? For better or for worse, I decided that it was not the appropriate "teaching moment" for trying to initiate Holly and Melissa into the complexities of derogatory group epithets. So I punted. "I'll explain it to you later, sweetheart." "Oh," she responded, "When I'm four?" (her three-year-old's translation of "later"). "Yes, when you're four," I answered, obviously not meaning it.

So much for the N word. But what lingers in my mind is a question—what else did that inquisitive little mind draw from whatever she incidentally saw about the O.J. Simpson trial? Or, for that matter, what else has she drawn, in her own way, from other chance meetings with multiculturally laden newscasts?

ROMANCE

Pocahontas, take two. As the girls' combination of fear and antipathy toward Indians receded, they readmitted that video into their multicultural curriculum. But the movie had taken on a new, more personal meaning.

One evening, without warning, Holly asked Laurel and me to leave the room. She didn't want us in the room during *that* part of the movie—the scene where Pocahontas and John Smith first express affection toward each other.

I don't want to get into cause-and-effect speculation. However, let me just say that Holly's desire for privacy with this video relationship—this intergroup relationship or, maybe in Holly's eyes, this inter–skin-color relationship—came at precisely the same time of her announcement of another relationship. Her two preschool boyfriends (twin brothers) had simultaneously asked her to marry them when they grew up. (Later she informed us that she *had* married them . . . both.) Had Pocahontas influenced Holly's reaction to their "proposal" or had their "proposal" influenced the way she viewed the Pocahontas–John Smith movie relationship?

Oh, let's not get carried away. After all, *Pocahontas* is just entertainment.

On the other hand, by the time she turned five, Holly had developed a fascination with the idea of romance, as well as with female traumas. Along with many of her kindergarten classmates, she was affected by the television coverage of Princess Diana's death. In fact, one day shortly thereafter she announced that she wanted to be a princess when she grew up. The girls became enchanted with *Sleeping Beauty* and, after they watched *The Karen Carpenter Story* with their mother, they felt the need to talk to us about her fatal eating problems. They loved Whitney Houston's 1997 multiracial television remake of Rogers and Hammerstein's musical, *Cinderella*, although Holly opined that the prince seemed a bit silly running around the country-side trying to jam the lost slipper on women who looked nothing like Brandy (who played Cinderella). I'm not sure what role skin color played in that observation, as neither Holly nor Melissa mentioned it.

But possibly the most surprising (to us) media event was the evening that Holly wandered into the den just after Laurel had begun watching the 1997 British TV remake of *Jane Eyre*. Before Laurel realized it, Holly had become mesmerized . . . and watched the whole thing. Her fascination with mediated dimensions of male–female relations revealed the powerful role that this multicultural curriculum was already playing in her personal development. The next day Laurel overheard Holly relating the plot to Melissa with great drama and considerable nuance.

THE LEARNERS

But enough description. Let's cast this discussion in a broader light. Holly and Melissa are just ordinary little girls. Well, not so ordinary. After all, they are *my* grandchildren.

But they are like other little girls and boys in that they are constantly learning—not just when, where, and what we adults want them to learn, certainly not just when, where, and what teachers, administrators, school boards, textbook publishers, or state curriculum adopters want them to learn.

And, like Holly and Melissa, much of what children learn outside of school, including through the media, will be multicultural—whether or not we want it, whether or not we notice it, whether or not we admit it.

The corresponding Chapter for this Selection can be found on pg. 53.

SEARCHING FOR PATTERNS:
A CONVERSATION WITH
CARLOS CORTÉS

C ORTÉS SPOKE WITH TEACHING TOLERANCE DIRECTOR JIM CARNES by phone from his home in Riverside, CA.

Multicultural education has been around long enough to have a history of its own. How has your perspective on the field changed over the past 20 years?

I started out as a historian, and, because my father was a Mexican immigrant, I became interested in the experience of Latinos in the United States, particularly Mexican Americans. But, as happened to a lot of us who began with an emphasis on one ethnic group, I soon realized that we had to take the next step, that focusing on my own group wasn't enough.

As I worked with diverse students and teachers, I became increasingly aware of the *intersection* of issues of race and ethnicity, language, religion, gender and sexual orientation, generation and age, and so forth, as they operate within each individual. These factors cross-cut and come out differently in every person. We have to look at the way the individual relates to the many groups to which she or he belongs, understanding that each person you come into contact with is influenced by a variety of groups.

The other dimension of my thinking that has changed is that I used to look at school as the engine that drove an understanding of multiculturalism. I don't any more. Schools don't

Source: Teaching Tolerance, No. 16 (Fall, 1999), pp. 10–15.

have a monopoly on teaching about diversity. My basic research interest has become the area that I call the "societal curriculum," which is the non-school teaching about diversity.

What elements does the societal curriculum encompass?

I break it down into four components. The first one I call the *immediate curriculum,* which consists of family, community, peers and those other immediate human influences around you. The second I call the *institutional curriculum*—things like churches, synagogues, YMCAs, Boy and Girl Scouts, the many institutions one comes across as one grows up. As you get older you might add groups like unions and professional associations.

Third is the *serendipitous curriculum*—the chance encounters that happen to everyone throughout their lives. For each person, there is a different set of chance events—they're not structured, they don't come out of a special institution. It could be a trip you went on, someone you met. It may be a particularly bad experience with someone of a certain ethnic background that suddenly changes your attitude toward that group of people.

Fourth is the *media curriculum,* which is my major research emphasis. I recognize that the media, too, is an institution, but it's so important that I consider it by itself as part of the larger societal curriculum.

Can you give some examples of how a teacher might use media images— negative or positive—constructively in the classroom?

Let's say as a part of *education,* as opposed to just in the classroom. I think it's more important to have students weigh the strengths and weaknesses of the media treatment of diversity, the contributions of the media to intergroup understanding or misunderstanding, than to have the teacher didactically assert, "This image is positive, this is negative." I try and keep students and teachers from simply talking about positive and negative because I think that ignores the nuances and complexity of the issue. It leads to trying to put every media treatment into one of those two categories—good and evil— which is a very American tendency.

I tell teachers, "Whatever you do, don't assign kids to go out and *look* for stereotypes, because then you've already given them the answer: 'You will find stereotypes.' Then every time they see an image or a depiction, they'll be likely to assume it's a stereotype." But if you have students look for *patterns,* then they can discover for themselves: "Aha! This looks like a pattern. We're not yet sure if it's a stereotype, but let's look further."

Concrete assignments work best. You could have students select one particular radio talk-show host and listen to the program regularly over a two-week period to determine if there's a pattern of treatment that the host uses when discussing members of a particular group.

I might say, "Collect all articles about women in two daily newspapers over a two-week period to determine if there's a pattern of the kinds of stories that they run. Watch TV news over a period of time to discover whether there's a pattern of treatment of religion. Make a list of the religious stories on the news and see if there's a pattern. Collect movie reviews for one month to see if there's a pattern of movies about a specific group. Is there a series of themes that continually come through?

This is fairly straightforward. By identifying patterns, students can come to their own conclusions about what the media are teaching and the kinds of possible stereotypes they should be aware of when they're reading or viewing media throughout their lives. This also reinforces the lesson that they're going to be lifelong learners about diversity through the media.

What role does the Internet play in the societal curriculum?

As many educators have claimed, the Internet allows people to converse with others of different backgrounds. Unfortunately, this interaction with others happens at a distance—you don't see them, you don't bump into them and live next to them.

Another drawback, I think, is that the Internet seems to encourage many people to focus only on intragroup communication with those of their own backgrounds or ideologies. We know that people tend to go back to the same sites over and over. I'm terrified of a future when people get most of their news and information simply by going to two or three basic ideological Web sites that filter the world for them. That could polarize us even further.

Increasingly, it seems, demographic predictions are being used to "scare" people into dealing with diversity. How can educators challenge that fear-based approach?

If you simply see demographic change as some huge flood of difference washing over the nation, then it can lead to fear, anger, antagonism. But if you see it as a series of changes with which we can work to build something better by drawing on its strengths, then it takes you in a different direction.

One issue that really galvanizes people in my workshops is the issue of intermarriage. I have to go off on a tangent here, or maybe it's a tantrum! Many multiculturalists today seem unwilling to deal with the growing factor of intermarriage. Too much of multicultural education is frozen into a kind of group purity paradigm, when, in fact, intermarriage is one of the enormous changes that are taking place in America. For example, one-third of all Latinos born in the U.S. now marry someone who is not Latino. That says an awful lot about what the next generation's sense of ethnic identity is going to be—it's going to be much more unpredictable. What will these cultural blends be like?

Once I bring up the topic of intermarriage, it's as if I've given people permission to come out of the closet! One after another they seem eager to talk about their background, their spouse, one of their kids who has married someone with a different racial or ethnic identity. Even in our multicultural society, many people—including some multiculturalists—are still frozen in that old single-group thinking that we were using 25 years ago.

I've been reading a lot of autobiographies of individuals who are finding new spaces that break down the starkness of traditional Black/White, Latino/Anglo and other ethnic dichotomies. Gregory Howard Williams' *Life on the Color Line: The True Story of a White Boy Who Discovered He Was Black* is a great example. We have an increasing number of people who are multicultural *within their own identity*. I find that very heartening. This is part of what I call an "ecological change" in the nature of diversity.

What other factors can you identify in that ecological change?

The traditional way of thinking has been about White communities becoming Black. The next phase was that of White Anglo communities becoming Black or Latino or Asian. What we're now seeing is the rapid evolution of two other kinds of communities. One is the bicultural community in which neither group is Anglo, and the other is the non-majoritarian community—where no group has a majority anymore. That's a big shift from the old majority/minority paradigm.

I recently read that 243 counties in the United States now have an Anglo numerical minority, and 42 of those counties have made that shift in the last five years. That's just *counties*. If you look at school districts and communities, you also see these ecological shifts. But what happens in places like the San Gabriel Valley of California, which used to be almost all Latino and then large numbers of Asians moved in? There's been almost no multicultural research on what it means when you get that inter-ethnic combination. What happens when 60 percent of Koreatown in Los Angeles becomes Latino, heavily Central American? We have limited research on these settings. They're truly multicultural, not traditional majority/minority.

We've got one community in California—Carson—that last year hit the magic moment when it was 25 percent Anglo, 25 percent Asian/Pacific Islander, 25 percent Black and 25 percent Latino. It was a monumental vision of the future! Of course, that's already changed this year, because at least one of those groups has grown and one has gone down. The old paradigms don't deal with these changes. A teacher in a Chinese/Latino school is going to encounter quite a different situation from a teacher in a White/Black school. Not to mention the mixed-race kids that might be in these schools.

That's why multicultural education has to keep growing to address these new kinds of issues. By looking at the intersection of immigration patterns, communication, cultural transfer and cultural maintenance, linkages to foreign nations and so forth, we can learn and help students learn how diversity in the United States is connected to diversity around the world.

How can teachers respond more effectively to the "diversity within diversity"?

To say "All students are different" is really an anarchic statement. It's not useful to look at 30 students in your class as entirely different from each other. The important questions are "Are there *patterns* of difference on which I can draw? Are there certain effective ways of dealing with different kinds of students? Can I develop a repertoire of five or six of approaches that help me reach more kids than I would in using just one or two techniques?"

Because of the fear of stereotyping, sometimes there's almost a terror of categorization. When a the teacher says, "I treat every student as a unique individual," my response is, "Then how do you get them to the proper bathroom?" We inevitably and classify by groups. The challenge is to use that group knowledge constructively, not destructively; subtly, not stereotypically.

In one workshop exercise, I divide the chalkboard in half, with "Generalization" on one side and "Stereotype" on the other. Then we compare the characteristics. For example, the generalizer will take a piece of group knowledge and use it as a clue to how an individual is likely to act. A stereotyper will take that same group knowledge and insist that people of that group will act a certain way. Instead of being a clue, that group knowledge becomes an assumption: "Latinos speak Spanish" is a stereotype. We know that 25 percent of Latinos speak little if any Spanish. "Latinos are more likely to speak Spanish than are other Americans" is a generalization—we're talking about a likelihood. Therefore, when I approach a child who's Latino, I should realize that there is a good likelihood that the parents speak Spanish or the child knows Spanish. Yet I need to avoid the stereotype, which would mean assuming that the child's family speaks Spanish or, worse yet, doesn't speak English, so I need to send home a note in Spanish.

A lot of material that's designed to help teachers deal with stereotypes actually ends up making them afraid to generalize. When I work with teachers, I try to remove the fear of generalizations. The irony is that we can't live without generalizations, which are the basis for a knowledge of the world. Yet we also have to fight continually to keep those generalizations from hardening into stereotypes.

The same goes for students. We know that prejudices exist. We know that beneath prejudices lurk lots of misunderstandings, fears and lack of knowledge about others. What I'm hoping—and I must admit that there's been little long-term research on this topic—is that as students become attuned to thinking about the patterns of treatment they see in the media and encounter in other parts of the societal curriculum, they'll step back and begin to resist those patterns that corrode their relations with other human beings. This is my hope.

The corresponding Chapter for this Selection can be found on pg. 55.

REFERENCES

Aboud, F. (1988). *Children and prejudice*. Oxford, England: Basil Blackwell.

Ansen, D. (1989, July 17). Gibson and Glover return: "Lethal Weapon 2" serves up sadism with a smile. *Newsweek,* p. 53.

Appleton, N. (1983). *Cultural pluralism in education: Theoretical foundations*. New York: Longman.

Atkinson, D. R., Morten, G., & Sue, D. W. (Eds.). (1979). *Counseling American minorities: A cross-cultural perspective*. Dubuque, IA: William C. Brown.

Bagdikian, B. (1983). *The media monopoly*. Boston: Beacon Press.

Bandura, A. (1977). *Social learning theory*. Englewood Cliffs, NJ: Prentice-Hall.

Banks, C. A. M. (1977). A content analysis of the treatment of Black Americans on television. *Social Education, 41*(4), 336–339, 344.

Banks, J. A. (1973). Teaching for ethnic literacy: A comparative approach. *Social Education, 27,* 738–750.

Banks, J. A. (Ed.) (1981a). *Education in the 80s: Multiethnic education*. Washington, D.C.: National Education Association.

Banks, J. A. (Ed.) (1981b). *Multiethnic education: Theory and practice*. Boston: Allyn and Bacon.

Bettelheim, B. (1976). *The uses of enchantment: The meaning and importance of fairy tales*. New York: Knopf.

Boorstin, D. J. (1961). *The image or whatever happened to the American dream?* New York: Atheneum.

Brookover, W., Beady, C., Flood, P., Schweitzer, J., & Wisenbaker, J. *School social systems and student achievement: Schools can make a difference*. New York: Praeger.

California State Department of Education (1983). *Basic principles for the education of language-minority students: An overview*. Sacramento: California State Department of Education.

California State Department of Education (1981). *Schooling and language minority students: A theoretical framework*. Los Angeles: Evaluation, Dissemination and Assessment Center, California State University, Los Angeles.

California State Department of Education (1971). *Report and recommendations of the task force to reevaluate social science textbooks grades five through eight*. Sacramento: Bureau of Textbooks, California State Department of Education.

Campbell, R. (1978). The ideology of the social consciousness movie: Three films of Darryl F. Zanuck. *Quarterly Review of Film Studies, 3,* 49–71.

Carnoy, M. (1974). *Education as cultural imperialism*. New York: David McKay.

Clark, R. M. (1983). *Family life and school achievement: Why poor Black children succeed or fail*. Chicago: University of Chicago Press.

Coleman, J. S., et al. (1966). *Equality of educational opportunity*. Washington, D.C.: U.S. Government Printing Office.

Comstock, G. (1977). *The impact of television on American institutions and the American public*. Honolulu: East–West Communications Institute, East–West Center.

Cortés, C. E. (1981). The societal curriculum: Implications for multiethnic education. In J. A. Banks (Ed.), *Education in the 80s: Multiethnic education* (pp. 24–32). Washington, D.C.: National Education Association.

Cortés, C. E. (1991). Hollywood interracial love: Social taboo as screen titillation. In P. Loukides & L. K. Fuller (Eds.), *Plot conventions in American popular film* (pp. 21–35). Bowling Green, OH: Bowling Green State University Popular Press.

Cripps, T. (1970). The myth of the southern box office: A factor in racial stereotyping in American movies, 1920–1940. In J. C. Curtis & L. L. Gould (Eds.), *The Black experience in America: Selected essays* (pp. 116–144). Austin: University of Texas Press.

Cuban, L. (1984). Transforming the frog into a prince: Effective schools research, policy, and practice at the district level. *Harvard Educational Review, 54*(2), 129–151.

Cullery, J. D. & Bennett, R. (1976). Selling women, selling Blacks. *Journal of Communication, 26,* 170–174.

Cummins, J. (1979). Linguistic interdependence and the educational development of bilingual children. *Review of Educational Research, 49*(2), 222–251.

Davies, M. M. (1997). *Fake, fact, and fantasy: Children's interpretations of television reality*. Mahwah, NJ: Erlbaum.

Davison, W. P. (1983). The third-person effect in communication. *Public Opinion Quarterly, 47*(1), 1–15.

Dinnerstein, L., Nichols, R. L., & Reimers, D. M. (1979). *Natives and strangers: Ethnic groups and the building of America*. New York: Oxford University Press.

Dower, J. (1986). *War without mercy: Race and power in the Pacific war*. New York: Pantheon.

Festinger, L. (1957). *A theory of cognitive dissonance*. Evanston, IL: Row, Peterson.

Fishman, J. A., & Keller, G. D. (Eds.) (1982). *Bilingual education for Hispanic students in the United States*. New York: Teachers College Press.

Forman, H. J. (1933). *Our movie made children*. New York: Macmillan.

Gans, H. J. (1967). The mass media as an educational institution. *Television Quarterly, 6,* 20–37.

Garcia, R. L. (1982). *Teaching in a pluralistic society: Concepts, models, strategies*. New York: Harper & Row.

Geertz, C. (1973). *The interpretation of cultures*. New York: Basic Books.

Giroux, H. A. (1996). *Fugitive cultures: Race, violence, and youth*. New York: Routledge.

Goodman, M. E. (1964). *Race awareness in young children* (2d ed. rev.). New York: Macmillan.

Greenberg, B. S. (1972). Children's reactions to TV Blacks. *Journalism Quarterly, 49,* 5–14.

Grossman, H. (1984). *Educating Hispanic students: Cultural implications for instruction, classroom management, counseling, and assessment*. Springfield, IL: Charles C. Thomas.

Hall, E. T. (1976). *Beyond culture*. Garden City, NY: Doubleday.

Halliburton, W., & Katz, W. L. (1970). *A syllabus of United States history for secondary schools.* New York: Arno Press.

Hanke, L. (Ed.) (1964). *Do the Americans have a common history? A critique of the Bolton theory.* New York: Knopf.

Harris, J. R. (1998). *The nurture assumption: Why children turn out the way they do; parents matter less than you think and peers matter more.* New York: Free Press.

Hatcher, R., & Troyna, B. (1993). Racialization and children. In C. McCarthy & W. Crichlow (Eds.), *Race, identity and representation in education* (pp. 109–125). New York: Routledge.

Hernton, C. C. (1965). *Sex and racism in America.* New York: Grove Press.

Hirschfeld, L. A. (1996). *Race in the making: Cognition, culture, and the child's construction of human kinds.* Cambridge, MA: M.I.T. Press.

Holmes, R. M. (1995). *How young children perceive race.* Thousand Oaks, CA: Sage.

Jacobs, L. (1939). *The rise of the American film: A critical history.* New York: Harcourt, Brace and Company.

Jencks, C., Smith, M., Acland, H., Bane, M. J., Cohen, D., Gintis, H., Heyns, B., & Michelson, S. *Inequality: A reassessment of the effect of family and schooling in America.* New York: Basic Books.

Jones, C. J. (1981). Image and ideology in Kazan's "Pinky." *Literature/Film Quarterly, 9*(2), 110–120.

Jordan, W. (1968). *White over Black: American attitudes toward the Negro, 1550–1817.* Chapel Hill: University of North Carolina Press.

Jowett, G. (1976). *Film: The democratic art.* Boston: Little, Brown and Company.

Kane, M. B. (1970). *Minorities in textbooks: A study of their treatment in social studies texts.* Chicago: Quadrangle Books.

Katz, P. A. (1976). The acquisition of racial attitudes in children. In P. A. Katz (Ed.), *Towards the elimination of racism* (pp. 125–154). New York: Pergamon Press.

Keen, S. (1986). *Faces of the enemy: Reflections of the hostile imagination.* New York: Harper & Row.

Kilpatrick, J. (1995). Disney's "politically correct" *Pocahontas. Cineaste, 21*(4), 36–37.

Kirby, J. T. (1978). D. W. Griffith's racial portraiture. *Phylon, 39,* 118–127.

Kirp, D. L. (1982). *Just schools: The idea of racial equality in American education.* Berkeley: University of California Press.

Kleinfeld, J. S. (1979). *Eskimo school on the Andreafsky: A study of effective bicultural education.* New York: Praeger.

Kohlberg, L. A., & Ullian, D. Z. (1974). Stages in the development of psychosexual concepts and attitudes. In R. C. Friedman, R. M. Richaret, & R. L. Warde Wiete (Eds.), *Sex differences in behavior* (pp. 209–222). New York: Wiley.

Lamb, B. S. (1975). The convenient villain: The early cinema views the Mexican-American. *Journal of the West, 14*(4), 75–81.

Lambert, W., & Klineberg, O. (1967). *Children's views of foreign people.* New York: Appleton-Century-Crofts.

Leckenby, J. D., & Surlin, S. H. (1976). Incidental social learning and viewer race: "All in the Family" and "Sanford and Son." *Journal of Broadcasting, 20*(4), 481–494.

Lepore, J. (1996). *The Scarlet Letter* and *Pocahontas. American Historical Review, 101*(4), 1166–1168.

Leslie, E. (1996). Pocahontas. *History Workshop Journal, 41,* 235–239.

Longstreet, W. S. (1978). *Aspects of ethnicity: Understanding difference in pluralistic classrooms.* New York: Teachers College Press.

Martinez, T. (1969). Advertising and racism: The case of the Mexican-American. *El Grito, 2,* 3–13.

Matabane, P. W. (1988). Television and the Black audience: Cultivating moderate perspectives on racial integration. *Journal of Communication, 38*(4), 21–31.

Medved, M., & Medved, D. (1998). *Saving childhood: Protecting our children from the national assault on innocence.* New York: HarperCollins.

Michalek, L. (1989). The Arab in American cinema: A century of otherness. *The Arab Image in American Film and Television, Cineaste, 17*(Suppl. 1), 3–9.

Miller, R. M. (Ed.) (1979). *The kaleidoscopic lens: Ethnic images in American film.* Englewood, NJ: Jerome S. Ozer.

Morris, D., Collett, P., Marsh, P., & O'Shaughnessey, M. (1979). *Gestures.* New York: Stein and Day.

Myrdal, G. (1944). *An American dilemma: The Negro problem and modern democracy.* New York: Harper & Brothers.

O'Hearn, C. C. (Ed.) (1998). *Half and half: Writers on growing up biracial and bicultural.* New York: Pantheon.

Omi, M., & Winant, H. (1994). *Racial formation in the United States: From the 1960s to the 1990s* (2d ed.). New York: Routledge.

Paredes, A. (1958). *"With his pistol in his hand": A border ballad and its hero.* Austin: University of Texas Press.

Parsons, T. W., Jr. (1965). Ethnic Cleavage in a California School. Doctoral dissertation, Stanford University.

Pearce, R. H. (1953). *The savages of America: A study of the Indian and the idea of civilization.* Baltimore: Johns Hopkins Press.

Perspectives on inequality (1973). *Harvard Educational Review,* Reprint Series No. 8.

Peterson, R. C., & Thurstone, L. L. (1933). *Motion pictures and the social attitudes of children.* New York: Macmillan.

Philips, S. U. (1983). *The invisible culture: Communication in classroom and community on the Warm Springs Indian Reservation.* New York: Longman.

Powell, P. W. (1971). *Tree of hate: Propaganda and prejudices affecting United States relations with the Hispanic World.* New York: Basic Books.

Purkey, S. C., & Smith, M. S. (1983). Effective schools—a review. *Elementary School Journal, 83*(4), 427–452.

Ramírez, M., III, & Castañeda, A. (1974). *Cultural democracy, bicognitive development, and education.* New York: Academic Press.

Ramsey, P. G. (1987). Young children's thinking about ethnic differences. In J. S. Phinney & M. J. Rotheram (Eds.), *Children's ethnic socialization: Pluralism and development.* Newbury Park, CA: Sage.

Raths, L. E., & Trager, F. N. (1948). Public opinion and "Crossfire." *Journal of Educational Sociology, 21*(6), 345–368.

Rist, R. C. (1978). *The invisible children: School integration in American society.* Cambridge, MA: Harvard University Press.

Robinson, C. (1963). *With the ears of strangers: The Mexican in American Literature.* Tucson: University of Arizona Press.

Root, M. P. P. (Ed.) (1992). *Racially mixed people in America*. Newbury Park, CA: Sage.

Rosen, I. C. (1948). The effect of the motion picture *Gentleman's Agreement* on attitudes toward Jews. *Journal of Psychology, 26,* 525–536.

Rosenstiel, T. B. (1989, August 7). Viewers found to confuse TV entertainment with news. *Los Angeles Times,* Sec. I, p. 1.

Samuda, R. J. (1975). *Psychological testing of American minorities: Issues and consequences*. New York: Dodd, Mead & Co.

Sardar, Z. (1996–1997). Walt Disney and the double victimisation of Pocahontas. *Third Text,* Winter, 17–26.

Schramm, W., Lyle, J., & Parker, E. B. (1961). *Television in the lives of our children*. Stanford, CA: Stanford University Press.

Shaheen, J. G. (1984). *The TV Arab*. Bowling Green, OH: Bowling Green State University Popular Press.

Singer, R., & Kazdon, R. (Eds.) (1976). Television and social behavior. *Journal of Social Issues,* Fall.

Sklar, R. (1975). *Movie-made America: A cultural history of American movies*. New York: Random House.

Smith, A. F. (Ed.) (1976). *Transnational linkages of ethnic groups*. Denver: Center for Teaching International Relations, University of Denver.

Spickard, P. R. (1989). *Mixed blood: Intermarriage and ethnic identity in twentieth-century America*. Madison: University of Wisconsin Press.

Stanley, R. H., & Steinberg, C. S. (1976). *The media environment: Mass communications in American society*. New York: Hastings House.

Starr, R. (1973). The great frontier thesis as a framework for the American history survey in secondary schools. *History Teacher, 6,* 227–232.

Tilton, R. S. (1994). *Pocahontas: The evolution of an American narrative*. New York: Cambridge University Press.

Trubowitz, J. (1969). *Changing the racial attitudes of childen*. New York: Praeger.

Vidmar, N., & Rokeach, M. (1974). Archie Bunker's bigotry: A study in selective perception and exposure. *Journal of Communication, 24*(1), 36–47.

Volkan, V. (1988). *The need to have enemies and allies: From clinical practice to international relationships*. Northvale, NJ: J. Aronson.

Webster, Y. O. (1992). *The racialization of America*. New York: St. Martin's Press.

Weinberg, M. (1977). *A chance to learn: A history of race and education in the United States*. Cambridge, England: Cambridge University Press.

Williams, G. H. (1995). *Life on the color line: The true story of a white boy who discovered he was black*. New York: Dutton.

Wollenberg, C. (1976). *All deliberate speed: Segregation and exclusion in California schools, 1855–1975*. Berkeley: University of California Press.

Wood, M. (1975). *America in the movies*. New York: Basic Books.

Wurman, R. S. (1989). *Information anxiety*. New York: Doubleday.

Zack, N. (1993). *Race and mixed race*. Philadelphia, Temple University Press.

Zanuck made movie despite criticism of racial theme (1949, September). *Ebony,* p. 25.

INDEX

Bold numbers indicate figures.

ABOUT THE AUTHOR

CARLOS E. CORTÉS is a Professor Emeritus of History at the University of California, Riverside. Since 1990 he has served on the summer faculty of the Harvard Institutes for Higher Education and is also on the faculty of the Summer Institute for Intercultural Communication.

Among his many honors are the 1980 Distinguished California Humanist Award, the American Society for Training and Development's 1989 National Multicultural Trainer of the Year Award, the California Council for the Social Studies' 1995 Hilda Taba Award, and the National Association of Student Personnel Administrators' 2001 Outstanding Contribution to Higher Education Award. A consultant to many government agencies, school systems, universities, mass media, private businesses, and other organizations, he has lectured on diversity throughout the United States, Latin America, Europe, Asia, and Australia and has written film and television documentaries.

His book, *The Children Are Watching: How the Media Teach about Diversity*, was published in 2000 by Teachers College Press.